William Strauss & Neil Howe
WITH PETE MARKIEWICZ

Millennials

AND THE

POP
CULTURE

STRATEGIES FOR A NEW GENERATION OF CONSUMERS
in Music, Movies, Television, the Internet, and Video Games

Millennials
AND THE POP CULTURE

Howe, Neil and Strauss, William
    Millenials and the pop culture

ISBN 0-9712606-0-5

Library of Congress Control Number 2005938032

Table of Contents

Preface

When we began writing our first book together, *Generations*, in the mid-'80s, not many people in any business looked at their products and markets through a generational lens. Among the few who did were pioneers in the popular culture—from director John Hughes to the creators of MTV and BET. In the years since, though, especially after the "discovery" of Generation X in the early '90s, nearly everyone looks at markets that way, in fashion, cosmetics, cars, colleges, the military, you-name-it.

Through the history of youth pop culture, people in that business have made earnest efforts to figure out what's going on in young minds. Usually, they get it right—as in, for example, the late '80s and '90s. The accelerated pace, technological edge, and brassy attitude of popular entertainment effectively served the young people then coming of age. But every two decades or so—when a new generation reaches college age—many of them get it wrong. This is nothing new. It happened in the early '60s, again in the early '80s, and it's happening again now.

Once you start looking at anything—including the pop culture—through the lens of generational change, the pieces start fitting together. Consider, for example, how the first stirrings of the modern pop culture arose among the men and women of a large and indulged postwar generation. We don't mean Boomers—no, we're referring to the "Missionary" generation of W.C. Handy and Scott Joplin (and Jane Addams, FDR, and Albert Einstein). Born after the Civil War, they came of age just as the "frontier" was declared over. The homesteads were gone, the west explored. Instead, many young people turned their attention to popularizing a culture, pulling together some late-nineteenth century threads. What came of it? Ragtime. The blues. Jazz. Tin

i

pan alley. The *original* nickelodeon. And, in time, the first films, movie stars, and radio stations.

Since then, five more generations have had a major hand in the evolution of pop, from the famous "Lost Generation" to Generation X, each with its own cadre of stars, writers, directors, and producers. Initially, they targeted their cultural products to people their own age. Then, as they matured, they had to target a new generation younger than themselves. Always, those younger generations set new trends. Some culture creators rode those trends—and prospered. Others stuck with the old formulas—and did not.

Today, we're seeing the emergence of the seventh generation of pop: Millennials. Here again, some will catch the new youth trends and prosper, and others will not. Since 1997, when Millennial middle schoolers triggered the music industry's tumble, the world of youth pop has moved to a newly uncertain ground.

In entertainment, and other fields, generational change does not come easily, given all the creative teams in place, products in the pipeline, and brand images wrapped around well-established concepts. Breaking out is hard.

In assembling examples, and crafting some of the "hands on" suggestions, especially in the realm of interactive entertainments, we've had the active help of Pete Markiewicz, whose company (Indiespace) has ridden the wave of the Internet revolution and Gen-X culture, marketing the works of fledgling artists, pioneering online music sales, and publishing extraordinarily perceptive Web essays on generational change. We would also like to thank our colleague of many years, Rick Delano, for his advice and support, and Marc Waddell of Trademark Artists Management for his contributions to our discussions about the Internet.

We know the world of collegians, teens, and 'tweens through nearly two decades of joint research, dating back to our earliest work on the book *Generations*, which we started writing when the first Millennials were in preschool. (That's when we first affixed that name to these children, who now are in their twenties.) We've been following their trend lines—and, just as important, tracing their place in history—ever since.

Once you look at today's generations from a cultural (and business) perspective, you may find them interesting in their fuller historical context, which we described in our prior books. *Generations* (1991) is the full history of America from the first New World settlers forward, told as a series of generational biographies. In *13th-Gen: Abort, Retry, Ignore, Fail?* (1993), we wrote a socio-biography of Generation X, published right around the time of its discovery by the media. *The Fourth Turning* (1997) applied our generational concepts to a larger theory about the seasonality of history, in America and elsewhere.

Millennials Rising (2000) is our book about the younger generation, which we afterwards supplemented with *Millennials Go to College* (2003) and a Millennials handbook we recently wrote for the U.S. Armed Forces recruiting command. We recommend *Generations* and *The Fourth Turning* to readers who wish to learn more about our methodology, and Millennials Rising and Millennials Go to College for those seeking further perspectives on the young people we describe in this volume.

Our foray into the popular culture, with this generation, seemed a natural consequence of Strauss's nearly quarter-century as a theater director and performing artist, as cofounder of the Capitol Steps (www.capitolsteps.com). Over the last six years, Strauss has combined these two interests by collaborating with some very fine theater teachers to launch The Cappies (www.cappies.com) a nationwide program through which teenagers are trained as theater critics, after which they attend and review each others' shows, and then become the voting judges for "Cappie" awards presented at Cappies Galas.

We each have Millennial children, two school-age Howes (11 and 13, at this writing), and two young-adult Strausses (21 and 22). Strauss also has two grown Gen-X children (24 and 28).

Whether our reader has children or not, we encourage you to start this book by asking: What teenagers do you know personally? What are they and their friends like? If they were given the time and resources, and left to their own creative devices, what kind of entertainment would they create? Would they want something different, something more barrier-testing, or (just as provocatively) something *less* that way from their entertainment?

We'll lay odds that whatever this "something" will be, it won't be what you often see in today's movies or TV shows, or hear about in songs. That's the problem, in a nutshell.

Every generation has some people who set trends, others who follow, and others who resist. In combination, all a generation's members lend it a unique cultural flavor. Each generation is historically necessary, as a corrective to the ones who came before. Each has strong and weak points, unique perceptions and blind spots, forces for progress and reaction. This has been true for Boomers and Gen Xers, and will surely be true for Millennials.

Our object is not to judge, but to understand. There is no such thing as a "good" or "bad" generation. Every generation in American history is or was what it had to be—and, in the end, each one has turned out to be what America needed at the time. We expect the same will be true of Millennials. Something new is arriving with today's rising generation. We ask our reader first to accept that, and then to apply whatever meaning you wish to it. We share the view of the great German scholar Leopold von Ranke, who wrote that "all the generations of humanity appear equally justified." In "any generation," he wrote, "real moral greatness is the same as in any other."

We invite you to share any comments with us, by email, via authors@lifecourse.com.

— Neil Howe and William Strauss

Foreword

Pop culture is my fascination, and I've spent many years in the arts and entertainment industry in Los Angeles. I began my company (and Web site) right around the time Doug Copeland provided the name "Generation X" to the kids raised on MTV, and—like many in the industry—I spent much of the '90s riding that wave.

Around 1997, I began to notice a gradual disconnect between our artist clients and the newer generation of teens. Increasingly, "new" music and film was little more than nostalgic revivals with a bit of an edge added. Our own sales data confirmed that the age of music purchasers had begun to rise.

In time, it became clear to me and others then marketing to Gen X, that an age creep was affecting the pop world. Artists were aging to a point where they were starting to miss new youth trends. By the late '90s, many of our twenty and thirtysomething artists and entertainment professionals seemed to be marketing to the rapidly receding memories of their own teen years.

What was the real youth culture? Nearly nobody—not musicians, writers, label execs, filmmakers, nor market researchers—seemed to have a satisfactory answer.

Strauss and Howe were the eye-opening exception. When I read their books, I realized that what I was witnessing in the entertainment culture was the early stage of the end game for styles that had been associated with Generation X since the early '80s. Their analysis demonstrated that a new "Millennial" generation was already replacing X in the early teen brackets, and was poised to turn the industry upside down in the years to come.

Look back at their first book, *Generations*, written in the '80s, to see what Strauss and Howe forecast, about what would happen to all generations, and to America, in the '90s. Look at *13th-Gen*, written in the early '90s, to see what they forecast about what Gen Xers would be like in their twenties and thirties. Look at *The Fourth Turning*, written in the middle '90s, to see what they forecast about the current "Oh-Oh" decade.

Their predictions have been stunningly accurate. When the oldest Millennials were just in second grade, Strauss and Howe described what they would later be like in high school and college—clearly and correctly. They also correctly predicted a national mood change of the sort America did indeed experience in the aftermath of September 11, 2001.

Everyone I know in the entertainment business who has read any of their five books has come away convinced that Strauss and Howe are alerting us about something very important, very large. When they asked me to help them with this project, I was delighted to contribute what practical knowledge I could.

The authors have a broad and far-reaching understanding of the problems faced by the business of pop culture. Howe has advised a wide range of investment firms, marketers, universities, government agencies, and others about the new youth trends. Strauss has been a major culture creator himself for more than two decades, during which he's perhaps best known as cofounder and director of the Capitol Steps. He's also a playwright who has written three musicals: *MaKiddo*, a lampoon on today's teen culture; *Anasazi*, a story about Hopi legend and prophecy (drawn from the Strauss/Howe book, *The Fourth Turning*); and—of special relevance here—*Free-the-Music.com*, a comedy about collegians who download and a big music company that will shrink from nothing to stop them.

Strauss and Howe know Millennials, like the saying goes, "up close and personal." Over the past three years, they have separately visited several dozen colleges and more than 60 high schools across the nation. In recent years, Strauss has spent hundreds of hours working with some of the most creative teens in the nation. Six years ago, in the wake of the Columbine tragedy, he joined with a theater teacher to found a nationwide program, The Cappies, to celebrate creative teenagers. Fifteen Cappies programs now exist nationwide, each of them culminating in a Tonys-style Cappies Gala. Every summer, more than forty "Cappie" winning teen performers from across the United States gather at the Kennedy Center, as the all-star cast of the Cappies National Theater.

These two authors know generations, they know history, they know the youth culture, and they have an astounding record of correctly forecasting societal changes.

Many of the entertainment executives I know here in L.A. follow local youth trends and are getting feedback from their own high school or college-age kids. Too often that feedback is: "Mom, dad, you're not quite getting it right."

If you read this book, you will.

— Dr. Pete Markiewicz

PART ONE

THE MILLENNIAL
GENERATION

1 | WHERE DID THE YOUTH MARKET GO?

"Our civilization is doomed if the unheard-of actions of our younger generations are allowed to continue."

—Cuneiform tablet found in the Sumerian city of Ur, written circa 2,000 BC

WHERE DID THE YOUTH MARKET GO?

There's a new generation gap in America. It's not between parents and children, teachers and students, or leaders and protesters. It's between executives in the business of pop culture and the young people they want to entertain.

Across much of the entertainment industry today, a crisis of confidence has emerged over how to win the imagination and excitement of youth. Across the young generation, a new confidence is growing that they will soon be in control of their entertainment choices, regardless of the products they're now offered.

Every pop culture executive knows how important the youth market is. Yet nearly all would concede that the industry is no longer as sure as it used to be about who these youths are, what motivates them, and how their tastes are changing.

Some entertainment leaders don't understand why today's young people aren't like they were at that age. Others, feeling a bit disoriented, admit that it's hard to get a real sense for a new product until they give it to their own teenage sons and daughters and ask what they think of it. "Our kids have become our canaries in the coal mine," Comcast CEO Steve Burke recently confessed.

As doubt and anxiety grow, storm clouds gather over the future of the pop culture. Hardly a year goes by, it seems, when the entertainment industry is not jarred by disturbing news about its difficulty in reaching today's younger audience.

* In 2001, advertisers were rocked by a free-fall in ad revenue across all media, much of which was attributable—especially in radio, news, and magazines—to a shrinking younger audience. "Kids just don't listen or read anymore," came the expert cry. No they don't, at least not in the way older people want them to.

* In 2002, the recorded music industry encountered its worst single year in a decade-long famine in youth sales. The alarm bells have been clanging ever since. In constant dollars per capita, the typical American under age 25 is today buying *barely half* the CDs and tapes that he or she bought fifteen years ago.

* In 2003, reports came of a dramatic drop in TV viewing by guys in their late teens and early twenties. Smart kids in particular were simply turning the tube off, or not really paying attention even when it's on. The evidence mounts of a long-term erosion in youth interest in television.

* In 2004, Janet Jackson's "wardrobe malfunction" triggered a blast of long-suppressed parental outrage over sleaze in the popular culture—which young people heard and absorbed. Today's teenage consumers tell pollsters they are six times more likely to trust parents than pop celebrities on important issues.

* In 2005, as spring wore on to summer, movie theaters sent out an S.O.S. about the declining number of teens at neighborhood movie houses, teens who increasingly spent their time and dollars elsewhere—often, in front of home entertainment systems. Largely due to growing youth resistance, U.S. box office receipts were down (from the prior year) for 19 straight weeks—the worst downturn in two decades.

Meanwhile, as the troubling news has accumulated, pop culture producers have been busily working to control two broader youth-related challenges that impact nearly all of their media. One is the digital IT ("information technology") revolution, which threatens to reshape and reshuffle the entire industry and which youth consumers are pushing faster than any other age group. The other is P2P file-sharing and downloading, which threatens to hollow out any medium that depends upon direct consumer sales.

Many in the industry, perhaps out of frustration, have responded to both challenges in a singularly defensive and uncreative manner. They apparently hope that the technology revolution can be legislated and litigated away. By hunkering down, the industry half-imagines it can protect the comfortable niches of all the traditional media (from CDs and DVDs to cable and newsprint) against a digital transformation that most youths understand is absolutely inevitable.

As for file-sharing challenge, the industry's dreary battle plan consists mainly of software locks, lawsuits, court rulings, legal penalties, and heated invective against the "immoral behavior" of millions of downloading teens, described by a top industry spokesman as "pirates" and "criminals." Is this how the industry plans to sweet talk a confident and savvy generation of teens back to its corner?

The damaging wake generated by this sort of PR strategy points to yet another large challenge for pop culture producers: the fact that today's youth just don't think very highly of them. In a recent Primedia survey, teens in middle and high school put the media (both "news" and "entertainment") in second and third place in a long list of "groups most responsible for current problems in society." The media were way ahead of state and local governments, business leaders, immigrants, environmentalists, religious groups, and women's groups. They also ranked near the tail end of the teen list of "groups which will cause most changes for the better in the future."

Dating back to the late '60s, when many entertainment executives were young themselves, the industry has thrived off a reputation for communicating with youth about sensitive lifestyle issues that no one else will touch. That reputation may be fading. In a recent survey from the National Campaign to Prevent Teen Pregnancy, teens were asked who influences their values about sex. Only 4 percent answered "the media," while 45 percent answered "my parents." The more visibly the industry attaches itself to the pop culture (for example, at the annual Oscar or Emmy or Grammy or MTV awards), the less youth seem to want to be there.

Surveys and ratings spell out the uncomfortable bottom line: Thirty or forty years ago the entertainment media had a much deeper reservoir of respect and trust among youth than they do today.

One might reasonably ask: How can kids have a problem with the media when kids are surrounded by media as never before? In 1999, according to a Kaiser Family Foundation report, kids lived in a "media rich" environment. In a 2005 update on that report, the authors' amended their findings to note that today's kids live in a "media saturated" environment—so crowded are their homes and waking hours with TVs, boom boxes, digital players, game consoles, radios, cell phones, and computer screens.

But media saturation says little about the young people themselves. For the most part, it's parents and other adults who have done that to their world. Although young people certainly spend a lot of time with pop culture, time alone says little about how much they focus on it, care about it, interact with it, interpret it, or would like to transform it. Familiarity is not the same as loyalty. Today's midlife Boomers grew up with far less media—and far fewer youth surveys. Yet most fiftysomething media executives can surely recall how strong the bonds felt between youth and the pop-culture icons of the late '60s and '70s.

One might also reasonably ask: Why do we have new and special problems understanding youth today when we didn't have such problems in the past? The answer here is simple: *Today's youth belong to a new and special generation, the Millennial Generation, born since 1982.*

The oldest, first-wave members of this generation entered the first grade in 1988, graduated from high school in 2000, and graduated from four-year colleges in 2004. The youngest (probably) are infants or toddlers. First-wave Millennials, born in the '80s, are mainly the children of Boomer parents in their mid-forties to early sixties (born, 1943 to 1960). Later-wave Millennials, born since the early '90s, are mainly children of Gen-X parents in their mid-twenties to early forties (born, 1961 to 1981).

By looking at today's youth from a generational perspective, we understand better how differently they see the entertainment industry—and which direction they may push it. Recall the moment in the 1967 film *The*

Graduate, when a suited middle-aged man whispered the word "plastics" into Dustin Hoffman's ear. That moment summed up how Boomer youth then perceived over-the-top 50-year-olds—the materialistic power elite who had fought and won World War II. What one word might sum up, for young Millennials, an over-the-top 50-year-old today? What one word might make them wince at the values-obsessed cultural-elite generation who once crowded into Woodstock? The word "media" would be a good bet.

Back in the 1960s, who called the rising generation "criminal?" Middle-aged political leaders, upset over anti-war youth protests. In recent years, who calls kids that? Middle-aged executives, upset over youth file sharing. Back then, who ultimately won the generational confrontation? The young, who wielded the culture to triumph over the hubris of their parents' technology. Who will win this time? The young, who will wield technology to triumph over the pretensions of their parents' culture.

A generational perspective also helps us understand the timing of some of the larger trends that have recently impacted the entertainment industry.

* Think back to the mid-1980s, when American moviegoers flocked to a new film genre about wonderful babies who inspired parents to be better people (*Raising Arizona, Baby Boom, Three Men and a Baby*).
* Next, think back to the mid-'90s—1994 was the pivotal year—when national leaders demanded that elementary school-age children be protected from edgy content, as talk of stricter ratings and v-chips and cops-in-shops became a national political issue.
* Next, think back to the late-'90s—1997, especially—when the recording industry began noticing a sudden taste shift toward "boy bands" among 13- to 15-year-old consumers along with a downward lurch in CD sales.
* Lastly, think about 2004 and 2005, when major Hollywood studios began focusing on changing viewing habits and ticket-buying softness among their prime movie-goers in the 18- to 24-year-old bracket.

Connect the dots between these ages and dates and you find something very interesting. They all refer to the *same group* of young people, the first-wave of the Millennial Generation, whose new attitudes, habits, and expectations are transforming every age bracket they enter. To anticipate the timing of other Millennial changes yet to happen and to better understand the Millennial changes that have already happened, we need to take a deeper look at just who these Millennials really are. Every new generation turns a corner on the social and cultural trends introduced by the generation who came just before. Boomers did that. So did Generation X. And so too, now, do Millennials.

Some people try not to think about generations. Teens will buy anything, they insist, so long as it's new and packaged right. That's self-delusional nonsense. Teens might — for a while, if only out of curiosity, much like Boomers bought Pat Boone LPs and tickets to beach movies in the early '60s. But if it doesn't strike a chord, they'll try to sneak a peek without paying for it, after which they'll move on and spend their money on things they do like.

Some people say the trick is to identify every nifty new youth trend ten milliseconds before your competition, without necessarily understanding what's driving these trends. That doesn't work well, either. From New York to Los Angeles, "cool hunting" marketers have seen many of their youth trends predictions turn out wrong.

All this is nothing new. Every older generation of producers, directors, writers, and performers tries its best to figure out its target youth market — sometimes trusting in intuition, other times in experts, trial and error, or sheer luck. Along the way, every older generation gets quite a lot right about young people, a fact no less true in recent decades than it was twenty, forty, or sixty years ago. What happens, though, is that what they "get right" will, at some point, be overwhelmed by what they get wrong. This happened in the early '60s, again around 1980, and it's happening again now.

Every twenty years or so — once in a generation — a new youth culture sneaks up on the business of pop. These days, the problem is hardly that no one is looking. To the contrary. Exit polls, surveys, focus groups, "trendsetter" analyses, and media ratings constantly monitor the heartbeat of the young. Youth gossip, demographics, and psychographics are regularly analyzed and compiled. Publicity and marketing outlays for feature films tripled in the '90s, while overall costs only doubled. Entertainment companies figure if they're spending this much on research and marketing, they must be getting a few things right—or, if not, that they're at least succeeding in shaping youth tastes to conform with what they're selling.

But are they? Along with others of their own age or generation, what many entertainment professionals know about teens reflects their own personal experience, supplemented by what they've seen in the media—in film, TV plots, and news stories—which often just reinforces those same collective memories. None of the above may have any connection with the real daily lives of the new youth generation coming on scene.

Let's start by asking our reader, how much do you know about today's teens? What has been the trend for U.S. teenagers in each of the following areas since 1995? Circle what you think, and then compare your responses with the correct answers shown in Table 1.1b (page 11).

Table 1.1a: Youth Trend Since 1995	up	unchanged	down
Fatal shootings in schools			
Violent crime rate, teens aged 14 to 19			
Percent of high school students who have had sexual intercourse			
Abortion rate, teen women under age 18			
Birth rate, teen women under age 18			
Tobacco use, high school students			
Percent of high school students who drink any alcohol			
Percent of high school seniors who take the SAT			
Average combined SAT score			
Percent of teens who say they like their parents' music			
Percent of teens who say they share their parents' values			
Average daily time spent doing homework, kids aged 12 to 17			
Average daily time spent watching TV, kids aged 12 to 17			
Percent of high schools giving course credit for community service			
Average daily time spent in unstructured & unsupervised activities			
Suicide rate, children/teens aged 18 and under			
Stranger abductions of children			
Illegal drug use, teens aged 18 and under			
Prescription drug use, children & teens			
Obesity and asthma, children & teens			

Taken as a whole, in recent years, nearly every entertainment media has failed to recognize how a new and truly different generation (of Millennials) is beginning to change the direction of trends established by the prior youth generation (of Gen Xers).

Why so? Consider who the front-line culture makers are. Most of them are young adults ranging in age from their mid-twenties to their late thirties, Gen Xers on the opposite side of the life cycle from teenagers. They don't have them as children, siblings, or social friends. At most, they may have a cousin or two in their teens. Aside from teachers, very few people in their twenties or thirties ever set foot in today's high schools.

This has been true for over 100 years, since the late-nineteenth century origin of the modern pop culture. The creators of the popular culture have usually been too old to have teenage siblings, but not old enough to have teenage children. When the youth culture is not changing very rapidly, as was true through most of the '70s or '90s, this is not so much of a problem. But when it is changing, as it did in the '60s, the '80s, and again now, it can be an enormous problem—or an enormous opportunity.

The entertainment industry's core dilemma is not economic or technological. No, it's something less familiar but more correctible—the need to understand the youth market, in a time of transition from one generation to the next.

Now let's return to Table 1.1b. For every trend except the last two, the correct answer is what a typical legislator, or principal, or parent, or teenager, would want it to be. The two exceptions are prescription drug use, and health problems resulting from physical inactivity, both of which are way up.

If you answered most of the questions correctly, you're on the road to understanding the Millennial generation. Maybe you're the mom or dad of teenagers. If not, you're at least in tune with their world (a bit like Madonna, as cutting edge as ever, dressing in florals, writing children's books, and celebrating family).

If you answered most of them wrong, you're not alone. Despite the fact that the questions are based on studies and statistics that are easily available and widely circulated, many in the entertainment industry think youth

Table 1.1b: Youth Trend Since 1995 (Correct Answers)			
	up	unchanged	down
Fatal shootings in schools			✓
Violent crime rate, teens aged 14 to 19			✓
Percent of high school students who have had sexual intercourse			✓
Abortion rate, teen women under age 18			✓
Birth rate, teen women under age 18			✓
Tobacco use, high school students			✓
Percent of high school students who drink any alcohol			✓
Percent of high school seniors who take the SAT	✓		
Average combined SAT score	✓		
Percent of teens who say they like their parents' music	✓		
Percent of teens who say they share their parents' values	✓		
Average daily time spent doing homework, kids aged 12 to 17	✓		
Average daily time spent watching TV, kids aged 12 to 17	✓		
Percent of high schools giving course credit for community service			✓
Average daily time spent in unstructured & unsupervised activities			✓
Suicide rate, children/teens aged 18 and under			✓
Stranger abductions of children			✓
Illegal drug use, teens aged 18 and under			✓
Prescription drug use, children & teens	✓		
Obesity and asthma, children & teens	✓		

trends are moving in directions exactly opposite to what the data show. If they're in their thirties, they might mistakenly assume that today's youth trends are a continuation of trends they themselves experienced as teens.

When informed which way the youth trends are really going, many might object that most of them apply only to affluent kids or white kids or suburban kids. But here too they would be mistaken. In fact, African-American teens in the inner-city are actually *leading* many of these trends in terms of percentage improvement. Second-generation immigrant teens, mostly Latinos or Asians, are also showing better-than-average improvement over the past decade.

The point here is not that most of the Millennials are pushing all but a few of the above behaviors in a positive direction—although most people who look at the data would say that is the case. The point is that they are pushing the behaviors *away* from personal risk-taking. Back in the Boomer youth era, nearly all of those trends were heading in exactly the opposite direction—toward the edge, toward risk. Over the span of two generations, there have been an enormous and measurable changes in the preferred sense of life direction among American youth.

College officials and military officers see these trends clearly, because they need to deal effectively with so many young people each day and because they need to meet annual admission or recruiting goals. People in marketing and culture trades are coming to this more slowly, but they're starting to see it too.

When you look at Millennials as a post-X generation, you can gain new insight into reasons for some of the broad pop-culture changes that have swept youth in recent years. Like why the new trend in kid-vid, from Barney to today's teen movies, has become so energetically team-oriented. Like why kids and teens in public places started moving in organized and supervised groups, often wearing the same T-shirts. Or why, in 1997, the heroic theme of *Titanic* struck such a chord among 'tweens—who, in that same year, stopped buying grunge albums. Or why teenagers became so reluctant to undress in front of adults (or each other) in gym locker rooms. Or why Erika Harold, Miss America for 2003, had to battle with pageant officials over her right to talk about teen chastity. Or why a teenager recently told a *New York Times* reporter that the "punk look is going away, all those bracelets up the arm.... Now it's clean-cut, like looking 'nice' for the day." Or why Harry Potter has become the biggest brand in the history of books.

This new youth mindset is, first and foremost, an American phenomenon. What is taking place with Millennials in the United States, and to a significant degree in Canada, is not yet apparent among 19- to 22-year-olds around the world, but it will be within a few years. Millennial-style trends among young 'tweens are already drawing comment in western Europe, in China, and in the rest of the English-speaking world.

In America and elsewhere, Millennials are rising. They will be the dominant youth consumers of pop culture over the next two decades, and they will continue to be important mature consumers of the pop culture for decades thereafter.

2 | MILLENNIALS RISING

"Meet the Millennials, and rejoice."

— Anna Quindlen, *Newsweek* (2000)

MILLENNIALS RISING

Today, we stand at a turning point in U.S. generational history. The Boomer Generation (their oldest turning 62 in 2005) is beginning to pass from parenting to retirement. Generation X (their oldest turning 44) is beginning to move into middle age. And a completely new youth generation, age 23 on down, is beginning to replace Gen-X in the young adult bracket. Meanwhile, Gen-X styles and lingo (along with the very name "Generation X") are beginning to seem tired and dated to teens.

When today's new youth generation was still just emerging as small children during the late '80s, it was already clear that they represented something very post-X. The name "Millennial" was coined in 1988, when the first small children of this new generation entered kindergarten. Immediately heralded as the high school "Class of 2000," they became the target of the "Goals 2000" educational reform movement, and their identity soon got wrapped up in thoughts about the coming new millennium.

What name does this generation itself prefer? According to teen polls taken by ABC-TV and by bolt.com, teens widely prefer "Millennial Generation" to all others. Their second choice is not to have a name at all.

Generation Y and Echo Boom are two other names that have been often applied to today's youth. "Generation Y" was first suggested in 1993, in *Advertising Age*, to refer to the 13- to 19-year-olds of that year, a group that most observers would today include in Generation X. The Echo Boom refers to their parents and the long-anticipated uptick in births (during the 1980s)

Six U.S. Generations and Nearly 120 Birth Years

YEAR BORN

	1883–1900	**1901–1924**	**1925–1942**
	LOST	**G.I.**	**SILENT**
Generation	The Lost Generation had to grow up fast—amidst urban blight, unregulated drug use, "sweat shop" child labor, and massive immigration. As children, their violence, independence, and low educational achievement worried parents. Most Lost males were draft-eligible for World War I. As twentysomethings, they were brassy flappers, union scabs, expatriate novelists, and nihilist "flaming youth." They also pioneered entire economic sectors—supermarkets, roadside commerce, radio and aviation—we take for granted today. After surviving a Great Depression that hit during their peak earning years, they slowed down and, during World War Two, delivered pugnacious midlife leadership. As crusty "Norman Rockwell" elders, they distrusted public power, gave generously to their world-conquering juniors, and asked remarkably little for themselves.	The G.I. Generation enjoyed a "good kid" reputation as the beneficiaries of new playgrounds, scouting clubs, vitamins, and child-labor restrictions. They came of age with the sharpest rise in schooling ever recorded. As young adults, their uniformed corps patiently endured Depression and heroically conquered foreign enemies during World War II. In a midlife subsidized by the G.I. Bill, they built suburbs, invented vaccines, plugged missile gaps, and launched moon rockets. Their unprecedented grip on the Presidency (1961 through '92) began with the New Frontier, Great Society and Model Cities, but wore down through Vietnam, Watergate and budget deficits. As senior citizens, they safeguarded their "entitlements" but had little influence over culture and values.	The Silent Generation grew up as the suffocated children of war and Depression. They came of age just too late to be war heroes and just too early to be youthful free spirits. Instead, this early marrying "lonely crowd" became the risk-averse technicians and professionals as well as the sensitive rock 'n' rollers and civil rights advocates of a post-Crisis era in which conformity seemed to be a sure ticket to success. Midlife was an anxious "passage" for a generation torn between stolid elders and passionate juniors. Their surge to power coincided with fragmenting families, cultural diversity, institutional complexity, and too much litigation. They are entering elderhood with unprecedented affluence, a hip style, and a reputation for indecision
Famous People	Al Capone, Raymond Chandler, Amelia Earhart, Ernest Hemingway, Dorothy Parker, F. Scott Fitzgerald, George Patton, Marcus Garvey, Harry Truman, Dwight Eisenhower.	John Kennedy, Ronald Reagan, John Steinbeck, Alex Haley, Ray Kroc, Jackie Robinson, Lee Iacocca, Ann Landers, Charles Lindbergh, Betty Friedan, John Glenn, Claire Booth Luce.	Martin Luther King Jr., Richard Cheney, Robert Kennedy, Sandra Day O'Connor, Colin Powell, John McCain, Jesse Jackson, Geraldine Ferraro, Neil Armstrong, Jack Welch, Gloria Steinem, Maya Angelou.
Famous in Entertainment	John Ford, Michael Curtiz, Frank Capra, Louis Armstrong, Irving Berlin, George Gershwin, Jimmy Cagney, Mary Pickford, Lillian Gish, Rudolph Valentino, Humphrey Bogart, Mae West, the Marx Brothers.	Walt Disney, William Wyler, Joseph Mankiewicz, Leonard Bernstein, Robert Wise, Bette Davis, Benny Goodman, Katharine Hepburn, John Wayne, Jimmy Stewart, Judy Garland, Bob Hope, Sidney Poitier, Charlton Heston.	Francis Ford Coppola, Mike Nichols, Mel Brooks, Woody Allen, Norman Lear, Shirley Temple, James Dean, Marilyn Monroe, Elvis Presley, Ray Charles, Barbra Streisand, Bill Cosby, Paul Newman, Paul Simon, Johnny Carson, Bob Dylan.

Except for many Boomers (who assume they must know), the first thing most folks want to know when you talk generations is: *Where do I fit?* This table puts the Millennials, and their five predecessor generations, into perspective. Think about your own family—your parents, your favorite aunt or uncle, your youngest brother, your great-grandmother. When were they born, and how did their generational membership shape them? Then think about some individuals who've inspired you—movie stars, great writers, even political leaders—and speculate whether they have ended up carrying out a key part of their own generation's "script."

YEAR BORN →

1943–1960	1961–1981	1982–Now
BOOM	**X**	**MILLENNIAL**
The Boom Generation grew up as indulged youth during an era of community-spirited progress. These kids were the proud creation of postwar optimism, Dr. Spock rationalism, and "Father Knows Best" family order. Coming of age, however, Boomers loudly proclaimed their antipathy to the secular blueprints of their parents; they demanded inner visions over outer, self-perfection over thing-making or team-playing. The Boom "Awakening" climaxed with Vietnam War protests, the 1967 "summer of love," inner-city riots, the first Earth Day, and Kent State. In the aftermath, Boomers appointed themselves arbiter of the nation's values and crowded into such "culture careers" as teaching, religion, journalism, marketing and the arts. During the '90s, they trumpeted values, touted a "politics of meaning," and waged scorched-earth culture wars.	Generation X survived a hurried childhood of divorce, latchkeys, open classrooms, and devil child movies. They came of age curtailing the earlier rise in youth crime and fall in test scores—yet heard themselves denounced as so wild and stupid as to put *The Nation At Risk*. As young adults, navigating a sexual battlescape of AIDS and blighted courtship rituals, they dated and married cautiously. In jobs, they embraced risk and prefer free agency over loyal corporatism. From grunge to hip-hop, their culture revealed a hardened edge. Politically, they have leaned toward pragmatism and non-affiliation and would rather volunteer than vote. Many have grown up facing a Reality Bites economy of winner-take-all markets and declining young-adult living standards.	The Millennial Generation first arrived when "Baby on Board" signs appeared. As abortion and divorce rates ebbed, the popular culture began stigmatizing hands-off parental styles and recasting babies as special. Child abuse and child safety became hot topics, while books teaching virtues and values became best-sellers. By the mid-'90s, politicians were defining adult issues (from tax cuts to PBS funding to Internet access) in terms of their effects on children. Hollywood replaced cinematic child devils with child angels; cable TV and the Internet are cordoning off child-friendly havens. Since 2000, with The No Child Left Behind Act trumpeting standards and accountability, rates of serious violent crime, pregnancy, smoking, and drinking have dropped to record lows among teenagers.
Bill Clinton, George W. Bush, Al Gore, John Kerry, Hillary Clinton, Tom DeLay, Rudy Giuliani, Bill Gates, Steve Jobs, Condoleeza Rice, Donald Trump, Russ Feingold, Carly Fiorina.	Mark Andreessen, Michael Jordan, Michael Dell, Jeff Bezos, Barack Obama, Mia Hamm, Tiger Woods, Venus Williams, Larry Page, Mary Bono, Kwame Kilpatrick.	Sarah Hughes, Jessica Lynch, Matt Leinart, Michael Phelps, LeBron James, Tara Lipinski, Freddie Adu, Megan Kanka, Danica Patrick, Michelle Wie.
Jim Morrison, Janis Joplin, Ron Howard, Steven Spielberg, George Lucas, Gilda Radner, Spike Lee, Oliver Stone, Oprah Winfrey, Diane Keaton, Howard Stern, Rush Limbaugh, Michael Jackson, Tom Hanks, Madonna.	Quentin Tarantino, Jodie Foster, Robert Rodriguez, Steven Soderbergh, Kurt Cobain, Jon Stewart, Johnny Depp, P. Diddy, Tupac Shakur, Tom Cruise, George Clooney, Brad Pitt, Jennifer Lopez, Britney Spears, Ricky Martin, Queen Latifah.	Frankie Muniz, Haley Joel Osment, Ashley and Mary-Kate Olsen, Hilary Duff, Kelly Clarkson, Amanda Bynes, Charlotte Church, Lindsay Lohan, Raven-Symone, Ryan Cabrera, Scarlett Johansson, Ashlee Simpson, Lil Bow Wow.

to Boomer mothers. Neither label is popular with today's youth for the simple reason that no new batch of teens and collegians want to be seen as derivatives of older people. Millennials are also sometimes referred to as the "digital" or "net" generation—names that are oddly narrow in scope but that do have the virtue of highlighting their affinity for, and mastery of, today's new information technologies.

The problem with the Generation Y label is not just its unpopularity among teens. The deeper problem, imbedded within the label, is the errone-ous assumption that every new generation is best understood as a simple continuation or elaboration of the last generation. Relying on this assump-tion, marketers who use data to track youth trends can easily miss what's going on. Most data analysis relies on static life-stage models, which assume individuals will act one way when young and in other ways when they get older. This sort of analysis is correct at times, but wildly incorrect at other times. In particular, it always misses the arrival of a new generation.

People carry with them the unique stamp of the eras in which they are born and raised. As they enter each new life stage (childhood, youth, middle age, elderhood), they change the societal role for that life stage. As elders, Boomers will behave very differently than their G.I. parents did at the same age. In midlife, whether as family heads or as national and corporate leaders, Gen Xers will behave differently from Boomers—a fact that any 35-year-old is likely to tell you. The same is true for youth.

Why Generations Matter

A generation is unique in acquiring a shared history that lends its members a social and cultural center of gravity. Like an individual, a generation can collectively feel nostalgia for the values of its youth, and can search for its ultimate destiny. As each new generation arrives, advances, and recedes, a unique "peer personality" reveals itself. Not everyone will share that persona, of course, but each person within that generation will have to deal with it, willingly or unwillingly, over a lifetime.

Proof of this abounds. In the late '60s, the share of Americans aged 65 and over who considered themselves big-government Democrats surged.

Then, in the early '90s, the share of older people who thought that way began to recede. The intervening era defined the high-tide of AARP activism and congressional action to expand old-age entitlements. Did seniors feel some profound political change of heart during those years? Not at all. Over that quarter century, the Americans who reached retirement age were the same civic-minded Americans who, as young voters for the New Deal Coalition, had come of age as big-government Democrats in the 1930s. More recently, the retirees have come from a very different generation.

To give another example, drug abuse has recently risen dramatically among middle-aged Americans, even as it has fallen among younger people. During the '70s, the mortality rate for substance-abuse overdoses among adults in their 50s was roughly the same as for teens. By the late '90s, it was over ten times higher. To understand why, you need to apply a generational perspective. Middle age was not associated with drug abuse until the Boomers entered this phase of life. It's the maturing of the Boom Generation, with its high percentage of lifelong drug users, that explains this finding—not some change in the intrinsic nature of midlife itself. (One might predict that, as Boomers move into retirement communities, drug abuse will follow them there as well—and recent news stories indeed confirm a rapid expansion in drug rehab programs for younger retirees in "active adult" communities.)

When pop culture writers and performers project their own life experience to youth culture, a generational mismatch can occur between entertainment and real life. In *Vanilla Sky*, the protagonist was clearly a member of Generation X. However, the soundtrack's music comes almost entirely from the '60s and early '70s, and the character's stored-up memories show scenes from over a decade before he was supposedly born.

In *Traffic*, a movie full of cynical, bored, angry, coked-out kids, including the daughter of the National Drug Czar who just happens to be both a National Merit finalist and a heavy-duty mainlining drug addict. *Traffic's* screenwriter, then age 35, told *USA Today* that the portrayal is absolutely accurate because he saw such behavior often as a teen. Maybe this was true during his own Gen-X youth, but it's far less often the case now. Teen drug use has dropped dramatically since the early '80s. When *USA Today* talked to today's teens about the movie, they found it off-base. "We get jaded at my school once in a while, but I would not say it is a constant thing," a New Jersey 17-year-old told the paper. "The depiction in the movie is an exaggeration," she said. "The top students are not the ones using drugs."

The TV show "Boston Public" has similarly projected a supposedly "real" concept that was more real to Gen Xers and Boomers than to Millennials. The show was (as of 2004) twice as popular among adults over age 40 than among teens of high-school age—who know, from first-hand experience, that behavior commonly displayed on that show would, in today's schools, get students suspended or expelled, teachers fired or arrested, and administrators humiliated by parents and the media.

The definition of "cool" held by twenty- and thirtysomethings now feels old-fashioned to teens. As Millennials come of age, the image of sullen, ironic, cynical, slacker, in-your-face, "X-treme" youth is becoming more cliché than reality, an old story, the stuff of '80s and '90s nostalgia pieces.

To many an older eye, the Millennial Generation is a good news story. Compared to teens of earlier decades, they tend to be more confident, optimistic, team oriented, rule following, and eager to achieve. To other eyes, though, they are worrisome in their blandness, group-think, and easy acquiescence to authority. However you view them, who they are reflects the hopes and fears of their parents who came of age during the 1960s and 1970s. Far more than the previous two generations when young, Millennials are closely tied to their parents, and their decisions about entertainment frequently result from a consensus across generations.

The oldest cohorts of Millennials reached their 'tween years in the middle '90s. In the 2003–04 school year, these cohorts filled all four years of college. Yet they are only the leading wave of this generation, whose main force will arrive when today's elementary and middle schoolers, born in the early '90s, become the primary culture consumers later this decade and next. Comprising the peak of the Millennial baby boom, their interests and attitudes will swamp any remaining Xer styles by sheer force of numbers. The trends described here are the beginning, not the culmination, of the Millennial generational shift.

The Changing Face of Youth

At regular intervals, when new youth trends reach a critical mass, any stale yet prevailing adult conceptions about the teen culture are swept aside—often along with out-of-touch entertainment creators—by a new batch of young people. In recent history, these generational surprises have arrived about once every twenty years.

The Silent Generation (born 1925–1942) came as a surprise. In 1946, about the time General George Marshall declared the nation's victorious G.I. Generation troops to be "the best damn kids in the world," Americans braced for fresh ranks of organized collegians who would join organize union strikes, join socialist parties, and accelerate the mass mobilizations of the New Deal and World War II. These new youths were expected to be just like the world-conquering generation just before them, different only in that they might carry familiar youth traits to a higher level.

This didn't happen. After the returning G.I.s—the soldiers, sailors, and airmen who had won the war—flowed quickly into and then out of the nation's campuses, older people were surprised to learn that the next generation of "teenagers" (then a brand new word) seemed uninterested in conquering the world. They kept their heads down, worried about their "permanent records," married very young, planned large families, and sought long careers with big organizations.

Rather than change the system, the new collegians wanted to work within it. Looking back, historian William Manchester wrote, "Never had American youth been so withdrawn, cautious, unimaginative, indifferent, unadventurous—and silent.... They waited so patiently for everything that visitors to college campuses began commenting on their docility." In music, this was the generation that fueled the early demand for "crossover" rock 'n roll and doo wop, then Bill Haley and the Comets, then Little Richard, Elvis, and the Motown sound. They gave birth to Mad magazine, the "beat" culture, the Playboy forerunners of the sexual revolution, and all the madcap Jerry Lewis alternatives to the conventional sort of TV show then preferred by older G.I.s.

People expected the young Silent Generation to be a linear extension of the G.I. Generation. It wasn't.

Boomers (born 1943–1960) came as a surprise. By the early '60s, Americans had grown used to talking about a "Silent Generation" of college students. As experts looked ahead to the onrushing bulge of children known as the "baby boom" who were about to arrive at college, they foresaw a new corps of technocratic corporatists, a Silent Generation to the next degree, even more pliable and conformist than the gray flannel "lonely crowd" right before them. "Employers are going to love this generation," Cal-Berkeley's Chancellor Clark Kerr declared in 1959, "They are going to be easy to handle. There aren't going to be any riots."

Wrong. Not even the biggest-name social scientists—not Erik Erikson or Margaret Mead—saw a hint of the youth explosion that was about to shake America. As the Boomers began their famous '60s rebellion, the record industry caught the generational wave. Music became the heartbeat of the new youth "counterculture." In film, many famous directors like Alfred Hitchcock found it increasingly difficult to speak to the changing mood, and genre staples (westerns, biblical epics, beach jiggle movies) faded. But new directors like Mike Nichols stepped up and defined the Boomer break-out in films like *The Graduate* and *Carnal Knowledge*. Television was the last to adjust, continuing to show a docile image of youth and family throughout the '60s, while campus riots, sexual liberation, drug use, and skyrocketing divorce rates took center stage.

People expected young Boomers to be a linear extension of the Silent. They weren't.

Generation X (born 1961–1981) came as a surprise. Move forward another twenty years. Around 1980, amid Boomer-fueled disco, the bell-bottomed strut, and lava-lamp love, youth experts began commenting on the emergence of the "Baby Buster" generation, whose members had no memories of the assassination of John Kennedy and no clear impression of Woodstock, Vietnam, or even Watergate. What would they be like? Once again, the expectation was linear, that these youths would be like Boomers, only more so. Demographic forecasters suggested that the teens in the '80s and '90s

Median Ages
of TV Viewers

The median age of TV viewers is, on the whole, considerably older than the median age of movie viewers (age 29) and the overall U.S. population (age 36).

In the fall of 2003, Nielsen Media Research reported the following to be the median ages of these networks and programs:

Nickelodeon	10	All TV (prime-time)	37
MTV	22	Fear Factor	38
Run of the House	25	Friends	39
VH1	26	E.R.	42
The Simpsons	26	NFL Monday Night Football	45
Malcolm in the Middle	29	Boston Public	45
O.C.	30	Frasier	47
Smallville	31	Law and Order	50
WWE Smackdown	31	West Wing	52
Gilmore Girls	32	CBS (prime-time)	53
WB (prime-time)	33	Threat Matrix	55
Arrested Development	34	Fox News	59
Total U.S. population	36	60 Minutes	59
Fox (prime-time)	36	CNN	62

would be more ideological, "holistic," and values-driven—extending what *American Demographics* termed "an ongoing trend away from material aspirations toward non-materialistic goals."

Those predictions were rudely overturned when the scrappy, pragmatic, and free-agent Gen-X persona emerged a few years later. Disco gave way to MTV, soul to hip-hop, as the residues of the Boomer hippie culture gave way to punk and grunge, hackers and gamers, gangsta rappers, professional soldiers, high-paid athletes, MBA dot-commers, and an ocean of struggling temp workers. The journey was no longer the reward.

Institutions that serve youth—from colleges to employers to the armed services—were thrown into disarray. Who got it right in entertainment? Not the writers featuring campus rebels or liberated fern-bar narcissists. Instead, fast-cut MTV videos and hip-hop broke the musical mold, and writer John Hughes caught the new youth attitude in a string of teen-oriented films, especially *The Breakfast Club* and *St. Elmo's Fire* (both 1985). Forsaking Boomer activism, his stories and characters celebrated the rise of an in-your-face, ironic, and apolitical youth culture, which, like *Howard the Duck*, was "trapped in a world it never made."

People expected young Gen Xers to be a linear extension of Boomers. They haven't been.

Millennials (born 1982–20xx) are coming as a surprise. Today, another 20 years have passed, and yet another generational change is on the doorstep. As a group, Millennials are unlike any other youths in living memory. More numerous, more affluent, better educated, and more ethnically diverse than those who came before, they are beginning to manifest a wide array of positive social habits that older Americans no longer associate with youth, including a new focus on teamwork, achievement, modesty, and good conduct.

Yet most people's perception of youth (especially among those who don't have regular contact with teens) still lags behind reality. As was true 20, 40, and 60 years ago, a common adult view is that today's teens are like the prior batch (Generation X), taken to the next degree (alias, Gen "Y"). A study recently published in the academic journal, *Social Policy Research*, finds American adults take a dim view of the younger generation. Among the findings:

* Only 16 percent of adult Americans agree that people under the age of 30 share most of their moral and ethical values.
* The three most frequently reported topics of youth news on the local stations are crime victimization, accidents involving young people, and violent juvenile crime, accounting for nearly half of all youth coverage.
* When asked to comment on recent unbiased news items about teens, adults consistently overlooked the positive data (which usually dominated the story) and focused instead on the few negative trends.

The data are clear—and reflect a profound disconnect between the good news about today's teens and the adult misperception of them. Part of this phenomenon is due to the tendency of people to be positive about their own lives and families (and the young people they know personally) while being very negative about the state of America in general (and youth in general).

When asked about their parenting skills, parents give themselves an A or B—but give all other parents a D or F.

This is starting to give way. When you gather parents of today's collegians and teens, from a variety of backgrounds, and ask them to describe their own kids and their kids' classmates and other friends, the picture they draw is very post-X.

On October 21, 2002, students in a theater class at Blue Spring South High School, outside Kansas City, Missouri, were asked to write one sentence that they would like media executives to read. Here is what they wrote:

* *"We are not as dumb as you think we are."*
* *"Don't portray us as really stupid, because we're not."*
* *"The teens in magazines and on TV are wearing inappropriate clothes, which attracts guys in a bad way."*
* *"Little kids shouldn't be allowed to see things."*
* *"We are not always like you make us look."*
* *"I don't think you understand us."*
* *"I would like the image of teens, on TV and in magazines, to not be so harsh."*
* *"Don't take advantage of me."*
* *"Be cleaner."*
* *"You need to start listening to our ideas and what we think would be good for people these days."*
* *"Teenagers are not as desperate for love as you make us look on TV."*
* *"Why do you make it look like something bad always happens to teens?"*
* *"Teenagers are smarter than most adults think."*
* *"You are all wrong."*

First-wave Millennials, born during the early '80s, transformed high schools through the late '90s, and are now doing the same to college campuses. They have brought their new style and attitude to every institution they touch. As they do, they are replacing the circa-'80s image of youthful alienation with a new image of connection—upbeat, engaged, and, especially, technologically advanced.

Thirtysomething creators of "hip" music, film, Web sites, or other entertainment are facing a new dilemma. What they are good at often looks flagrantly "Gen-X" to Millennials, who increasingly feel that their styles, attitudes, and values don't speak to them nearly as well as do their own emerging artists.

In fashion, the term "contemporary" has become an unpopular expression, presumably because it refers to a look Millennials associate with Gen-X. Their preferred styles (and terms, as reported by *The New York* Times) are "classic" and "retro," in other words, modern adaptations of a look that is pre-Gen-X—and is, for that matter, pre-Boom and pre-Silent as well.

Will Millennials bring a "return" of the youth style of any decade? While they are throwbacks to no other time, given their high-tech modernism, their new mindset does embody the sensibilities of another era: the 1930s. Over the next few years, just as the raucous '20s morphed into the smoother "swing" '30s, the edgy youth styles of the '90s will become just a memory.

Millennials are rebelling, as all generations do. In politics, economics, and world affairs, their rebellion is mostly against Boomers in their fifties on up. In the culture, for the most part, their rebellion is against those in their thirties.

This problem has arisen many times before. Yet the flip side of many a generational problem yields clues to its solution. As has happened so many times before, astute writers and performers of the older generation will lend a fresh new voice that connects with the new youth attitude. Frank Sinatra and Rosemary Clooney did that for the Silent, Bob Dylan and Paul Simon did it for Boomers, Madonna and Michael Jackson did it for Gen Xers, and some Gen Xers will surely do it for Millennials. Meanwhile, those who persist in the old styles will increasingly be rejected by the young.

Today's Youth and the Digital IT Revolution

For pop-culture producers, it's not enough to know that this rising generation is new and different, and that Millennials are advantaged—and feel advantaged—in technology to a degree that older generations never were or felt at the same age. Something else must be added: Nowhere do Millennials perceive this advantage more strongly than in their sense of mastery over how technology can be applied to the pop culture. To be familiar with software and broadband and graphics and microprocessors and digital mixers is one thing. But for most youths, the pop culture—buying it, creating it, downloading it, manipulating it, sharing it—is where all the pieces come together at the center of a *whole new lifestyle*.

Many of the smartest Millennials believe that their generation is capable of redefining society's relationship to technology. If they're right, the pop culture is where their generation will start. Some would say it's where their generation is already starting.

Leaders in the entertainment industry need to keep this in mind as they grapple with the challenges of the digital IT revolution. Yes, these challenges are

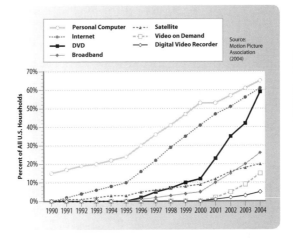

Source: Motion Picture Association (2004)

◀ **Figure 2.1**

Type of Consumer Media Capability as a Share of all Households, 1990–2004

daunting. The industry is indeed undergoing a technological upheaval, the most seismic in at least a century. Industry leaders often assume, however, that getting the new technology right is a very different problem from getting the new generation right. Not so. They are in fact the same problem. Getting one right will automatically mean getting most of the other right as well.

To understand why, let's look at the overall dimensions of this revolution.

Historically, nearly all of the goods and services marketed by the entertainment industry have been *analog*, *media-bound*, and *passive*. This was true with the first communications technologies of the late-nineteenth century. It was true with the boom in motion pictures, radio, and electronics in the 1920s. And it continued to be true through the late 1990s. Each product consisted of analog data that could only be created and enjoyed with highly specialized equipment that was specific to one medium: a vinyl record, a celluloid film, a TV studio signal. Entertainment was passive because there was little the consumer could do with it except sit, watch, and listen. Few major innovations appeared over time, except perhaps the ability to listen to recorded music in your car or to view a movie of your choice at home.

About once a generation, to be sure, the invention of a more convenient new medium sent waves of innovation washing over the entertainment world. Usually, the new winners outnumbered the losers, and most sectors of the industry ended up benefiting by all the new media and devices that consumers had to buy. New markets and new fortunes followed the introduction of LPs, 8-tracks, cassette tapes, VHS tapes, CDs, and DVDs. Consumer retooling around CDs helped buoy the music business during the '90s, and retooling around DVDs has done likewise for the movie business over the last few years.

The entertainment paradigm, however, remained basically unchanged. The producers defined, created, and marketed the pop culture product. The consumers merely bought, watched, listened, and enjoyed.

Today that paradigm is crumbling. The pop culture is entering a new era in which most entertainment services and products will be *digital*, *media-free*, and *interactive*. Whenever the pop culture turns digital (translated into strings of 0's and 1's), it unfastens itself from any particular medium. It can be transmitted through anything, stored anywhere, enjoyed at any time by anybody and with any (or even with no) equipment. Once digital, the pop culture naturally lends itself to interactivity. Anyone can learn how to cut and splice it, alter it, do something new and creative with it, even if they aren't invited to do so by those who originally made it.

The impact of this digital IT technoquake is causing the historical structure of the entertainment industry to shudder and sway. Entire sectors within this structure, each wed to the some until-now changeless medium, face stark choices. Scenarios of enormous gains and total ruin are equally plausible. No one in the business can afford to feel merely comfortable.

Increasingly, every part of the entertainment industry is competing with every other part. This never used to happen. Makers of computers (Dell's flatscreen TV), of software (Microsoft's Xbox 360), and of cell phones (online phone games) now freely compete in the consumer electronics sector, which itself is not afraid to fight back against all comers (Sony's PS3, touted as a

Product Placement & Branded Entertainment

Most older Americans are surprised—and annoyed—to discover a connection between commercial messages and the song or movie or TV show they sponsor. Most Millennials, having grown up in an era in which advertising has fused with entertainment, aren't at all surprised and often find it amusing. They are familiar with a much broader variety of tactics by which media can pay for itself—including the growing practice of "product placement" and "branded entertainment."

Compelled by the digital IT revolution to seek out new revenue sources, the entertainment industry can build on this familiarity in the years to come, but should do so with care.

Thirty years ago, in film and TV shows, cars were merely cars, drinks were drinks, and shoes were shoes. If a product appeared onscreen, that was purely to add color, not profit. That has changed over the past quarter century. What kind of car appears in a high-speed chase is now more of a marketing than a creative decision. Whether filmgoers realize it or not, today's on-screen stories include a barrage of products, services, brands, logos, and slogans, all of which come with a price.

Product placement dates back to the second-stage James Bond films of the 1970s (AMC cars were everywhere in *The Man With The Golden Gun*), but the tactic really didn't catch on and grow until the Millennial childhood era. In 1982, *ET* broke new commercial ground by showcasing Reese's Pieces, pushing that product's sales up by 65 percent. In the 1990s, as product placement spread from films to TV shows, it began to encompass increasingly irreverent pitches in order to get attention. *Home Alone* portrayed John Candy as a villain who drove a Budget Rent-a-Truck. A "Seinfeld" episode featured a Junior Mint candy getting stuck in a tooth cavity. *Wayne's World* turned over-the-top endorsements into a joke (and a profit) for Pizza Hut and Nuprin.

In recent years, the tactic has been the object of a much negative commentary. A line may have been crossed with *Goldeneye* (1995), described by Dale Buss, writing for *Business Week* online, as "one long-running commercial." Two years later, another Bond film, *Tomorrow Never Dies*, featured so many products (Visa, Avis, BMW, Smirnoff, Heineken, Omega, Ericsson, L'Oreal) that a *New York Times* critic complained that "The world's top-secret agent has lent his name to more gadgets than Tiger Woods." In 1998, "The Truman Show" depicted life as a 24-hour reality program funded entirely by product placement. Novelists Douglas Coupland (*Shampoo Planet*) and David Foster Wallace (*Infinite Jest*) wrote darkly satirical novels about a world gone ad-amuck.

Lampooned or not, product placement has today grown into a major fixture of mainstream entertainment. Movie producers now acknowledge that the appeal of a story line to marketers can now determine whether it goes to production. On TV, those "Desperate Housewives" all drive Fords. Those "Sex in the City" women all use Apple computers. Spooked by time-shifting audiences armed with DVRs, TV producers are hungry for any revenue that can replace their traditional advertisers—prompting *Variety* magazine to note that "product placement is like crack cocaine to the networks." In 2004 alone, product placements generated $1.8 billion for the TV networks, an impressive 46 percent gain over the previous year.

When TV shows like "The Apprentice" are structured as unabashed product placements in and of themselves, they begin to enter another territory: "branded entertainment." This refers to artists, films, CDs, TV shows, or magazine issues that are exclusively funded by one commercial sponsor. To underwrite branded entertainment, a sponsor either contracts with an established media company, or it commissions the entertainment all by itself—a rapidly growing trend that has been facilitated by low-cost digital production, editing software, and broadband Web transmission. BMW has produced its own short films. Diesel, Intel, Nike, Sony, and Honda have all hosted short-film contests.

As multi-taskers comfortable with multimedia, Millennials tend to be more comfortable than today's older generations with these multi-messaging media tactics. While they are less responsive than Boomers or Gen Xers to traditional saturation advertising, they are more responsive to "infotainment" and "advertainment" approaches that wrap messages inside other messages—and they are less offended to see commerce overlapping with art. To many Millennials, there is nothing wrong with entertainment that includes cues about how to shop, dress, talk, and act around peers. These cues could consist of product placements—or be part of a broader, thematic approach intended not so much to advertise a specific good as to brand and promote an entire youth lifestyle.

There is good news here for the entertainment industry—with two important caveats. First, message packaging must be expertly and seamlessly executed in order to work. Millennials have no patience for the rude or tacky "come on." Second, the practice of self-commissioning by sponsors could become a major threat to established media companies, unless the latter start competing seriously and creatively in the growing market for "branded entertainment."

"home media hub"). Cable, DSL, cellular, and wireless are all battling each other for the profitable privilege of being the household's premier digital pipeline and programmer. Fox, Time Warner, Viacom, Sprint, SBC, Microsoft, and Verizon all want to be full-service entertainment companies. Entire new daisy chains of predation are emerging, with movie theaters at risk from chain-store DVD rentals, who are at risk from for-sale DVDs, video-on-demand, and online rentals, who are in turn at risk from BitTorrent piracy.

Vast corporations face the threat of overnight irrelevance—consumer electronics companies of becoming just cheap gadget-makers, cable and wire-less companies of becoming just "dumb pipes" and utilities, software companies of getting outmaneuvered by Linux-type open sourcing. Vast sums are spent on campaigns to lobby state and local legislatures, and the U.S. Congress, to outlaw rival technologies (as broadband telecomm companies are now doing against low-cost municipal Wi-Fi).

In many cases, producers of entertainment content aren't even sure who's the ally and who's the enemy. Will Apple's iPod and iTunes help or hurt them in the long run? What about media-player cell phones? Or TV webcasting? Or Internet on home entertainment systems?

Many industry leaders view this as the long-awaited "convergence" between all of the major technology sectors that deliver entertainment—the quarter-trillion dollar consumer electronics sector, the one-trillion dollar computer sector, and the two-trillion dollar communications sector. "Convergence is finally really happening," said Gottfried Dutine, the executive VP at Phillips. "Digitalization is creating products that can't be categorized as tech or consumer electronics. The walls are coming down." Even non-tech sectors will be caught up in the big shake, from music stores and movie theaters to concert promoters and Broadway musicals. "This is going to be the most disruptive period in the past fifty years," declared Hossein Elslambolchi, president of AT&T Laboratories.

The rising generation has a very large stake in all this.

Over the next ten to twenty years, the attitudes, habits, skills, and dreams of the Millennial Generation will exercise a decisive—even overwhelming—influence over determining the winners and losers of this digital IT revolution.

Anyone worried about the technological direction of the entertainment industry has all the more reason to worry, and learn, about Millennials.

Pop-culture content is only part of the issue here. As has been true with every new youth generation, today's young consumers will steer the look and feel of songs and movies. What's unprecedented about Millennials is their influence over pop-culture delivery. The IT revolution plays directly into this generation's greatest strength. The Millennial mastery of applied hi-tech overlaps precisely with that aspect of entertainment that is entering an era of historic flux.

A clear advantage will go to those who understand the new Millennial mindset before it arrives in full force. Imagine how useful it might have been, in preparing for new thematic messages in the pop culture by the year 1975, to have earlier understood young Boomers (big ideals being a lifelong Boomer strength). Imagine how useful it might have been, in tooling up for the new commercial style of artists and studios by the year 1995, to have earlier understood young Gen Xers (free agency being a lifelong Xer strength). Now imagine you need to tool up for the new technological infrastructure of the pop culture by the year 2015. What should you do?

To answer that question, a good place to start is to reflect on three core challenges the IT revolution poses for the entertainment industry. For each, let's look at how Millennials may determine how it is ultimately handled.

New Flexibility in Modes of Pop Culture Delivery

In the pre-digital era, when each type of entertainment was attached to its own medium, delivery was inflexible. This enabled companies to set durable profit centers at each media bottleneck. In the new era, as digital content becomes re-routable and re-programmable through any transmission or display device, delivery is becoming more flexible with each passing year. The old discrete media bottlenecks no longer matter as much. Facing a winner-take-all pressure to either expand or perish, every player must compete on all fronts to stake out a lasting position in the newly "converging" industry.

To figure out which strategy will work best in the Millennial youth era, think "team tech" and reflect on a few of the early winners. Look at the spectacular early success of online music stores, which offer a whole new way to think about music sales. This could have been foreseen several years ago, had anyone noticed the emerging Millennial desire for a portable, customizable, sharable listening experience. Look at the recent explosion of ringtone, ringback, and wallpaper sales for cell phones (now estimated at $4 billion worldwide)—almost entirely driven by young users. This too could have been foreseen, had anyone noticed how much Millennials like to meet and talk and celebrate their gatherings with tech-enhanced social rituals.

Another "team tech" trend now gathering speed is the transforming of the typical game from a solo to a group experience. This too was foreseeable for a generation which began revealing its team orientation in the K-8 schools of the mid-'90s. Back then, when 'tweens really liked a movie, all they could do afterwards was buy a game in which they could take on the bad guy one-on-one. Today, networked games allow them to join with all their friends and build an empire or wage entire battles together. The demand for entertainment as a networked experience (through Internet, LAN, or cell phone) is being pushed by Millennials more than any older generation.

New Difficulty in Capturing the Return on Creative Property

"Piracy," within the domestic U.S. market at least, is a new industry challenge that has been triggered almost entirely by the shift to digital media. Plenty of young Boomers and young Gen Xers tried to copy and share music in their time, but the available methods (usually taping) were so troublesome that they never became a significant threat to the sales of music products. Over the past several years, copying and sharing has become widespread. With the inexorable spread of higher bandwidth, it will soon encompass video as well as audio programming.

This challenge too will be settled on Millennial terms. Industry leaders have tried to preserve the status quo by filing suits, by pushing for new laws, by installing irksome DRM protection software, and by disparaging young people for lack of principles. They may succeed in the occasional courtroom or state house, where older generations have home-field advantage, but Millennial culture sharing is not going to stop. In time, the hunker-down defense is doomed. Like King Canute, industry leaders might as well try standing on the seacoast and ordering the tide to retreat.

To profit from Millennial consumers, industry leaders need to think creatively and redesign their entire way of doing business. They should focus much more on *branding*, *packaging*, *portability*, and *interactivity*. Millennials are a "big brand" generation, more willing than Gen Xers to allow a small number of well-regarded brands to simplify their lives. They are very open to non-traditional packaging concepts, such as tuning in each week to a favorite singer (like a TV serial), rather than waiting each year for one big CD purchase. Because they're so often busy and on-the-move, they want their audio and (soon) video entertainment to be portable. They also like the action-response aspects of anything interactive, which in youth eyes makes them fun. And with Millennials, fun can always compete with free.

Finally, the entertainment industry needs to find new customers. It needs to adopt business models that enable companies to generate revenue through *advertising* (the traditional TV and print media model), *promotion* (using content as come-ons for shows or for other products), and *direct synthesis* with other products (such as video games and cell phones). Among the three, advertising seems the most traditional—yet in the digital age it is the most open to stunning new innovations, such as pinpoint targeting and interactivity. It is also merging with content (for example, as product placement and branded entertainment) in ways that Millennials, more than older generations, are willing to embrace.

While the digital IT revolution may make it harder to sell pop culture directly to consumers as stand-alone products, it makes it easier to sell pop culture as imbedded components of an all-encompassing lifestyle. This new opportunity nicely matches the shift in generational personalities. Where today's Boomers like to stop their daily activities to focus on an authored work of art (a book by a favorite author or a CD by a revered rock group), tomorrow's Millennials may be more inclined to mix daily activities with a branded media experience (blending the talents of various artists).

New erosion of barriers to entry in the entertainment business

In the old days, the only way an artist could deliver a new product to a large market was by lining up a whole series of well-capitalized and professional players—agents, managers, studios, producers, distributors, lawyers, networks, and marketers. These players dominated the choice of artists and together demanded a very large share of the revenues.

In the new era, all this is changing.

If there is a nightmare sci-fi scenario that haunts the sleep of many media CEOs, it is a future in which everyone will possess a cheap but intelligent handheld device that is wirelessly connected to the Internet. This device will be able to scan thousands of artist Web sites, each with its own hi-tech programming, and reproduce any with magnificent audio and holographic video. In such a scenario, every player between the artist and the final consumer becomes superfluous—owning no bottleneck, adding no value, and earning no fee.

The pop culture world is nowhere near that yet, of course, and may never get there. But recent trends are moving in that direction. Cable companies and TV networks are anxious about the spread of IPTV ("Internet Protocol" TV), especially when hooked up to home entertainment centers. Mobile "WiMax" promises, in few years, to put everyone within range of the Internet. Radio networks worry about the growth of Internet "podcasting," even as they transform their own programs (especially news and interview shows) into downloadable podcasts. Turning the new trend around by playing rather than making podcasts, Infinity recently created "the world's first-ever podcasting radio station," entirely programmed by listeners in the San Francisco Bay Area.

The music industry worries about downloadable songs, even when prices are charged, and for good reason. Someday, prominent artists—and countless others trying to gain an audience—may be able to go directly to Apple, AOL, and Microsoft, and push the present-day music industry into irrelevance. The more negatively Millennial consumers view the established recording industry brands, the more likely (and sooner) newcomers like orchard.com will actually make this happen.

Today's youth, meanwhile, are actively promoting this democratization of the pop culture. They love downloads and direct Internet access. They flock to TV programs and Web sites that allow them to choose or "vote" for their favorite performers. Many teens are patching together software that allows them to produce their own songs, movies, or programs. They enjoy sharing their creations or discoveries with each other, and they naturally prefer to do this with few or no commercial intermediaries.

In the long run, it's unlikely that the entertainment industry will be any less substantial, or less profitable, than it now is. By their very nature, pop culture products have to be produced and marketed, and hardly anyone will want to search the virtual globe in their quest for each good song or show. Even so, Millennials are seeking—and will ultimately get—a pop culture that enables talented performers to make themselves known, audiences to get directly involved, and fans to reshape content. In the future, the successful culture creator will think less in terms of polishing a finished artifact and more in terms setting a stage, mingling with the audience, and creating a community.

Current players in the entertainment world can lead these trends, join them, or battle against them. Plenty of money will be made, but not the same way as it is today, and not necessarily by the same people.

Getting to Know the Millennial Generation

Anticipating how a single person will behave, over time, requires a thorough familiarity with that person. The same is true for entire generations. Any forecast about where Millennials are likely to steer the pop culture—for example, how they might push the IT revolution toward interactivity, big branding, and social ritual—must be based on familiarity with Millennials as a generation. Such a forecast should also be informed by historical understanding of how other generations like Millennials have typically matured from childhood into adulthood.

The rest of Part I, accordingly, is devoted to a closer look at these young people and to the telling their story.

At this writing, Millennials stand at a key moment in their life cycle, vis-à-vis the popular culture.

* On November 22, 1963, the first Boomers were turning 20. The Beatles arrived in 1964.
* On January 20, 1981, the first Gen Xers were turning 20. MTV arrived in 1982.
* In 2005, the first Millennials are turning 23.

What's coming? No one can say, exactly—but by the end of this book, a reader may be ready to make a very good guess.

3 | A NEW GENERATION OF AMERICANS

"We like to let people in on a little secret. These kids are less likely to take drugs, less likely to assault somebody else, less likely to get pregnant, and more likely to believe in God."

—Vincent Schiraldi, Justice Policy Institute (2000)

A NEW GENERATION
OF AMERICANS

According to a recent national survey, barely one adult in three thinks that today's kids, once grown, will make the world a better place. To believe the newspapers, you'd suppose our schools are full of kids who can't read in the classroom, shoot one another in the hallways, spend their loose change on tongue rings, and couldn't care less who runs the country. A few years ago, in an otherwise positive campaign by Apple Computer featuring true-to-life adults, a teenage girl was depicted as stoned, clueless, and scarcely able to put two words together. Not surprisingly, she had twenty- and thirtysomething "fan clubs" talking about her "authenticity"—betraying an underlying cynical contempt for the young.

How depressing. And how wrong.

Current youth indicators reveal attitudes and behaviors among today's teens that represent something very new and unfamiliar.

They're optimists. Nine in ten describe themselves as "happy," "confident," and "positive." Teen suicide rates are declining for the first time in the postwar era. A rapidly decreasing share of teenagers worry about violence, sex, or drugs, and an increasing share say that growing up is easier for them than it was for their parents.

They're rule-followers. Over the past ten years, rates of violent crime among teens has fallen by 70 percent, rates of teen pregnancy and abortion by 40 percent, rates of high school sexual activity by 15 percent, and rates of alcohol and tobacco consumption are reaching all-time lows. As public attention to school shootings has risen, their actual incidence has fallen. Even including such shootings as Columbine, there have been fewer than half as many killings of students by students on school property since 2000 (averaging around 10 per year) as there were in the early '90s (over 40 killings per year).

They're gravitating toward group activity. Twenty years ago, community service was rare in most high schools. Today, it is the norm, having more than tripled since 1984, according to the U.S. Department of Education. A 1999 Roper survey found that more teenagers blamed "selfishness" than anything else when asked about "the major cause of problems in this country."

They trust and accept authority. Most teens say they identify with their parents' values, and more than nine in ten say they "trust" and "feel close to" their parents. A recent survey found 82 percent of teens reporting "no problems" with any family member—versus just 48 percent who said that back in 1974, when parents and teens were far more likely to argue and oppose one another's basic values. Half say they trust government to do what's right all or most of the time—twice the share of older people answering the same question in the same poll. Large majorities of teens favor tougher rules against misbehavior in the classroom and society at large.

They're the most watched-over generation in memory. The typical day of many a

Figure 3.1 ▶

Suicide Rates for Youth, Aged 15–19 and 20–24, 1970 to 2002

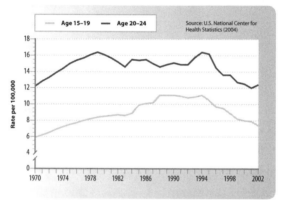

Figure 3.2 ▶

Serious Violent Crime, Rate of Offenders and Victims Aged 12–17, 1980 to 2003

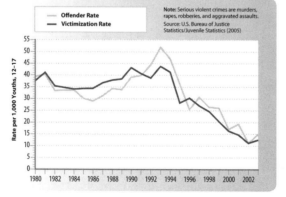

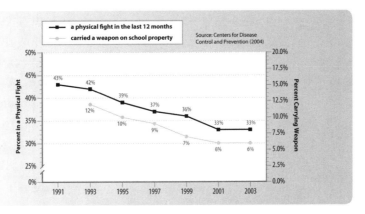

◀ **Figure 3.3**

Share of High School
Students from
1991 to 2003 Who
Report Having...

child, tween, or teen has become a nonstop round of parents, relatives, teachers, coaches, babysitters, counselors, chaperones, minivans, surveillance cams, and curfews. Whether affluent or not, kids have become more closely managed. Since the mid-'80s, "unstructured activity" has been the most rapidly *declining* use of time among pre-teens.

They're smart. Since the late '80s, grade school aptitude test scores have been rising or (at least) flat across all subjects and all racial and ethnic groups. The number of high school students who take and pass an Advanced Placement test has more than doubled in the past ten years. Fully 73 percent

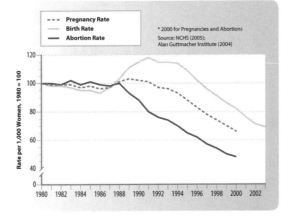

◀ **Figure 3.4**

Rates of Pregnancy,
Abortion, and Birth for
Girls Aged 15–17,
1980 to 2003*

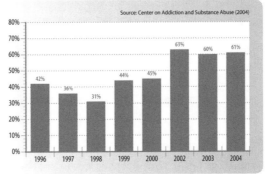

◀ **Figure 3.5**

Percent of Teens
Reporting That They
Attend "Drug-Free
Schools," 1996 to 2004

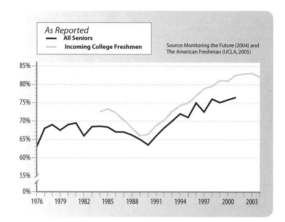

Figure 3.6 ▶

Share of High School
Seniors Who
Volunteer:
from 1976 to 2004

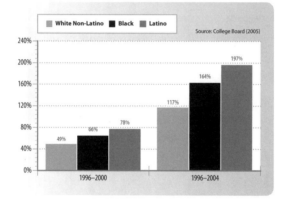

Figure 3.7 ▶

Number of AP Exams
with Grade of 3, 4, or
5, in all U.S. Public
Schools: % Increase
Since 1996

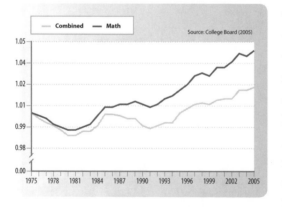

Figure 3.8 ▶

SAT Scores of College-
Bound Seniors,
1975–2005
(1975=100)

of high school students today say they want a four-year college degree. A growing share is taking the SAT. Even so, the average SAT score is the highest in 30 years. Eight in ten teenagers now say it's "cool to be smart."

Not all Millennials reveal these traits, of course. Every generation has all kinds of people, but so too does every generation have core traits that drive new trends and construct a new overall persona.

These Millennial traits reflect the fact that this generation was, from the start, more wanted than the one that came before. Born in an era when Americans showed a more positive attitude toward children, the Millennials are the product of a birthrate reversal. During the Gen Xer childhood, planned parenting meant contraceptives. During the Millennial childhood, it has meant visits to the fertility clinic. In 1998, the number of U.S. children surged past its previous Baby-Boom peak. Over the next decade, college freshmen enrollment is due to grow by roughly 40,000 per year.

Once you appreciate how Millennials have been regarded as special since birth and have been more obsessed-over at every age than Gen Xers, recent adult trends come into sharper focus. Falling divorce and abortion rates begin to make sense. You can understand why harms against children (from child abuse and high school gunfire to bloody video games and child kidnappings) are far less tolerable today than twenty years ago. You can clue in to why nearly every political issue of the '90s was recast as what newsweeklies call "kinderpolitics," as in: If it's good for children, do it—and if it isn't, don't. Year by year, for officeholders in both parties and at all levels, America's kids became not just a political trump card, but something like public property.

The Millennial Location in History

One way to define a generation's location in history is to think of a turning point in the national memory that its earliest birth cohorts just missed. Boomers, for example, are the generation whose eldest members have no memory of VJ Day. Gen Xers are the generation whose eldest members have no memory of John Kennedy's assassination. Millennials are the generation whose eldest members have no memory of sitting in school watching the space shuttle *Challenger* disintegrate.

Let's trace the historical location of each of the generations described earlier.

The Silent (born, 1925 to 1942) arrived during the Great Depression and World War II, events they witnessed through the eyes of childhood, tending their Victory Gardens, while the next-older G.I. generation built and sailed in the Victory Ships that won the war.

Boomers (born, 1943 to 1960) arrived during the "Great American High" that followed the war, a childhood era of warmth and indulgence that marked them forever as a "postwar" generation, while the next-older Silent compliantly entered the suburban and corporate world.

Gen Xers (born, 1961 to 1981) arrived during the "Consciousness Revolution," amid the cultural, societal, and familial turbulence of the Boomers' young adulthood.

Millennials (born, 1982 and after) arrived during the recent era of the "Culture Wars," while Gen Xers embarked on their young-adult dot-com entrepreneurialism.

America could now be entering a new post-9/11 era. How the "War on Terror" will affect Millennials over time, as they become young adults, is a matter of speculation. So far, the mood is reinforcing several Millennial traits and desires that were already apparent—including their orientation toward personal safety, family closeness, community action, applied high-tech, and long-term planning.

Millennials live in a world that has taken trends Boomers recall from their childhood and turned them upside down. Boomers can recall growing up with a homogenizing popular culture and a wide gender-role gap in an era when community came first and family stability was strong (though starting to weaken). Millennials have grown up with a fragmenting pop culture and a narrow gender-role gap in an era when individuals came first and when family stability was weak (though starting to strengthen).

As a postwar generation, Boomers arrived just when uniting, conforming, and building communities seemed the nation's logical priority. As a post-awakening generation, Millennials began to arrive just when diverging, liberating, and building strong lives as individuals seemed preferable. Such reversals reflect a fundamental difference in the two generations' location in history.

Millennials also represent a sharp break from Generation X. Gen Xers can recall growing up as children during the '60s and '70s, one of the most passionate eras of social dissent and cultural upheaval in American history, an era in which the needs of children were often overlooked or discounted. All this has left a deep impression on most of today's young Gen-X adults.

But Millennials can recall none of it. They have no personal memory of the ordered Cold War world (when only large and powerful governments had weapons of mass destruction). They only know about a post-Cold War era of multilateral confusion and power vacuums (when terrorists and rogue states are seeking these weapons). This generation has been shaped by such formative collective experiences as Waco, Oklahoma City, Columbine, the World Trade Center, and now 9/11 and the War on Terror. In all these instances, the real danger seems to come not from out-of-control institutions, but from out-of-control individuals, or small groups of conspirators, who have become a menace to humanity because national or global institutions are not strong enough to control or even monitor them.

For young Boomers, untethered individuals were the solution. For Millennials, they are more likely to be the problem.

How Boomers and Gen Xers have responded to their own location in history is a story that is mostly written, a story replete with ironies and paradoxes. How Millennials will respond to theirs is a drama waiting to unfold. Yet if you know what to look for and why, certain themes in this drama can be anticipated, and their implications pondered.

How Millennials Will "Rebel"

Over one hundred and fifty years ago, Alexis de Tocqueville observed that in America "each new generation is a new people." The question arises: Does some pattern or dynamic determine how each generation will be new?

Yes.

Three basic rules apply to any rising generation in nontraditional societies, like America, that allow young people some freedom to redefine what it means to be young, and to prod older people to change social mores—in other words, to "rebel."

* First, each rising generation *breaks with the styles and attitudes* of the young-adult generation, which no longer functions well in the new era.

* Second, each rising generation *corrects for what it perceives as the excesses* of the current midlife generation—their parents and leaders—sometimes as a protest, other times with the implicit support of parents and leaders who seek to correct the deficiencies of the adult world.

* Third, each rising generation *fills the social role* being vacated by the departing elder generation, a role that now feels fresh, functional, desirable, even necessary for a society's well-being. Through the living mem-

ory of everyone else, this dying generation has filled a social role so firmly as to prevent others from claiming it. Now, with its passing, it's available again to the young.

When you apply these rules to the generational dynamic in America, you can see what's been happening, and will continue to happen even more powerfully, with Millennials.

Millennials will rebel against Gen-X styles and attitudes, correct for Boomer excesses, and fill the role vacated by the G.I.s.

Stylistically, today's teens are breaking with today's thirtyish Gen Xers and the whole "X" (and "X-treme") attitude. Expect teamwork instead of free agents, political action instead of apathy, technology to elevate the community and not the individual, on-your-side teamwork in place of in-your-face sass.

Gen Xers in their late twenties and thirties often regard themselves as the trend-setters of the teen culture, but often they know little about what actually goes on there. After all, they haven't seen the inside of a high school in many years. So they fall out of touch and, in time, a new batch of teenagers breaks with their culture. This happened in the early '60s, again in the early '80s, and it's starting to happen again.

Meanwhile, Millennials will correct for what teens see as the excesses of today's middle-aged Boomers: narcissism, impatience, iconoclasm, and a constant focus on talk (usually argument) over action. In their "rebellion," Millennials will opt for the good of the group, patience, conformism, and a new focus on deeds over words. When they argue among themselves, they will value finding consensus more than being right. When they argue with older generations, they will try to persuade by showing how more than by explaining why. With adults of all philosophical stripes yearning for "community," the Millennial solution will be to set high standards, get organized, team up, and actually create a community. Unlike Boomers, Millennials won't bother spending three days at a retreat to figure out how to rewrite a mission statement.

The third rule of rebellion may be the key to understanding not just what Millennials are now doing, but where they see their clearest path in the years ahead.

Remember those whom Tom Brokaw christened the "greatest generation"—the ones who pulled America out of Depression, joined unions, conquered half the globe as soldiers, unleashed nuclear power, founded suburbia, and took mankind to the moon. The most important link this "G.I. Generation" has to today's teens is in the void they leave behind: No other adult peer group possesses anything close to their upbeat, high-achieving, team-playing, and civic-minded reputation. Sensing this social role unfilled, today's adults have been teaching these (G.I.) values to Millennials, who now sense the G.I. "archetype" as the only available script for correcting or complementing the Boomer persona.

In his 2001 *Atlantic Monthly* cover story, David Brooks gave the label "Organization Kids" to these Millennials, a tacit reference to the original G.I. "Organization Man" and about as far as you can get from the "Bourgeois Bohemians" (or "Bobos") Brooks finds so common among today's middle-aged. Today's Millennial teens often identify the G.I.s as their grandparents. When asked in surveys to assess the reputations of older generations, Millennials now in college say they have a much higher opinion of G.I.s and a somewhat lower one of "Generation X" than they do of either generation in-between—Boomers (the children of the postwar American High) or the Silent (the children of World War II). Many speak glowingly about G.I.s as men and women who "did great things" and "brought us together as a nation."

Today's teens don't rebel against midlife Boomers by being hyper-Xers—not when the oldest Xers are themselves entering their mid-40s. They rebel by being G.I. redux, a youthful update of the generation against which the Boomers fought 30 years ago. No one under the age of 70 has any direct memory of teens, or twentysomethings, who are G.I. in spirit. Millennials are, and will be. That's why what's around the cultural corner is so profound that it might better be called a youth revolution. Rebellions peter out—but revolutions produce long-term social change.

Millennial Origins

Recall the last twenty years of American childhood. If you're a Boomer, this era may seem like only yesterday, because you may recall it as a parent. If you're a Gen Xer, in all likelihood, you will know this era through a cloudier prism, since you were neither a child nor were raising children yourself.

The February 22, 1982, issue of *Time* published a cover story about an array of thirtysomething Boomers choosing (finally) to become moms and dads. This same year, bright yellow "Baby on Board" signs began popping up on the windows of minivans, a new-fangled "family oriented" vehicle.

In the 1983 holiday season, adult America fell in love with Cabbage Patch Kids—a precious new doll, harvested pure from nature, so wrinkly and cuddly-cute that millions of Boomers wanted to take one home to love. Better yet, why not produce your own genuine, live Millennial?

After twenty years of wanting more distance between themselves and their children, new parents now wanted closeness. From 1974 to 1990, the share of fathers present at the birth of their children rose from 27 to 80 percent—an historic shift helped along by hundreds of Lamaze teachers. By 1990, the "attachment parenting" childrearing style of William and Martha Sears became the vogue.

The *era of the wanted child* had begun.

In September 1982, the first Tylenol scare led to parental panic over trick-or-treating. Halloween suddenly became a night not merely of celebrating silly scary things, but also of hotlines, advisories, and statutes—a fate that soon befell many other once-innocent child pastimes, from bicycle-riding to BB guns.

A few months later came national hysteria over the sexual abuse of toddlers, leading to dozens of adult convictions after what skeptics liken to Salem-style trials.

All the while, several influential new books (The Disappearance of Childhood, Children Without Childhood, Our Endangered Children) assailed the "anything goes" parental treatment of children since the mid-'60s. Those days were ending. The family, school, and neighborhood wagons were circling.

The *era of the protected child* had begun.

In the early '80s, the national rates for many behaviors damaging to children—divorce, abortion, violent crime, alcohol-intake, and drug-abuse—reached their postwar high-water mark. The well-being of children began to dominate the national debate over most family issues: welfare, latchkey households, drugs, pornography.

In 1983, the federal *Nation at Risk* report on education blasted America's K-12 students as "a rising tide of mediocrity," prompting editorialists to implore teachers and adults to do better by the next batch of kids.

In 1984, *Children of the Corn* and *Firestarter* bombed at the box office. These were merely the latest installments in a child-horror film genre that had been popular and profitable for well over a decade, ever since *Rosemary's Baby* and *The Exorcist*. But parents suddenly didn't want to see them. Instead, they begin flocking to a new kind of movie (*Baby Boom, Parenthood, Three Men and a Baby*) about adorable babies, wonderful tykes, and adults who would themselves become better people by choosing to look after them.

The *era of the worthy child* had begun.

In 1990, the *Wall Street Journal* headline—"The '60s Generation, Once High on Drugs, Warns Its Children"—was echoed by The New York Times: "Do As I Say, Not As I Did." Polls showed that Boomer parents did not want their own children to have the same freedom with drugs, alcohol, and sex that they themselves had once enjoyed.

By the early '90s, elementary-school kids were in the spotlight. During the Gulf War Super Bowl of 1991, children marched onto the field at halftime amid heavy media coverage (unseen during the Vietnam War) of the children of dads serving abroad.

Between 1986 and '91, the number of periodicals offered to young children doubled, and between 1991 and '94, the sale of children's music also doubled. In tot-TV fare, "Barney and Friends" (featuring teamwork and what kids have in common) stole the limelight from "Sesame Street" (featuring individualism and what makes each kid unique).

During 1996, major-party nominees Dole and Clinton dueled for the presidency amid much talk about "soccer moms" and the safety of young teens (smoking, curfews, limitations on first-time drivers licenses).

During 1997, Millennials began to make an impression on the pop culture. Thanks to the Spice Girls, Hanson, and others, a whole new musical sound appeared—happier, brighter, more innocent. "They like brands with heritage. Contrived, hard-edged fashion is dead. Attitude is over," MTV president Judy McGrath said of her company's new teen interns." They like what's nice and fun in fashion and sports. They like the Baby Gap ads. They're simple and sweet."

The *era of the perfected child* had begun.

Actually, those MTV interns were late Xers, born a little before 1980. But the big change—the revolution in youth—is coming from those 1982-86 birth cohorts. Other key trends await the Millennials' second wave, born later in the '80s. Test scores, though improving gradually for first-wavers, are likely to ramp up steeply once today's heavily homeworked, super-tested 'tweens enter high school. By the time the preteens of 2001 reach college age, and campuses are a hotbed of Millennial styles, the true Millennial persona will reveal itself in full force.

Boomers started out as the objects of loosening child standards in an era of conformist adults. Millennials have started out as the objects of tightening child standards in an era of nonconformist adults. By the time the last Millennials come of age, they could become the best-educated youths in American history, and the best-behaved young adults in living memory. But they may also have a tendency toward copying, consensus, and conformity that educators will want to challenge, as well as many other new personality traits that will require broad changes in the world of higher education.

Through the late '90s, these same much-watched children passed through high school, accompanied by enormous parental, educational, and media fascination—and headlines, not all of them positive. After the April 1999 Columbine tragedy was replayed again and again on the news, this adult absorption with Millennial safety, achievement, and morality reached a fever pitch. Eighteen months after Columbine, these wanted, protected, worthy, perfected children began entering college.

Twenty years ago, the arrival of Generation X on campus took many institutions of higher learning by surprise. Professors and administrators began noticing that incoming students were less interested in the protest movements that had driven college life throughout the '60s and '70s.

The Gen-X attitude toward knowledge was more instrumental. In history classes, students were less likely to ask about which wars were moral than about how you win one. The most highly motivated students gathered in professional schools, where the object was less to change the world than to enable grads to make a lot of money. A good student was one who could get the best transcript with least possible expenditure of effort—a bottom-line focus which Gen Xers maintained as entry-level workers in the late '80s and '90s, with wondrous consequences for the economy's productivity.

Institutions of higher learning had to adjust to fit this style of student. *In loco parentis*, already under assault during the '60s and '70s, virtually disappeared. Pass/fail grading options became available for many if not most classes, and core curricula requirements relaxed. Widespread use of drug and alcohol forced colleges and universities to build new relationships with local police. Speech codes were enacted to counter uncivil discourse. Large, school-wide events became less common, as cynicism about school spirit and campus community spread. Students took longer to earn their degrees.

College clientele changed as well. More foreign, older, and "continuing education" students were enrolled. To meet shifting demand driven by changing economic conditions, business and law schools expanded, while science and engineering departments were increasingly the province of international students.

Now, with the arrival of the Millennials, campus life is undergoing another transformation. Policies needed to accommodate or manage college students in the '80s and '90s have become inappropriate. Instead, in the current decade, college administrators have been adjusting their institutions to a new crop of students who are:

* Close to their parents.
* Focused on grades and performance.
* Busy with extracurricular activities.
* Eager to volunteer for community service.
* Talented in technology.
* More interested in math and science, relative to the humanities.
* Insistent on a secure, regulated environment.
* Respectful of norms and institutions.
* Ethnically diverse, but less interested in questions of racial identity.
* Majority female, but less interested in questions of gender identity.

They also are very numerous and very intent on going to college, which are making these trends all the more consequential.

In the fall of 2004, the first Millennials entered law schools, medical schools, and others post-graduate programs. As they flood into the highest student reaches of academe, every aspect of university life is revealing a new young-adult mindset.

4 | THE NEW TEEN MARKET

"It's great! Nobody is plain white, or plain black, or plain anything. Eventually I'm hoping every place will be like this."

— Liz Short, teenager at a mixed-race symposium at Wellesley College (2000)

THE NEW TEEN MARKET

The teen market is not what it used to be, even when measured purely by the numbers. To demographers and economists, each new generation brings with it a new batch of data trend lines. One good test of whether we can draw an accurate qualitative profile of a generation is whether this profile matches the quantitative data. Let's take a new look at Millennials by the numbers: their size, their diversity, the dollars they spend, and the hours they work.

The Millennial Bulge

The best-known single fact about the Millennial Generation is that it's large. Already, America has well over 80 million Millennials. By the time future immigrants join their U.S.-born peers, this generation will probably top 100 million members, making it nearly a third bigger than the Boomers. In native births per birth year (expected to average 3.9 million), Millennials will tower over Gen Xers, Boomers, and every earlier generation in America.

Some demographers refer to Millennials as America's "Baby Boomlet" or "Echo Boom." In two key ways, these terms are misleading. First, the 1990s-born Millennials—the larger half of the generation—are primarily the children of Gen Xers, not Boomers. And, second, these terms imply that the large number of Millennials is mainly a matter of arithmetic, as though a "baby boomlet" mechanically had to issue from a "baby boom" of parents. Yes, that happened, but the echo effect accounts for only a small part of the rise. Most of the boomlet reflects higher fertility—the greater likelihood by the mid-'80s over the mid-'70s that the typical woman of childbearing age will have a baby. For the most part, what gave rise to the large number of Millennials was the desire of their parents to bear and raise more of them.

The larger-than-expected size of this generation resulted from the early-'80s shift in adult attitudes toward children that greeted their first-born members. The arrival of Generation X in the early '60s coincided with an era of decline in the U.S. fertility rate and a society-wide aversion to children. And so it remained for the following 20 years, as small children seldom received positive media coverage, and adults complained to pollsters about how family duties hindered their self-discovery. Children became linked to new adjectives: unwanted, at-risk, throwaway, homeless, latchkey.

By 1975, when annual births had plunged to barely three million—versus over four million in the late '50s—newspapers talked about Gen Xers as America's new "Baby Bust" generation. Baby-goods companies, like Gerber Products, were hit hard. Starting in 1977, annual births tilted back up again, slowly at first, and the baby industry began bouncing back. By the early '80s, Gerber (and others) were rescued by a floodtide of new babies, who also brought good cheer to the manufacturers of cribs, strollers, rockers, safety seats, PJs, dolls, safety gadgets, and toddler books and videos.

Figure 4.1 ▶

Total U.S. Births, in Millions, 1950 to 2003

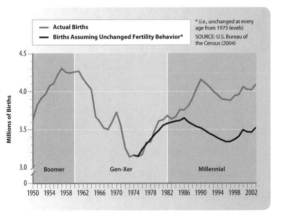

Most experts at the time contended that the late-'70s birth surge would be short-lived, but they were in for a surprise. After leveling off at about 3.6 million during 1980–83, the national birth rate did not drift back down. Instead, it rose-to 3.8 million in 1987, 4.0 million in 1989, and 4.2 million in 1990. In many regions, hospitals delivery rooms became overcrowded and pediatricians hard to find. During the '90s, the annual number of births again drifted below the 4.0 million benchmark, until 2000 produced another surge in the fertility of young (this time, Gen-X) women. Overall, Millennial births have been roughly 20 percent higher than if the fertility of women at each age had remained steady at mid-'70s rates.

During the '60s and '70s, the era of Gen-X babies, adults went to great efforts not to produce children, driving up demand for contraceptive technologies and for sterilization and abortion clinics. By contrast, during the Millennial baby era, adults have gone to great efforts to conceive and adopt babies. Sterilization rates, which rose sharply in the '60s and '70s, plateaued in the middle '80s and have since fallen. The annual abortion rate, after ramping up during the Gen-X baby era, hit a peak in 1980 and declined sharply through the '90s. Meanwhile, the share of all births declared to be "unwanted" by their mothers has also declined—with an especially sharp drop in unwantedness by African-American mothers.

What's important about the "baby boomlet" is how sustained it became, and how it reflected a resurgent adult desire to have kids. As a share of the population, America actually had more grade-school children during the tail-end years of the postwar "baby boom" than it does today. But back when those last Boomers were in elementary school, around 1970, the number of schoolchildren was trending downward—and steadily fewer adults wanted to give birth to them, make films or TV shows for them, or pay much public attention to them.

Keep an eye on this Millennial bulge, the 25 million Americans born between 1987 and 1992, who are now mainly in high school. As they move up the age ladder, they will lend mass to new movements launched by the older (but slightly smaller) cutting edge of this generation.

Keep special watch on those born in 1990, the peak of the Millennial birth bulge. They were first-graders in 1997, the "tweens" in 2002, the high school class of '08, and the college class of '12. They also mark the approximate midpoint of this generation, the divide between the mostly Boomer-parented '80s cohorts and the mostly Gen-X-parented '90s cohorts. By the time they enter college and assert themselves as full-scale pop culture consumers with less parental input, the impact of Millennial consumers on the pop culture mindset will be very clear.

Colors of the World

Millennials are the most racially and ethnically diverse, and least Caucasian, generation in U.S. history. As of 2004, non-whites and Latinos accounted for 40.3 percent of the 22-or-under population, a share half-again larger than for the Boomer age brackets, and more than three times larger than for today's seniors.

Ethnically, what differentiates Millennials from what Boomers recall of their own college years is the much vaster range of global diversity. The issue of color can no longer be defined in clear black-white (or even black-white-Latino) terms. A class full of Millennial collegians, even when one looks just at Americans, can include young women and men whose ancestors come from nearly every society on earth, including regions (Central and South America, sub-Saharan Africa, the Arab crescent, South Asia) that were far less represented on the campuses of the '60s.

Figure 4.2 ▶

Nonwhite Race and Hispanic Ethnicity, by Generation, in 2004

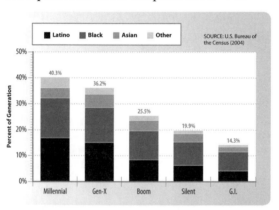

Figure 4.3 ▶

Interracial Dating?

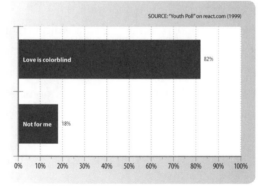

To this point, Millennials are less often immigrants themselves than the children of immigrants. In 2003, just under 5 percent of Millennials were immigrants themselves, versus 17 percent of Gen Xers and 12 of Boomers. Yet one Millennial in five has at least one immigrant parent, and one in ten has at least one non-citizen parent. Containing more second-generation immigrants than any earlier twenty-year cohort

Generations of Hip Hop

For Millennials, hip hop is a dominant pop culture presence. "Rap/urban" has become the biggest-selling CD genre—and the hottest source of underground "mixtape" releases. Hip hop themes are appearing in a growing variety top-selling movies, from Eminem's *8 Mile* to Ice Cube's funny and family-friendly *Are We There Yet*. In "Grand Theft Auto," it has inspired the new millennium's best-selling video game. As the look and feel of hip hop has spread to white, Latino, and Asian celebrities, its influence has extended to sporting events, radio and TV shows, and even ads for the most mainstream products. General Motors has sponsored a "King of Bling" contest for their Hummers and Cadillac Escalades. Ads for Formula 50 vitamin water have shown 50 Cent reading *The Wall Street Journal*.

Yet even as Millennials participate in the new pop-culture triumphs of hip hop, they do so as an inheritor generation and not (as Gen X was) the generation that was present at its creation. As such, they will revise hip hop, play with it, satirize it, invert it—and, in the end, change it. As they begin retooling hip hop for Millennial consumers, Gen-X performers are shifting away from the lone-wolf toughness and brutality so popular in the mid-90s. Instead, they are moving toward such witty lampoons as Austin Powers in *Goldmember*, slapstick humor, and new themes like community, success, and self improvement. Today's rapper is about "gettin' my executive on" and "makin' it right." As hip hop's fan base shifts from Gen-X fans to a new round of Millennial fans, the underlying focus is transforming from what-I-want-now to what-we've-got-now.

The rise of hip hop parallels the rise of rock 'n roll—except that it arrived one full generation (a little over two decades) later.

Rock 'n roll originated in the 1950s with Silent Generation performers (Bill Haley, Elvis Presley, Little Richard), was popularized around 1960 by legendary Silent promoters like Motown's Berry Gordy, Jr., and grew explosively in the '60s, fueled by a new Boomer generation of teens. Hip hop originated in the 1970s with Boomer performers ("old school" MCs like Kool Herc, Grandmaster Flash, Sugarhill Gang), was popularized around 1980 by legendary Boomer promoters like Def Jam's Russell Simmons, and grew explosively in the '80s, fueled by a new generation of Gen-X teens.

The parallel continues for the triumph of both genres. In the late 1960s, as Boomer performers (Jim Morrison, Pete Townshend, Neil Young, Janis Joplin) took over, rock 'n roll became the pop culture's hottest item. In the early '70s, it was still controversial, but a decade later—when the Beach Boys starred at a Fourth of July concert on the National Mall in Washington, D.C.—rock 'n roll had become part of the establishment. In the late 1980s, as Gen-X per-formers (Dr. Dre, Ice Cube, LL Cool J, Mike D) took over, hip hop became the pop culture's hottest item. By the early '90s, it remained controversial, but a decade later—when McDonalds (alias "Micky D's") introduced rap and break dancing themes into its national advertising—hip hop had become part of the establishment.

The obvious contrast between the sound and feel of the two genres reflects the difference in generational origins: Boomer versus Gen-X. While rock 'n roll originated as a passionate, idealistic, and playful sound, hip hop projected a pragmatic, cynical, and "all business" attitude. Rock 'n roll celebrated a new feminism, while hip hop vaunted a new masculinism. Rock 'n roll often idealized rural community settings and drew inspiration from racial crossover in the South and Midwest, while hip hop idealized urban commercial settings and drew inspiration from all-black areas in New York ("New Jack City") or Los Angeles ("Straight Outta Compton").

Like rock 'n roll, hip hop has told a decade-by-decade story of generational change among stars and fans. During most of the 1970s, when it was performed by Boomers for Boomers, hip hop remained an informal and largely unprofitable "street fad"—with a huge emphasis on spontaneity and ethnic authenticity. In the 1980s, as Platinum "rap" albums began making real money selling to Gen-X youth, the genre began pushing the edge on violence, sex, and drugs. That's when it acquired its trademark hedonism and harshness. Late in that same decade, Boomer performers like Ice T and Public Enemy's Chuck D (along with some first-wave Gen Xers like Dr. Dre) harnessed hip hop to a critique of white racism and calls for a new-style black assertion. Hip hop had become a national "wedge" issue.

In the early '90s, a new and younger batch of Gen-X performers emerged who would eclipse the remaining Boomers, dominate the rest of the decade, and take hip hop to unprecedented levels of notoriety and, ultimately, acceptance. All were born between 1968 and 1972—including MC Ren, Ice Cube, Queen Latifah, Jay-Z, Tupac Shakur, Snoop Dogg, P. Diddy, Notorious B.I.G., Eminem, Missy Elliott—and thus came of age at the height of the violent urban crime wave of the early '90s. In their first hit CDs, many glamorized "gangsta rap" and pushed the hip hop lifestyle to outrageous extremes of brutality and cynicism. Several (most famously, Tupac and B.I.G.) perished in shootouts.

The tone started changing in the late '90s, with the rapid decline in urban crime and the arrival a new generation of Millennial fans. The most popular hip hop artists began blunting their edges, lightening their messages, accepting their prestige, and taking pride in—even boasting of—their success and affluence.

Since 2000, a gradually aging galaxy of rap artists has been performing to virtually all-Millennial youth audiences. Later-wave Gen-X performers (born in 1973 to 1981, including 50 Cent, Nas, Ja Rule, Ludacris, Kanye West, Mase, The Game) are just now emerging from the shadow of their fabled "elders," who are now in their mid-30s.

Regardless of the age or generation of the performers, hip hop is changing during the Millennial youth era in a direction sometimes chided as "hip pop" or "pop rap." While rappers like Nelly or Lil' Kim remind listeners that the genre clearly remains on the dangerous side of the Millennial experience, down and dirty is no longer cutting edge. In theme, the new style is more open to humor, to manners, to commitment, to religion, and to success. In sound, it has a denser and more digitally overdubbed "produced" feel. Background melodies are returning. The mood is often playful. Often, today's rap is hard to distinguish from rhythm and blues.

The Millennial impact on hip hop has just begun. Today, Millennial fans are making their mark. By the 2010s, Millennial performers will do so. Come the 2020s, Millennial performers of hip hop (or whatever it will then be called) will develop a new style for a new young generation. This genre is a work in progress, its full story yet to be told.

group in U.S. history, Millennials embody the "browning" of American civilization. Thanks to the Cold War's end, satellite news, porous national borders, and the Internet, they are also becoming the world's first generation to grow up thinking of itself, from childhood forward, as global.

Indeed, American (and Canadian) students mark the leading edge of a new worldwide generation. Since World War II, the leading edges of new European generations have arrived roughly five years or so after those in America. Euro-teens still resemble Gen-X more than their American counterparts, but some observers in Europe and Asia are describing the emergence of a Millennial-style shift among young teens. In Germany, these new kids have been called the *Null Zoff* ("no problem") generation—in Sweden, *Generation Ordning* ("ordered generation").

As always, America is expected to play a large role in determining how this rising generation is perceived around the world, just as it did with global Generation X. As Lee Siew Hua observes in the Malaysian *Straits Times*, "The Millennial Generation will in time produce a mightier imprint on American life and decency standards, and possibly globally, as long as the United States exports trends."

Although generational patterns vary somewhat around the world, given each country's own particular history and culture, it is likely that most of today's 20-year-old foreign students may in fact be part of a different generation than 20-year-old American students. But that will probably not be true five years from now, and certainly not ten years from now. The lagged age-location of Gen Xers abroad has been helping the explosive recent growth MTV Networks' viewership in Europe and Asia, where the irreverent, apolitical, and cosmopolitan style that is MTV's trademark still has huge appeal. Down the road, as Millennials entirely replace Xers abroad in the target youth market, MTV Networks will face the same kinds of questions America-based media are asking today.

In many respects, urban non-white youths—especially African-Americans—are bigger contributors to this generation's emerging persona than white youths. Ask yourself these questions: Which kids are most likely to be wearing school uniforms? Urban non-whites. Whose schools are moving fastest on back-to-basics drilling and achievement standards? Urban non-whites. Whose neighborhoods are producing the swiftest percentage decline in rates of teen crime, teen pregnancy, child poverty, and school violence? Urban non-whites.

Dating back to Emancipation, African-Americans have long been an out-sized cultural contributor to generational currents. In recent decades, we have seen this in civil rights (Silent), black power (Boomers), and hip-hop (Gen Xers). That contribution continues, albeit in new forms, with today's urban schoolchildren, who are far more likely than suburbanites to wear standard-issue clothing, learn by rote, and jointly shout upbeat slogans like "I'm going to succeed!" in the classroom.

Millennials are the first American generation in which Latinos outnumber African-Americans. With over half having at least one immigrant parent, many young Latinos face a future full of hard challenges. One-third live in poverty, in substandard housing, and without health insurance. The share of Latinos in grades 10–12 who drop out each year (9 percent) is much higher than for non-Latinos (5 percent). Problems are particularly acute for Latino boys, who have lower expectations for the future than their female counterparts.

Latinos and Asians are making their mark on the core of the Millennial persona. Asian teens in particular are also a rapidly growing presence. With parents even more attached to "family values" than the white adult majority, both the Latino and Asian youth cultures are setting a distinctly Millennial tone—positive, team-playing, and friendly—in schools and neighborhoods from Seattle to Boston, Miami to San Diego. Latino pop icons provide a distinctly Millennial feel with upbeat lyrics, colorful clothes, dancing in couples, and close family ties. Likewise, the Asian and mixed-race pop vocalists tend to present songs with affirming messages.

If there is one part of this generation that is lagging somewhat behind many of the new Millennials trends, it is the largely Caucasian youths in rural and small-town America. In recent years, rural youths have shown the *least* decline or even a rise in the use of alcohol, cigarettes, marijuana, and many harder drugs (like methamphetamine). Their cultural tastes may also lag behind their peers elsewhere, to whom they may look for signals.

The unprecedented ethnic diversity and mixed-race aspect of this generation, combined with the fact that they are precursors of new generations elsewhere in the world, makes them globally powerful.

Teens as a Target Market

Much of the interest in Millennials, as a generation, has been commercial—how to make them watch an ad, how to make them buy, how to use them to make their parents buy. Driving this interest is in part their sheer numbers and the overall affluence of the '90s—but also in part a sudden awareness, among teen marketers, that generations matter. In the early '90s, marketers awoke to the realization that they had never fully targeted Gen X, and they were determined not to let this mistake recur with the next batch of teens.

Today, a lot more cash is being spent on young people than ever before, as anyone who has recently visited a typical teen bedroom can attest. Purchases by and for children age 4 to 12 tripled during the '90s, and teens hit their stride at the decade's end.

In recent years, however, the more troubled economy and growing indebtedness among college-bound teens seems to be dampening the spending fire. One youth marketing firm finds that the purchasing volume flowing through the hands of Americans aged 12 to 19 shot up from $153 billion in 1999 to $172 billion in 2001. Since then, it's basically been moving sideways. In 2002, after 9/11, it edged down to $170 billion; in 2003, back up to $175 billion; in 2004, back down to $170 billion.

Older kids of course spend a lot more than younger kids. Per person, the typical 12-year-old runs through about $100 per month. A high school freshman, $50 per week. A high school senior, maybe $100 per week.

All of these figures must be interpreted with care. Whether a family is affluent or not, it's increasingly hard to tell where a kid's own spending stops and where other spending on his or her behalf begins. In recent years, people of many age brackets have been spending more on children and teenagers—youths themselves, parents on their own kids, and grandparents and other non-parents on their young friends and relatives. Many Americans worry that all this spending is spoiling young people who have been raised in an era of nonstop affluence. But no one can say these kids are collectively neglected. Rightly or wrongly, adults are favoring this new generation by steering more money toward its wants and less toward their own, and by identifying its wants with their own.

At the moneyed end of the spectrum, there's truly no limit to what parents are willing to spend on their children. Witness the boom in pricey summer camps (for which weekly bills can top $2,000), lavish overseas teen travel adventures, teen-driven SUVs, and the daily crowds of rich Manhattan teens with Prada handbags and designer clothes.

In the middle class, teens have been stocking up on enough electronic gear to fill every available inch of their bedrooms and dormrooms, willingly paid for by parents who see this as a path to college and future success in a dot-com economy. Beyond that, major companies keep adding new product lines just for Millennials, such as Kids' Aquafresh, Pert Plus for Kids, Dial for Kids, Ozark Spring Water for Kids—the list is endless.

Plainly, not all teens have shared equally in the recent prosperity, nor in the commercial side of the child absorption that has come with it. In 2001, child poverty rates in every racial and ethnic group reached record lows, but since then have begun inching back up. Millennials in the bottom quarter of the household income distribution are, in absolute terms (poverty, housing, diet, and so on), much better off than they were in the '80s or '60s. However, their sense of relative deprivation may be at least as acute as ever. Kids from low-income families are more likely to compare themselves to affluent kids—and affluent kids to hyper-wealthy kids (whose lifestyle is the focus of so much media attention). Middle-class kids—and, especially, collegians—feel much more economically vulnerable than in other eras, given the higher cost of higher education and starter homes.

Low-income African-American youths face an extra burden. The large and highly visible number of extremely wealthy people of their race, especially in sports and entertainment, tends to conceal their needs, especially in the eyes of their peers.

The Parent-Child Co-Purchase

Most of the Millennial spending boom has been fueled by parental money, not their own. Over the past 15 years, the types of kid income that have risen the most are the types that parents most firmly manage (gifts, joint purchases, and paid household work). The types that have risen the least—or even declined—are the types they least control (weekly "allowances" and paid employment). Both trends defy the free-agent "proto-adult" youth stereotype of the Gen-X youth era.

The fastest-growing source of teen cash has been the direct ad-hoc payment from parent to child, often for a specific purchase on which parent and child confer. Since such payments are neither child spending nor parent spending, these consensual transactions resist the categories favored by many marketing experts. One teen in three now says ad-hoc cash from parents is their biggest source of income. Supplementing parental payments are gifts from grandparents, 55 percent of whom say they've given their grandkids one or more gifts in the prior month.

Another rapidly growing teen cash source is income earned through household chores, which often mingles with the parental "gift" category. Through the Millennial child era, more parents have been working longer hours—too long, in the eyes of many Millennials, who want to lead a more balanced life. Living in homes with such hardworking parents, Millennials have been spending substantially more time than Gen Xers

Figure 4.4 ▶

Share of Kids Age 6–17 Who Say They Influence the Purchase of…

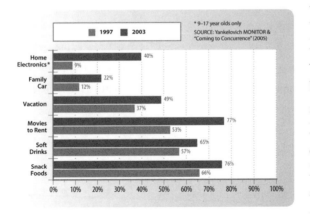

did on tasks previously performed by a parent, from food shopping to cooking to laundry to caring for siblings. And they're being paid for it. From 1991 to 1997, money from teen chores more than doubled.

Other income sources are falling in importance, including "allowances" unrelated to specific tasks. To many a Boomer and Gen-X parent, each dollar in "allowance money" seems wasted when that same dollar might be used to reward, instruct, punish, cajole, or moralize. Teen income from paid employment outside the home is also falling, reflecting the view of teens and parents that other uses of time (being on a school soccer team or in a school musical) could be more influential to college admissions committees.

For all of these reasons, teens are buying more things jointly with their parents. Teens ask parents for money to buy something, they together discuss whether it's worthwhile, the parents hand out the money, and teens go to the store (or online) to make the purchase. Officials at the Center for a New American Dream have noted a new "nag factor" driving many youth purchases, with 10 percent of 12- and 13-year-olds saying they ask their parents more than 50 times for products they've seen advertised.

While parents are often paying in full for major teen purchases (like expensive tickets to rock concerts) that in times past were more financed by youth work and savings, parents also appear to be influencing lesser teen purchases through rules, advice, and earmarked cash. At the same time, teens are influencing parental purchase decisions on big-ticket items like cars, houses, and vacations (by voicing their opinion) and on small-ticket items like groceries and take-out food (by saving their parents' time).

Thus has emerged the era of the parent-teen "co-purchase."

Twenty years ago, the big new trend in youth marketing was the independent child purchase. Today, the big new trend is the child purchasing only after receiving a parent's approval, alias the "co-purchase." The corollary of this is the "co-target," where marketers treat the child and parent as influencers of each other's purchases, from a teen's school clothes to mom's new car. To close the sale, you have to market to, and persuade, both parties.

Teens frequently consult with parents on buying decisions. "Today's working parents feel so guilty about not spending time with their children that they try to compensate by offering them more consumer power," *The Financial Times* reported in 1997. "Others believe today's child-rearing practices fit in with Boomers' respect for individual desires. And others say children's participation in purchasing decisions reflects, in part, parents' uncertainty about high-technology items."

The co-purchase is a new, Millennial-era phenomenon. In the early '80s, Nickelodeon successfully promoted itself to Gen-X 'tweens as a "parent-free zone." A decade later, when the focus-group reaction was no longer favorable, Nick dropped the slogan.

Organization Kids

For Millennials, job time, job experience and job income are a weakening presence in the lives of teens.

Year to year, teen employment usually tracks the patterns of adult employment. In a recession, when one peaks, the other typically does so at about the same time. Yet over the longer term, teen employment shows little relation to the employment of older age brackets. For example, you would think the stagflationary '70s would have been a shakeout time for teen workers, and the roaring '90s a growth time. But very much the opposite occurred. From one generation to the next, shifting parental and youth attitudes have played key roles in pushing teen employment up or down. Teen employment was low for the Silent, rising for Boomers, and high for Gen Xers—and now, for Millennials, falling again.

For Boomer teens, the "right" to work was a newly won youth freedom. Then Gen Xers came along and pushed teen workloads higher. Summer and after-school teen work grew strongly and almost continuously from the mid-'60s to the early '80s, when late-wave Boomers and first-wave Xers (girls especially) pushed paid teen employment to a postwar peak. Xers kept it near these high levels for the rest of the decade.

Throughout the Gen-X youth era, the purpose of teen work was shifting away from supporting families and toward personal spending money, career-building, or self-fulfillment. One of every six 15-year-olds held an after-school job, one of every three a paid summer job, and, for the first time ever, employed girls outnumbered employed boys. Later in the '80s, as adult immigrants began moving into the service sector, teen employment began to ebb slightly. By the late '80s, employment rates for 16- and 17-year-olds were roughly 5 percent below those of the late '70s. Rates for 15-year-olds were 20 percent lower.

In the Millennial youth era, employment has continued to fall among teens, especially younger teens, despite an economy that through the year 2000 desperately wanted young workers and was willing to pay plenty for them. Then came another recession and 9/11. In 2001, the share of teens aged 16 to 19 working or looking for work fell to the lowest levels ever recorded since recordkeeping began in 1948, according to the U.S. Bureau of Labor Statistics. In subsequent years it has continued to fall, hitting 44 percent in 2004.

What accounts for the ebbing popularity of paid work for teenagers? Attitudes have

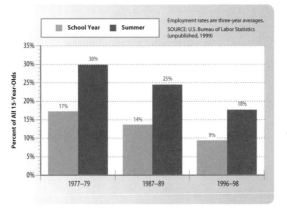

◄ **Figure 4.5**

Employment Rate of 15-Year-Olds, Late '70s to Late '90s

changed, among teens and their parents. During the '90s, parents and educators began to have second thoughts about whether too many teens might be wrapping tacos when they should be wrestling with math. And more teens themselves now question whether unskilled work is a good use of time. When the bottom line is getting into college (more than paying for it), time spent on computer lessons, select soccer, community service, or SAT prep courses seems more valuable, long-term, than nearly any kind of job. As a result, many of the service jobs Gen-X teens once held are now held, not by Millennial teens, but by older Gen-X immigrants.

This does not mean that Millennials are averse to gainful employment. To the contrary: Millennials like to plan, are focused on the future, and believe any work they do today should be a planned and preparatory investment for the permanent kind of life they wish to lead tomorrow. Compared to Gen X, they are more likely to find summer jobs that serve the community or teach new professional skills—and less likely to bother with jobs that simply generate spending money. Today's collegians are broadly interested in finding internships, semester or summer, private or public, paid or unpaid, as long as they advance their long-term plan.

Busy 24/7

Millennial teens may be America's busiest people.

Long gone are the old days of Boomer kids being shooed outside to invent their own games—or of Gen-Xer kids being left "home alone" with a "self-care" guide. For most of today's kids, such a hands-off nurturing style would be considered dangerous, even abusive.

The new reality is structure, planning, and supervision. From 1991 to 1998, according to University of Michigan researchers, eighth and tenth graders showed sharp reductions in their share of those who engage "every day" or "at least once a week" in such open-ended youth activities as going to movies, cruising in cars and motorcycles, or walking around shopping malls. Vast majorities of high-school seniors say they are more looked-after and have less free time than their older brothers and sisters at the same age. During the 1990s,

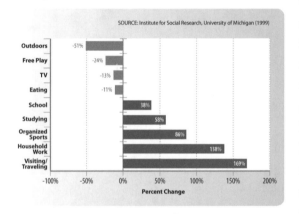

Figure 4.6 ▶

Weekly Hours of Children Aged 3–12, by Activity Percent Change, from 1981 to 1997

the sale of student day-planners soared from one million to 50 million. As 10-year-old Stephanie Mazzamaro told *Time* magazine: "I don't have time to be a kid."

In a survey on pre-school and elementary-school kids aged 3 to 12—now age 10 to 19—comparisons of time diaries between 1981 and 1997 revealed a stunning 37 percent decline in the amount of "unstructured" free time, from 52 to 33 hours per week. Beyond Internet-use, here is where this time is going.

* **School:** *Up by 8.3 hours per week.* This is the single most expanded child activity. More kids aged 4 and 5 (known in earlier generations as "pre-schoolers") are now in school. More grade schools have early morning classes, after-school programs, hobby groups, prayer clubs, "extra learning opportunity" programs, and summer school, which is now mandatory in many districts for kids who score low on certain tests and don't want to repeat a grade. Federal spending on after-school programs is growing rapidly, although 74 percent of elementary and middle-school parents say they would pay for such programs out of their own pocket, if necessary.

* **Household chores:** *Up by 3.5 hours per week.* Many more chores are done by today's kids, either alone or (as with grocery-shopping) with a parent.

* **Personal care:** *Up by 3 hours per week.* Showering, hair care, tooth care, dressing, and other cosmetic items are taking more time.

* **Travel and visiting:** *Up by 2.5 hours per week.* This includes visits to non-custodial parents, who sometimes live in distant cities, or time spent in transit to soccer games, music lessons, and other scheduled events.

This was a survey of small children, but high school students are just as busy—and often not in ways that today's adults can recall of their own youth. Millennials are less likely to spend time lying on their backs imagining stories as they clouds roll by, and more likely to spend time learning how to excel at standardized tests. They are less likely to play self-invented "pick-up" games with made-up rules, and more likely to play on select teams with adult referees, professionalized rules, and published standings.

The Decline of the "Youth" Obsession and the Return of Big Brands

In teen purchasing power and youth market trends, a new generational universe is emerging. Millennials are beginning to reconnect the youth and adult markets, to reverse the inflow of school-age youths into paying jobs, and to reunite the splintered and narrowcast buying habits inherited from Gen X. They are transforming the commercial role of youth through positive peer pressure, cooperative choice-making with parents, and easily accessible new teen media. With e-stores, chat rooms, and IM buddy lists, they are the first youth generation in which virtually any member can keep up hour-to-hour with the opinions and tastes of peers across the nation.

Millennial coolness to exclusive and obsessional "youth" targeting is reflected on a number of fronts. In politics, for example, the weird argot of "rock the vote" campaigns that once amused Gen-Xers is less interesting to Millennial activists, who would rather join forces with like-minded adults and change the national outcome. As a result, Millennials are voting much more than Xers did: From 1996 to 2004, the 18-to-29 voter participation rate climbed from 34 to 54 percent nationwide. In employment, Millennials are less eager to seek out "teen jobs." They prefer well-chosen stepping stones (paid or unpaid) to high-value adult careers. In the pop culture, the new teen comfort with retreaded old movies and songs—or with exotic ethnic genres that have no "youth" subcategory—is well known.

During the Boomer youth era, the new secret of successful pop culture marketing was targeting and packaging "youth" as a special and magical idea. Marketing to Gen-X youth typically followed suit. But to succeed with Millennials, it may be necessary to reverse course and to re-integrate certain aspects of the youth and adult worlds. Imagine a favorite new entertainment show in the 2010s that resembles—in breadth of age bracket targeting—the "Radio Hour" of the 1940s more than the "Saturday Night Live" of the 1970s.

Another big Boomer-to-Xer youth trend has been the push toward market fragmentation—and that trend too is turning around. The niche is foundering. Big brands are back. Aided by new technologies, from Web chat to cell phones, Millennials pay keen attention to what's happening at the gravitational center of their peer group, whether online at one of the new multi-user game sites, or in person at Target and Wal-Mart (both of which enjoyed post-9/11 boosts in teen buying). Mass fads, big brands, group focus, and a lower-profile commercial style are ready for a comeback. Meanwhile, "the edge" has peaked—along with weak product loyalties, hyper-commercialism, and the focus on risk and self.

Mass marketers have taken full note of this. In the April 1998 issue of *American Demographics*, Texas A&M professor James McNeal—probably the most eminent national authority on the youth market—foresaw that "advertising that encourages children to defy their parents, make fun of authority, or talk unintelligibly will be replaced with informative ads describing the benefits of products." That was seven years ago, so you can now substitute the word "teenagers" for "children" in that forecast. The "informed" children of the early '90s are now in college, and are trending in this direction. Calvin Klein and Abercrombie & Fitch, faced with softening demand for their labels, have recently retooled, replacing the ultra-edgy "in your face" approach that worked so well in the '90s with a friendlier in-store attitude clearly aimed at Millennials.

Whatever you're marketing, whether soap, cars, colleges, or pop culture products, the best way to make the Millennial sale is to brand your image, target the mainstream, wrap yourself around the upbeat new mindset of youth, and make room for parents in your message.

5 | SEVEN CORE TRAITS

"With their emphasis on teamwork, achievement, modesty and respect for authority, today's high school graduates bear little resemblance to their more nihilistic Gen-X siblings and even less to their self-indulgent baby boomer parents."

— Milwaukee Journal Sentinel (2004)

SEVEN CORE TRAITS

Every generation contains all kinds of people. But each generation has a persona, with core traits. Not all members of that generation will share those traits, and many will personally resist those traits, but—like it or not—those core traits will substantially define the world inhabited by every member of a generation.

The following are the seven core traits of the Millennial Generation. On the whole, these are not traits one would have associated with Silent, Boomers, or Gen Xers, in youth. Far more closely, they resemble the era of G.I. Generation teens.

* **Special.** From precious-baby movies of the mid-'80s to the media glare surrounding the high school Class of 2000, now in college, older generations have inculcated in Millennials the sense that they are, collectively, vital to the nation and to their parents' sense of purpose.

* **Sheltered.** From the surge in child-safety rules and devices to the post-Columbine lockdown of public schools, to the hotel-style security of today's college dorm room, Millennials are the focus of the most sweeping youth-protection movement in American history.

* **Confident.** With high levels of trust and optimism—and a newly felt connection to parents and future-Millennial teens are beginning to equate good news for themselves with good news for their country.

* **Team-Oriented**. From Barney and soccer to collaborative learning and a resurgence of Greek life on campus, Millennials are developing strong team instincts and tight peer bonds.
* **Conventional**. Taking pride in their improving behavior and quite comfortable with their parents' values, Millennials provide a modern twist to the traditional belief that social rules and standards can make life easier.
* **Pressured**. Pushed to study hard, avoid personal risks, and take full advantage of the collective opportunities adults are offering them, Millennials feel a "trophy kid" pressure to excel.
* **Achieving**. With accountability and higher school standards having risen to the top of America's political agenda, Millennials are on track to becoming the smartest, best-educated generation of adults in U.S. history.

Millennials and Specialness

Millennials first arrived in the early '80s as the offspring of "yuppie" parents touting "family values"—of Boomer supermoms opting to have in vitro babies (a historical first) and Boomer dads demanding to be to be present at childbirth (another historical first). When this first Millennial wave entered grade school, the nation suddenly mobilized (in 1989) around a national school reform movement. A few years later, with the end of the Cold War, the fate of children became the central focus of political speeches, new legislation, and a gathering culture war. By 1998, more than half of all Americans (a record share) said that "getting kids off to the right start" ought to be America's top priority. National issues having nothing directly to do with children—Social Security, the war on terror, unemployment—began to be discussed in terms of their impact on children.

As Millennials have absorbed the adult message that they dominate America's agenda, they have come easily to the belief that *their* problems are *the nation's* problems, that *their* future is *the nation's* future, and that, by extension, everyone in America will naturally be inclined to help them solve those problems. Ask Millennials about their preferred choice of community service, and most often they will tell you it's helping other people their own age, either at home or abroad.

Millennials are more willing than other recent generations to acknowledge the importance of their own personal choices and actions. When asked about violence in schools, for example, the vast majority insist it's purely the fault of students—not of the culture, guns, or anything (or anyone) else.

When asked which groups will be most likely to help America toward a better future, teens rank "young people" second, behind only "scientists." When asked whose generation can have the greatest impact on what the global environment will become 25 years from now, 86 percent say their own, and only 9 percent say their parents'. When asked the same question, their parents mostly agreed, 71 percent saying their children's generation will have the most impact. When asked which of today's living generations has the highest reputation and which would they most like to emulate, Millennial high school seniors say (by lopsided majorities) say their grandparents' generation—the can-do war-winning "greatest generation."

Even as Millennials begin leaving home, their parents find it hard to let these special kids go. On college campuses, administrators are expanding their "empty nest" orientation programs for doting moms and dads, complete with teddy bears for them to hug. With catchy titles like "What Have You Done with My Child?" (University of North Carolina at Wilmington) and "May They Follow Your Path, and Not Your Footsteps" (Ohio Northern University), they are designed to assure audiences that the colleges are merely adding the final touches on their wonderful progeny.

Even looking ahead, parents want to stay close. One-quarter of Boomers say they expect their children or grandchildren to live with them at some point during retirement, and developers of active-adult communities say one of the biggest design shift has been the addition of extra rooms for visiting (or live-in) kids. Compare this to the attitudes of the Boomers' own parents, whose yearnings for escape and independence gave rise to age-exclusive senior communities like Sun City and Leisure World.

Over the past quarter-century, the attitude of every age bracket toward multigenerational households has become more favorable. In 1973, only 33 percent of young adults felt it was a good idea for older people to share a home with grown children, and 56 percent felt it was a bad idea. By 1994, those proportions had reversed, to 55 percent thinking it good and 28 percent thinking it bad. Over the past few years, surveys by MonsterTrak, an online job site for young adults, have shown that between 50 and 60 percent of college graduates plan to move back in with their parents, at least temporarily. The new popularity of extended family households has coincided with a growth in size (and cost) of an average family home. For reasons of lifestyle, cultural tastes, simple economics, it today makes far more sense for young adults to share homes with their parents than it did when Boomers were young. Once frowned upon by young and old alike, it is becoming a new norm in twenty-first century America.

Millennials and Sheltering

Americans have been tightening the security perimeters around Millennials ever since they first arrived, over twenty years ago. As adults, they've been gradually pulling down per-capita rates of divorce, abortion, alcohol consumption, and other dangers to children. As worried parents, they've become avid consumers for a child-proofing industry that has snapped up new patents for everything from stove-knob covers to safety mirrors. As voters, they've triggered a crusade for programs to look after their children—and, between 1988 and 1999, reduced the rates of child abductions (by 23 percent), runaways (by 25 percent), substantiated child abuse (by 43 percent), and missing children (by 51 percent).

The sheltering trend pushed in the reverse direction from what today's older generations recall from their own youth eras, when adult protectiveness was being dismantled (for Boomers) or not really there at all (for Gen Xers).

For Millennials, the edifice of parental care has been like a castle that keeps getting new bricks added—V-chips and "smart lockers" last month, carding at the movies this month, graduated licenses and bedroom spy cams next month. The Internet remains a refuge of teen freedom, to some degree, but the servers and software designers are constructing new castle walls there too. The older '80s-born Millennials recall a world with more open sky, while the younger '90s-born kids look up at the growing walls, unable to imagine what could be seen in their absence. A late-'90s survey on pre-school and elementary-school kids aged 3 to 12—now age 11 to 20—compared time diaries between 1981 and 1997 revealed a stunning 37 percent decline in the amount of "unstructured" free time, from 52 to 33 hours per week.

Younger Millennials, the ones still in elementary and middle school, appear to be even more supportive of extra protection than older ones in high school or college. A few months after Columbine, older teens wanted to increase rather than decrease school security by a two-to-one margin, while younger teens said the same by a four-to-one margin. When sweeping new rules such as school uniforms or student identity cards are first proposed, the usual experience is initial student resistance, but only until those measures are put in place, after which many students change their minds and become supportive. And, by huge majorities, Millennial teens support harsh punishments (including expulsion) for those who misbehave.

This adult obsession with security follows them wherever they go. A butter knife or aspirin tablet can land students in suspension. Every activity is structured, supervised, and enclosed—and before, during, and after activities, kids must be carefully strapped in or helmeted to prevent injury. Most schools have lifted bans on cell phones (now being marketed as "Barbie" phones for pre-teens) so parents can place check-up calls between classes.

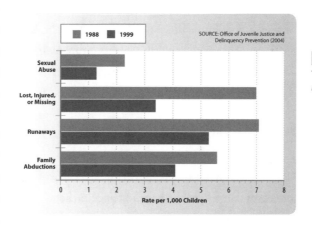

◀ **Figure 5.1**

Trends in Child Harm, Age 0 to 17

Summer camps boast email links and daily video downloads to home. Hi-tech devices now allow parents to record the speed at which the family car is drive or to snoop on drug use in the bedroom.

To some extent, the urge to shelter has created some real health problems for Millennials. Consider, for example, the dramatic decline in physical activity—especially unstructured activity outdoors. In 1969, half of all 18-

year-olds walked or rode a bike to school. Today, hardly any teens do that, making kids six times more likely to play a video game than ride a bike on a typical day. Just since 1995, bike riding is down one third—as is the share of children ages 7 to 11 who swim, fish, canoe, or play touch football. Since 1997, overall baseball playing is down 28 percent. Meanwhile, PE classes at schools are being cut back to make room for more academics. Most experts agree that this decline in physical activity has contributed to the quadrupling (from 4 to 16 percent) in the share of kids technically classified as "obese" and perhaps also to the rising incidence of ADHD. Increasing body weight (along with the new fixation on cleanliness) may also be pushing the rising incidence of asthma among kids.

Since 9/11, the protective boundaries have drawn even closer—with national TV coverage of "amber alert" warnings for missing children and the marketing of "home security" devices that allow parents to track their kids via GPS. Subcutaneous microchips have recently been seriously discussed by law enforcement and medical experts. With Millennials entering college, administrators are reporting a huge increase in "helicopter parents" who constantly phone and email faculty and deans to talk about grades, moods, foods, or whatever. These special kids, parents figure, will always require extra care.

True to the wishes of adult America, Millennials are protected, feel protected, and expect to be protected—even, some might say, overprotected.

Millennials and Confidence

In May 1997, Canadian journalist Deborah Jones dubbed Millennials the "Sunshine Generation," recognizing that on both sides of the border, 'tweens and teens comprised the happiest age bracket. For over thirty years, until the mid-'90s, the teen suicide rate marched relentlessly upward. Over the last decade, it has declined by 30 percent. Where polls show adults believing that being a parent is getting harder, they show Millennials believing that being a kid is getting easier. Among teens, this is a very recent development. As late as 1994, 70 percent of (Gen-X) 13- to 17-year-olds said it's "harder" to grow up now than in their parents' time. By 1999, among Millennials, that percentage had dropped to 43 percent.

Millennial Obesity

One Millennial health trend that is glaringly and disturbingly negative is the rising incidence of youth obesity, combined with a lack of fitness. Among children and teens aged 6–19 years, 16 percent (over 9 million children and teenagers) are now considered "overweight," which is defined as having a body-mass index of over 25. That's up from an estimated 4 percent in 1960. The data indicate that most of the deterioration has occurred since 1980, as Millennials have been appearing as children.

Americans in older age brackets (20 to 65 years) have also been getting plumper over the past two decades. However, the climb in obesity among Boomers and Gen-Xers has not been as dramatic—and, especially, did not start as early in life. Many health experts worry that the rising prevalence of childhood obesity could trigger higher rates of chronic illnesses, from heart problems to diabetes, as Millennials grow older. The fear is growing that the modern trend toward childhood obesity could even trigger a decline in the average lifespan of today's children, compared with today's adults. Some experts regard childhood obesity as a public health "epidemic" on par with cigarette smoking.

There are many reasons for these weight and fitness problems, the two most important of which are, first, too much of the wrong kind of food, and, second, not enough exercise.

Children ages 8 to 10 spend an average of six hours a day watching television, playing video games, and using computers, according to recent surveys by the Kaiser Family Foundation. As children and teenagers have grown fond of screen-based sedentary activities, whether done at home (TV, video games, computers) or elsewhere (movies, concerts), their new habits have measurably decreased their amount of exercise. A recent survey found that 25 percent of 'tweens and teens do not do vigorous activity on a daily basis, and another 14 percent report that they do not even do "light to moderate" activity on a daily basis.

This trend toward sedentary play has recently extended to college campuses. In a recent USA Today article, Mike Morris, a 20-year-old pole vaulter at DePauw University said that the introduction of Nintendo 64, in 1996, was a life-altering event for many in his circle of friends, shifting neighborhood play from outdoors to indoors. He described how, every day after working out, he returns to his dorm to play Halo combat games against 20 fellow students sitting in their various dorm rooms—few of whom are getting the same daily exercise he does. "My college memories are more likely to be a great move I put on to kill someone in Halo than a great move in pick-up basketball," he says. "It's kind of sad, in a way."

In the years to come, the U.S. government, and the nation's schools and physicians, are likely to launch a vigorous assault on the childhood obesity problem. Some are urging a campaign as vigorous and far-reaching as the one against tobacco products in the 1990s. If this happens, there are likely to be two clear targets: the food industry (the too-much-diet side), and the technology and entertainment industries (the too-little-exercise side).

The video game industry stands in the best position to address the fitness question. The popular "DDR" (Dance Dance Revolution) game was the first to demonstrate the potential for using game technologies to promote rather than hinder vigorous youthful activity. Other games are following suit, including Nintendo's Donkey Konga, which requires banging and clapping, Sony's EyeToy, which uses video cameras to track how well players dribble a soccer ball or make Kung Fu moves, or PowerGrid Fitness' Kilowatt, designed with a giant joystick that must be isometrically pushed or pulled. Other novel test products include shoe pedometers that transmit daily stats to computers or digital body sensors that allow users to improve baseball pitches or golf swings. If priority were given to the task, software could be developed for many more video games and internet devices that can be directly linked with participation in sports or exercise.

In subject matter, films and TV shows can play a positive role here by addressing the child and teen obesity problem in fresh, constructive, and entertaining ways—even if the act of viewing them is, by definition, sedentary.

A lesser, but rising, problem among Millennials is repetitive stress injury (RPI) to fingers, hands, wrists, arms, sometimes even shoulders and necks, caused by constant use of, and play on, a computer keyboard and mouse—and, to a lesser extent, with a video game joystick. Carpal tunnel syndrome is the best known RPI. To protect against this, a rising number of teens and collegians are wearing wrist guards.

"Why are kids so confident?" asked a recent KidsPeace report." Significantly, the word 'crisis' seems not to appear in the teen lexicon." The Cold War is over. The War on Terror is winnable. And even if the economy grows in fits and starts and the federal budget is deep in the red, well, the Internet keeps getting faster and cell phones cheaper.

More than half of all teens agree that "people my age should be optimistic about their chances of having a good job." Among those in families earning less than $30,000, 54 percent believe the world holds "many opportunities for me." Among those in families earning over $75,000, that proportion rises to 78 percent. More than four in five teens (including 95 percent of Latinos and 97 percent of African-Americans) believe they will be financially more successful than their parents—a percentage that rose sharply during the '90s.

The teen view of success has become better-rounded and less exclusively focused on one life goal. Over the last decade, "marriage/family" and "career success" have each declined in importance as "the one thing" in life. What's now more important is the concept of *balance*—between work and play, academic life and social life, and, down the road, between work life and family life. A rising share of high school seniors say "making a contribution to society" is "extremely" or "quite" important, while a declining share (though still a majority) say the same for "having lots of money."

In a turnabout from Gen-X teens of the '80s, Millennial teens have faith that the American Dream will work not only for them but for their own children. They see the future with a far longer view than their parents did at the same age. The share of teens who define success as "Being able to give my children better opportunities than I had" has reached an all-time high.

The events of 9/11 and the prospect of related economic shocks have shaken the confidence of many Millennials, but much less so than older Americans. Of all age groups, moreover, Millennials have proved to be the least perturbed by the new war rules, including violations of civil rights and intrusions against privacy. The reason: They already had their own 9/11, more than three years earlier, in April of 1999, at Columbine High School in Littleton, Colorado. In the remaining six weeks of that traumatic school year, students learned what would happen if they kept a sharp object in their pocket, played with a toy gun, or cracked a joke about student shooters. Come 9/11, they were already familiar with scanners, cameras, detectors, see-through backpacks, and unlockable lockers.

More than adults, Millennials have grown accustomed to the sight of aggressive security. And more than older generations, they tend to associate such shows of force with safety (rather than with threats to liberty). In this sense, teenage Millennials appear to be better prepared, functionally and emotionally, for the new mood of post-9/11 America.

Millennials and Team Orientation

Surrounded by individualistic older people, yet optimistic about their own abilities and prospects, Millennials have stepped into an Xer-styled teen world that, in their new view, lacked cohesion. They're now busy trying to make all the pieces fit together better.

The team ethic shows up in a new youth aversion to disorder within their own social setting—starting with classrooms. When public school students are asked what most needs fixing in their schools, most of them mention teaching "good manners," "maintaining discipline in the classroom," and making students "treat each other with respect." Forty percent want something to be done about unruly student behavior that interferes with schoolwork. Back in the Gen-X youth era, educators disliked peer pressure because they associated the concept with rule-breaking. Today, educators are discovering that peer pressure can be harnessed—through group projects, peer grading, uniforms, student juries, and the like—to enforce rules better.

The new team orientation has broadened their search for peer friendships, drawing them to circles and cliques. Only three teens in ten report that they usually socialize with only one or two friends, while two in three do so with groups of friends. The proportion of eighth- and tenth-graders who feel lonely or wish they had more friends declined sharply from 1991 to 1998. A rising share would prefer to stay with their buddies after graduation (and, thanks to cell phones, many do). Teachers report that, compared with students of a decade ago, those of today feel less close to teachers but closer to each other.

The Millennials' team ethic also shows up in their choice of friends. Honesty and hard work are now the highest-valued personal qualities among young people, even though teens admit that those virtues do not necessarily lead to popularity. Ninety-five percent report that "it's important that people trust me." In choosing their peer leaders, Millennials say they look for maturity, friendliness, and quality of moral character ahead of an imaginative or independent mind.

This Millennial cliquishness has made peer pressure a much bigger teen issue than before, yet Millennials see it more positively than adults do. Many see peers as a source of help, comfort, and power. Only about one-third of teens say they are under "a great deal" or "some" pressure from peers to "break rules," although a larger share report being teased about clothing, and bullying (especially verbal aggression among girls) is reported to be a rising problem.

Millennials are adapting new cell phone, networking, and social software technologies (like MySpace) to increase their level of interconnection. They're less interested in the anonymous freedom of the Internet and more interested in its ability to maintain peer networks. Roughly one half (34 million) of all U.S. kids under age 18 were online in 2003, comprising one-fifth of all U.S. Internet users. Of those online, nearly all use Instant Messaging (IM) services to talk to friends. A typical Millennial can have one or two hundred "buddies" on her IM list.

This team ethic reveals itself the emerging political views of this generation. When Millennial teens were asked to identify "the major causes" of America's problems, their seven most popular answers all pertained to what they perceived as an excess of adult individualism. Reason number one (given by 56 percent of all teens) was "selfishness, people not thinking of the rights of others." Reason number two (given by 52 percent) was "people who don't respect the law and the authorities." Reason number four, "lack of parental discipline of children and teens," was an answer very few Boomer teens would ever have given.

Where Millennials do see division, they don't see it in the same place as earlier generations. The Boomer rebellion of the '60s and '70s was energized by the perception of vast and unfair gap between gender roles and black-white racial stereotypes. Young Boomers perceived America's middle class as monolithic and powerful, maybe too powerful. Much of the subsequent Boomer agenda, in the '80s and '90s, has been to overcome sexism and racism and to weaken the middle class.

For Millennial youth today—a multiethnic generation bursting with nonwhite achievers and parented by "supermoms"—issues of gender and color no longer carry anywhere near the same voltage. A rising issue for them is the spreading income and wealth inequality of their parents, which they notice (especially in college) as the enormous opportunity chasm separating the kids of rich families from those of poor families. They see America's middle class as weak and endangered—leaving dangerously little room to plan a "balanced" life between poverty and opulence. Issues of class and money (taxes, estates, wages, debts, health-care, pensions, entitlements) could well become a lifelong priority, and political flashpoint, for this generation.

Millennials and Convention

Boomer children felt overdosed on norms and rules, and famously came of age assaulting them. Millennials show signs of trying to re-establish a regime of rules. Where Boomer teens had trouble talking to their parents—a major cause of the late-'60s "generation gap"—Millennials have far less trouble doing so. Their rebellion lies in moving to the ordered center, rather than pushing the anarchic edge.

Why this Millennial move to the center? Having benefited from a re-norming of family life following the turbulent '60s and '70s, today's teens are inclined to feel trust in the core aspects of their daily lives. Compared to Xers, Millennials bask in the sense of being loved by parents. In 1995, 93 percent of 10- to 13-year-olds felt "loved" all or almost all the time. In a 1997 Gallup survey, nine in ten youths reported being very close to their parents and personally happy—much closer than 20 years ago.

Millennials describe closer ties with their parents than any teens in the history of polling. Two-thirds of today's teens say their parents are "in touch" with their lives, and six in 10 say it's "easy" to talk with parents about sex, drugs, and alcohol. In a 1998 teen survey, 80 percent reported having had "really important talks" with their parents, and 94 percent mostly or totally agreed that "I can always trust my parents to be there when I need them." Back in 1974, more than 40 percent of Boomers flatly declared they'd "be better off not living with their parents." Many parents report that their Millennial children tell them everything about their lives, way beyond what Boomers ever dared tell their own moms and dads.

Far more than anything Boomers or Gen Xers can remember, today's teens and parents share tastes in clothes, music, and other entertainments. Revivals of Boomer-era music classics can be Millennial hits, and teens think nothing of introducing their parents to the latest Weezer album. Part of what has made "American Idol" so successful has been all the parents and teens rooting together for shared favorites. Behind this trend lies a deeper agreement on underlying cultural values. The share of teens reporting "very different" values from their parents has fallen by roughly half since the '70s, and the share who say their values are "very or mostly similar" has hit an all-time high of 76 percent.

While Millennials are broadly willing to accept their parents' exacting values (and spacious homes), they are also starting to think they can apply these values, and someday run the show, a whole lot better. When asked whether "values and character" will matter more or less to their own generation when they're parents, they answer "more" by a two-to-one margin. Revealingly, today's young people are far more trusting than their parents of the capacity of large national institutions to do the right thing for their generation and for the country. When teens are asked who's going to improve the schools, clean up the environment, cut the crime rate, they respond—without irony—that it will be teachers, government, and police.

"One of the macro-trends we're seeing is neo-traditionalism," says teen-marketer Kirsty Doig. "These kids are fed up with the superficialities of life. They have not had a lot of stability in their lives. It's a backlash, a return to tradition and ritual." This doesn't mean Millennials are a generation of conservative throwbacks—their very tolerant views on gay rights conflicts with that agenda—but rather a generation of modernists who believe every person has a place.

Millennials and the Entertainment Economy

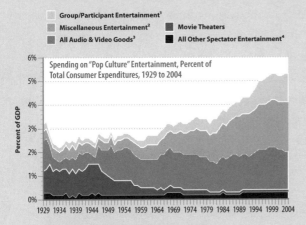

Group/Participant Entertainment[1]
Miscellaneous Entertainment[2]
All Audio & Video Goods[3]
Movie Theaters
All Other Spectator Entertainment[4]

Spending on "Pop Culture" Entertainment, Percent of
Total Consumer Expenditures, 1929 to 2004

Percent of GDP

6%
5%
4%
3%
2%
1%
0%

1929 1934 1939 1944 1949 1954 1959 1964 1969 1974 1979 1984 1989 1994 1999 2004

SOURCE: Bureau of Economic Analysis, Department of Commerce
[1] (e.g., theme parks, casinos, golf, bowling, skiing, sports rentals)
[2] (e.g., all rentals and access fees [movies, internet], camps, lotteries)
[3] including computer games
[4] (e.g., concerts, spectator sports)

As a share of Gross Domestic Product (GDP), consumer spending on what might reasonably be called "pop culture" held roughly stable at around 3 percent of GDP from the late 1920s until the early 1980s, or over half a century. Thereafter, it rose dramatically, from 3.4 percent of GDP ($71 billion) in 1982 to 5.4 percent of GDP ($361 billion) in 2000. The entire Millennial childhood has coincided with an explosive entertainment spending boom fueled by their (Boomer and Gen-X) parents and older siblings.

Since 2000, total spending has stopped rising. This occurred just as Millennials were poised to become the new booming youth market—one more sign that, in hindsight, pop culture producers erred if they took these young people for granted. More of the same simply did not impress a generation that has only known more of the same.

A close look at long-term spending reveals some interesting trends. During the early post-war period, from the late 1940s through the '50s, a dramatic decline in movie-going was compensated by a rise in spending on TVs, stereos, and record albums. Since the early '60s, there has been little overall change in spending on spectator activities, including movies. Instead, all the increase—which became especially rapid after 1980—has been generated by further growth in activities done at home (home entertainment centers, videogames)

and interactive entertainments (amusement parks, camps, lotteries, casinos).

Qualitative shifts have also been at work. Over the past 40 years, adults have reshaped the demand curve for youth pop, as new generations have taken over the business side of entertainment.

Back in the Boomer child era, the 1950s, the older generation that was then culturally dominant—G.I.s—did not consider culture, especially youth culture, as being central to American life. Whether music or film or TV, they viewed the pop culture as nice, but superfluous to the essentials of life: maintaining national defense, or building highways, suburbs, schools, or cars. That was a time when the national income and wealth distribution was far narrower than it was forty years before (in the 1920s) or would become forty years later (today). The gaps between the earnings of a school teacher or lawyer

or recording star—or the size or number of their houses—was far narrower than today.

When Boomers were young, it was difficult for an entertainment company to price any pop culture product at a higher level than what G.I.s considered fair. On a concert tour, a ticket to see the most popular stars, a Bing Crosby or Bennie Goodman, was well within the means of a middle-class family. That attitude remained in place, through the 1960s, as younger performers replaced older ones on the concert tour.

Now, all that is reversed. From youth forward, Boomers have regarded the pop culture with reverence, as something more central to national life than the physical infrastructure (highways, refineries, factories) that had been their parents' hallmarks. As Boomers have aged, they have put their rising purchasing power behind their cultural preferences. They are willing to pay hundreds of dollars to see a famous old rock star in person, to pay thousands to be part of a "fantasy camp" or spend personal time with a legend of their youth. Meanwhile, the business leaders of their generation have seen their ability to command top dollar for entertainment products as an appropriate expression of individualism in the unfettered "experience economy" marketplace. Thus has this generation fueled the demand for such luxury-level enjoyments as high-end rock concerts, pro sports suites and loge seats, closed circuit programming, and premium tickets at theme parks.

Entertainment companies will face a real marketing challenge, and perhaps some short-term income loss, in reversing this Boomer-driven trend toward price-differentiated markets. Yet a flatter price structure will appeal to a new youth generation with a more community-oriented outlook and a keener desire to see the pop culture as something to share. The long-term upside will be regaining the loyalty of a generation of consumers who have many decades of purchases still ahead of them.

Older people are often blindsided by the new traditionalism (or at what some less accurately call the "new conservatism") of today's teens. Few would guess that the share of college freshmen who say raising a family is an "important" life goal has risen to an all-time high of 75 percent today—up from only 59 percent in 1977. Even parents are sometimes surprised. Nearly half, when interviewed, believe it must be embarrassing for teens to admit they are virgins, yet only a quarter of teens themselves think so. The burgeoning "youth chastity" subculture has recently attracted much incredulous coverage from media with older readerships—for example, a 2005 *Rolling Stone* feature, entitled "The New Virgin Army: Life Among the Young and Sexless."

George Gallup, Jr., recently summed up the evidence as follows:

> *"Teens today are decidedly more traditional than their elders were, in both lifestyles and attitudes. Gallup Youth Survey data from the past 25 years reveal that teens today are far less likely than their parents were to use alcohol, tobacco and marijuana. In addition, they are less likely than their parents even today to approve of sex before marriage and having children out of wedlock. Teens want to reduce the amount of violence on TV; seek clear rules to live by, and promote the teaching of values in school. They are searching eagerly for religious and spiritual moorings in their lives. They want abstinence taught in school, and they think divorces should be harder to get.*

Researchers would not have said anything close to this about Boomers 40 years ago. On several of these topics, they would have said much the opposite.

Millennials and Pressure

Millennials feel pressured. A growing number of teens believe that near-term achievement determines long-term success—and that what a high-school junior does this week determines where she'll be five and ten years from now. This is a new teen perception. And it's a reversal of a 40-year trend.

In their youth, Boomers felt *decreasing* pressure to achieve. Back when JFK-era hopes of a gleaming technocracy ran aground on Vietnam, youth riots, credibility gaps, and energy crises, Boomers perceived their future growing more chaotic, less linked to work or credentials, and less subject to institutional rules. A common youth view was that you could do almost anything you wanted in high school or (especially) college and not expect that your life would be all that affected by it.

Gen Xers inherited those trends and stepped into this mindset. While they were in school, the defining symptom of teen alienation was the widespread perception that success was pretty much random in a fast-moving, risk-rewarding economy that offered a lot more opportunities than guarantees to young people. To this mindset, long preparation was often a waste of time, and a quick move or gamble was what often spelled the difference, good or bad.

For Millennials, the connection between today's behavior and tomorrow's payoff is returning. Rather than breed a sense of entitlement, the buoyant economy has placed them into a pressure cooker. A rising population of well-credentialed high school seniors increases competition for the best college slots. Technology, with its constant demands for response to phone calls, email and instant messages, is putting additional demands on a teenager's time. Schools are passing out Day Timers, teachers are starting classes in "time management for kids," and parents are giving their teenagers Sean Covey's bestselling *The 7 Habits of Highly Effective Teens: The Ultimate Teenage Success Guide.*

The common formula for today's youth is: Success in life is the reward for effort plus planning. That's why many of today's "organization kids" feel stressed in ways that many of their parents never felt at the same age. It's also why the classic Xer doctrine—that a person can always rebound from failure—no longer seems as plausible. As Millennials apply to college with essays about personal hardships and community service, their credentials and reputation (in testimonials from school counselors) matter more than ever before. Resume-building has become a stressful arms race, SAT Saturday a day of high anxiety.

If many college-graduating Millennials are coming home to live with their parents (unlike Xers, they can't be called "boomerang kids" since many never really left home to begin with), it's not because they want to mooch. It's because they want to avoid hurt or damage. They want to do it right—and first get their careers totally on track.

Constant pressure keeps Millennials moving, busy, and purposeful—as a *New York Times* story from 2000 makes plain:

> *"For the first time this year, New York City... will use the results of the fourth-grade test to help determine whether children will be promoted to the next grade. Last year, 67 percent of New York City fourth-graders and 43 percent of fourth-graders in the rest of the state failed the test." Sylvia Wertheimer, an assistant D.A. in Manhattan and mother of a fifth-grader, told the Times the new testing regime "really categorizes kids in the sense of a hierarchy, and kids are aware of it." Ms. Wertheimer went on: "[W]hat used to happen to us at the college level has now been brought down to fifth grade. The whole feeling is much more pressure, pressure, pressure."*

Grade inflation is continuing its three-decade-long trend. By 1998, one-third of all eighth graders, and one-fourth of all tenth graders, reported receiving an "A" or "A-" average. The impact of all those A's is simply to magnify the penalty of the occasional B or C—reinforcing the Millennials' fear of failure, their aversion to risk (and to out-of-the-box creativity), and their desire to fit in to the mainstream. It's common to hear long-time teachers observe that today's students are better prepared and organized than Generation X, and often know more stuff, but also that they're less willing to take risks, be creative, and "think outside the box."

To many Millennial teens, it's as though a giant generational train is leaving the station. Each of them believes they'll either be on the platform, on time and with their ticket punched, or they'll miss the train and never be on that platform again.

Millennials and Achievement

Thirty years ago, many a Boomer had big plans. So do many a Millennial today—but that's where the similarity ends. Young Boomers often charted their future course by their own internal compasses, asking how a path felt more than what all the signposts said. Millennial teens are turning that around, preferring timetables and milestones to mere inspiration.

The majority of today's high school students say they have detailed five- and ten-year plans for their future. Most have given serious thought to college financing, degrees, salaries, employment trends, and the like. Often, they start thinking about colleges and employers before the end of the ninth grade.

Millennials see these preparations as serious and important, but not exactly fun. The share of students who "try to do my best in school" keeps going up, but so does—among boys especially—the share who don't like school either "very much" or "at all." All their lives, many Boomers have been driven to choose specialties and careers that in some way feel like personal vocations. Millennials would rather strike a balance between what they have to do and what they want to do, rather than merge the two (common among Boomers) or compartmentalize the two (common among Gen Xers).

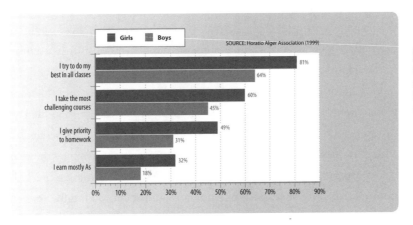

◄ **Figure 5.2**

Survey of Students Aged 14–18 in 1998–99, Answers by Gender

In college, young Boomers made their biggest mark in the arts and humanities. As young professionals, they became precocious leaders in the media, teaching, advertising, religion—anything having to do with the creative rearrangement of values and symbols. Millennial teens show the opposite bent. Surveys reveal that they like math and science courses best, social studies and arts courses least—and like to spend free time in shared activities with friends, instead of doing imaginative, creative tasks on their own.

Their collective ambitions have a rationalist core. According to a LifeCourse Class of 2000 Survey, teens have a great deal of confidence in their generation's lifelong ability to improve technology (97 percent), race relations (77 percent), and the economy (55 percent)—all public and benchmarkable spheres of social life—but far less confidence in their prospects for improving more subjective areas such as the arts (31 percent), family life (20 percent), and religion (14 percent). Other surveys reveal teens as more likely than adults to value friendships, but less likely than adults to value the ability to communicate feelings.

One might expect this rationalism to favor boys over girls. Thus far, that has not happened. Boys score as well as (or better than) girls on pure aptitude tests, but by nearly every measure of applied effort women now come out on top. Summarizing the data, the Horatio Alger Association's "State of Our Nation's Youth" report concluded: "Females challenged themselves more frequently to take the most difficult courses available...[and] worked harder at their course work and received better grades than males." Anyone who today peruses a high school yearbook, or goes to a high school awards assembly or honors class, will be struck by the preponderance of girls. Coming out of high school, moreover, more women than men apply for college; of those, more women than men are accepted; and of those, more women than men avoid dropping out in their freshmen and sophomore year. Fully 58 percent of all college freshmen are now women, a proportion that is rising by the year.

To explain this powerful "girl power" advantage, some experts have pointed to all the new stress on teamwork and social skills and "zero tolerance" of what some might call typical boy behavior. Young Millennial males feel at a disadvantage—and by the time they leave high school, many develop an aversion to educators who (they think) regard them primarily as problems. In college, young men focus more exclusively on—and continue to dominate—the most economically rewarding fields, such as business and technology. Out of college, many believe that learning on the job and avoiding costly student loans is a superior long-term choice. Whatever the reason, the gender gap in achievement shows how Millennials are redefining "conventional" standards in a very unconventional way.

The recent evidence of student achievement is still mixed, with greater success shown by girls than boys, and with gaps across racial and ethnic groups persisting but also shrinking. Minority male dropouts remain a major concern. In college, the cost (along with the burden of student loans) has become a major problem for young people whose families are not affluent.

Amid all the data, Millennials appear to be getting smarter by the year. This year's average national SAT score is the highest since 1974, a 27-year record. And even that achievement understates the trend. Today a much larger share of high school graduates (just over 45 percent) are taking the exam than took it back in the early '70s (roughly 30 percent)—including millions of poor and nonwhite youths, and the offspring of recent immigrants, who in earlier generations never would have tested at all. Recent national test scores are confirming that the '90s-born Millennials may, in time, do even better in school than those born in the '80s.

In high schools and colleges, the quality of extracurricular (what some call "co-curricular") programs is rising rapidly. From student governments to yearbooks and newspapers, from religious clubs to gay-straight alliances, from sports programs to student-run businesses, Millennial students are accomplishing and organizing and just *doing* more than earlier generations—and more than like-aged youth elsewhere in the world. This is particularly true for school theater programs, bands, orchestras, and choruses, whose graduates, in time, will provide many of the future performers, writers, directors, and producers of the pop culture. The exceptional training and hi-tech know-how of these budding professionals represents a vast resource—yet also perhaps a threat—to the entertainment industry as it is presently organized.

6 | THE MILLENNIAL MAKEOVER

"This generation is characterized by their adoption of new media, and new media serve both as a tool for them and as a way for them to define themselves. Young people often lead the way with new technology, and this is a source of pride for the Millennial Generation."

— *Born to be Wired*, Harris Interactive (2003)

THE MILLENNIAL MAKEOVER

What, exactly, does one do with a generation that is rebelling in the directions we're seeing with Millennials?

For anyone in the entertainment industry, other questions arise: Where is the *edge*? Where is the *art*? How can one be innovative in design around a generation that is already doing so much with technology on its own? How can anyone be *creative* in content around a generation that, at times, expresses annoyance at the very uncreative way the industry itself insists upon distributing and selling its content?

To answer those questions, you just have to think outside the box—while remembering that what once was "outside the box," all those trends that summed up youth culture over the last two decades, is now squarely *inside* it. That's nothing new. It happened in the early '80s, and before that in the middle '60s, and several times before that, as well.

The Millennial Makeover—When Will It Happen?

Every modern generation has staged a pop culture makeover. The Millennials have already begun theirs.

To prepare for what's ahead, you first need to look back and recognize a regular historical pattern. Every makeover has unfolded according to a timetable that is determined by the new generation's lifecycle relationship with those who are older and younger.

* **Tremor.** As 'tweens and teens, the breaking wave of a rising generation consumes the popular culture supplied by the next-up generation, many of whose "culture creators" range in age from their late twenties to their late thirties.

* **Breakout.** During its twenties, this breaking wave moves from consumer to primary producer of popular culture, aimed at its own generation's younger cohorts. At the end of this period there is maximum unity between the culture creators and youthful consumers.

* **Dominance.** During its thirties, the breaking wave consolidates its hold on popular culture, but falls increasingly out of touch with the youngest "tween" consumers who are the vanguards of the next generation. In the meantime, some of its younger members serve as stylistic role models for new youth trends. Sometime during this decade, the next generation begins actively rejecting the culture of a generation now entering middle age.

* **Rear Guard.** In its forties and fifties, the fully middle-aged generation creates less entertainment, and much of what it does create is either aimed at its own members, or a late-life effort to resurrect its own styles for new youth tastes.

Table 6.1 shows how this was true through the twentieth century for music, and how it is likely to remain true into the twenty-first.

The Millennials' impact on popular music will stretch across three decades, suggesting that the recent assault on the music industry (with downloads) is just an opening salvo.

Music—and its special vulnerability to shifting youth tastes—highlights the second reason why the Millennial breakout will not happen at one time. Music tastes frequently show their first change in purchasing habits of "tween" and young teen consumers, while other entertainments have artists and audiences who are considerably older.

As the popular culture has evolved, each entertainment media has its own main-target age bracket, a different life phase that drives tastes. Go into a record store, a movie cineplex on a Saturday night, or a Broadway theater lobby. The ages of people in each of those places will be quite different.

Table 6.1: Title?				
Decade	Makers	Buyers	Music	Star
1920s	Lost	G.I.s	gin fizz jazz	Louis Armstrong
1930s	G.I.s	G.I.s	big band	Benny Goodman
(TREMOR: teen canteens and sock hops)				
1940s	G.I.s	Silent	crooning	Frank Sinatra
1950s	Silent	Silent	crossover	Elvis Presley
(TREMOR: American Bandstand and the twist)				
1960s	Silent	Boomers	protest rock	Bob Dylan
1970s	Boomers	Boomers	disco	Bee Gees
(TREMOR: MTV and new wave)				
1980s	Boomers	Gen Xers	alternative	Madonna
1990s	Gen Xers	Gen Xers	grunge, rap	Nirvana
(TREMOR: downloading and boy bands)				
2000s	Gen Xers	Millennials	synthetic pop	'N Sync
2010s	Millennials	Millennials	—	—

Since the dawn of pop and the emergence of each new media technology, people of different ages have exercised varying degrees of influence over each aspect of the entertainment media. At the current time, these are the types most influenced by (and most popularly associated with) each age bracket:

* 'Tweens: music
* Teens: music, pop radio, film, rock concerts
* College-aged: film, rock concerts, video games
* Young singles: film, video games, clubs, TV comedy
* Young householders: TV comedy/drama/niche-cable
* Middle-aged people: TV drama/news/niche-cable, talk radio, theater
* Older people: TV news, theater, fine arts

The college-aged years of a new generation's breaking wave provide an important fulcrum for cultural change, because those are the years when they start to have a significant impact on forms of entertainment beyond music. During the 2003–2004 school year, Millennials occupied all four collegiate years for the first time. This suggests that the next several years will be particularly important for the Millennial cultural breakout.

Through their childhood and teen years—and even now, as they fill the ranks of collegians—Millennials have been almost entirely "consumers" of the culture created for them by Gen Xers. In their young adult era—now arriving—Millennials will move on to become primary culture creators: artists, musicians, writers, and interactive media authors, gradually replacing Gen Xers in these areas.

Here's the full time line for their breakout.

* Music: late 1990s to mid-'00s
* Film: mid- to late '00s
* Video games: mid- to late '00s
* Rock concerts: late '00s
* TV: late '00s to '10s
* Theater & fine arts: '10s and beyond

What's hitting Waxie Maxie a few years ago is just starting to hit the cineplex, Xbox, and PS3. In a few years, it will hit the satellite dish, and Broadway and Lincoln Center not long after that. Whatever the timing, the trend lines are clear.

This brings us to the core question:

The Millennial Makeover—What Will It Be?

The Millennial makeover will not take the form many in the entertainment industry have been wanting or expecting.

Millennials are poised to use civic life to rebel against the dominant culture. That's similar to what the G.I. Generation did in the 1930s—and very unlike what their Boomer parents, who used the culture to rebel against the then-dominant civic life, did in the 1960s. Boomers often saw pop culture celebrities as co-conspirators in their rebellion against a powerful establishment. Gen Xers often saw them simply as talented people who did their thing and got paid for it. Millennials, on the other hand, often see them as a powerful establishment that someone needs to rebel *against*.

How can this be?

Let's look briefly at recent trends in the major entertainment media categories—music and live entertainment, film and television, and Internet and video games—and examine how the Millennial makeover is already beginning to change each one.

Music and Live Entertainment

Like earlier teen generations born in the twentieth century, Millennials have been the nation's major retail consumers of music. Unlike earlier teen generations, however, they have entered into a quarrelsome, even hostile, relationship with a music industry that is dominated by the styles and products of Gen Xers and by the commercial and legal strategies of Boomers. The bottom line is that the music industry has done precious little—either in content, marketing, packaging, or technology—to capture the Millennial imagination.

It's widely known that the industry has not performed well lately. For four consecutive years, from 1999 to 2003, total U.S. sales of recorded music fell steeply. In 2004, total sales rose slightly (to $12.2 billion), but not enough to brighten a very dark picture. Sales that year remained lower in constant dollars than sales in every prior year since 1992, before Bill Clinton was

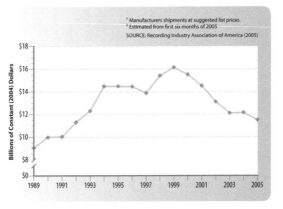

[1] Manufacturers shipments at suggested list prices
[2] Estimated from first six months of 2005
SOURCE: Recording Industry Association of America (2005)

◀ **Figure 6.1**

Total U.S. Recording Industry Sales,[1] 1989–2005[2]

elected to the White House. The estimates for 2005 show a renewed ($600 million) decline in sales of physical product, only partially offset by a ($125 million) rise in digital on-line sales.

What's less well known is that just about all the damage can be attributed to declining youth music purchases—which (through age 24, in constant dollars) were one-third smaller in 2004 than in 1989, when Ronald Reagan was still President. Over the same period, the youth share of total music purchases fell from 25 to 11 percent. Millennials are the first generation of 'tweens and teens in living memory to look at the music they see on the shelves and just say no thank you. Without midlife Americans replacing their older music libraries by purchasing lots of new CDs, the industry would be on the brink of collapse.

Many industry spokesmen have charged that the reason youth aren't buying music is that they're downloading it illegally. Yes, downloading is a problem. But Millennials stopped buying before they started downloading. The drop in youth purchases was steepest in the late '90s, before Napster and Gnutella and all the big early P2P services got underway. Millennials have no problem paying for music when it's purchasable in a format or product (online stores, ring tones, video games) that they like. On-line sales are indeed the one bright spot in the picture, with sales tripling in 2005 alone. To meet this new demand, many in the industry would have to change their business model, which they are reluctant to do. Major music labels have been far slower than other parts of the entertainment industry, especially video-game companies, in developing new ways to monetize the value of branded artists among young consumers.

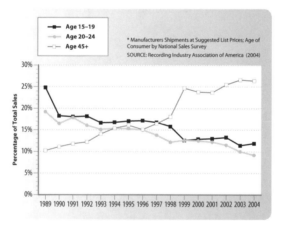

Figure 6.2 ▶

Share of U.S. Recording Industry Sales by Selected Consumer Age Brackets, 1989–2004

Further evidence that the music industry's Millennial problems run deeper than file sharing is the remarkable decline in the popularity of live concerts among youth. From 1976 to 2000, according to Gallup Polls, high school teens became 44 percent more likely to attend ballet, opera, and symphonies. Meanwhile, they became 22 percent less likely to attend rock concerts. Through 1992, teen rock concert goers outnumbered teen museum goers. Now, teens who go to museums considerably outnumber teens who go to rock concerts. One bright spot is the growing share of teen concertgoers who bring ticket buying parents with them.

The Graying of the Rock Concert

Over the last thirty years, the average age of the rock concert crowd, both performers and audience, has been getting older.

The explosive growth of rock concerts—their birth as a modern pop culture institution—came during the 1960s. It started with the Berkeley and Cambridge "folk revival" concerts in the very early '60s (featuring the likes of Joan Baez and Bob Dylan), gathered steam with the British invasion of the mid-'60s (the Beatles were able to sell out Shea Stadium in 1965 merely by word of mouth) and the emergent "counterculture" on display at San Francisco's Fillmore Auditorium. It reached a crescendo late in the decade with such iconic youth festivals as Monterey Pops in 1967 and Woodstock and Altamont in 1969.

The roster of performers at these events included few beyond their twenties (recall the motto: "don't trust anyone over 30"), and hardly anybody over 35. Films of those concerts reveal an audience nearly all of whom appear to have been under 25—a trend that persisted through the late '60s and into the '70s, with the mass of Boomer teens and collegians pushing their new "youth culture."

From the 1980s forward, the age of concert-goers has continuously risen. Now on the verge of retirement, aging Boomers continue to stage and attend rock extravaganzas. The youthful passion that once enlivened rock concerts gradually declined among Gen Xers, through the "Live Aid" '80s and "Lollapalooza" '90s. Since 1976, the share of teens who say they have attended a rock concert has declined from 40 to 31 percent.

Today, in a reversal of the 1960s, there are very few rock concert performers *under* age 35. In order, the Billboard Boxscore top ten grossing tours of 2004—ranging from $125 million (Madonna) to $44 million (Toby Keith)—are shown in Table 6.2.

The average age of these ten performers was 50. To be sure, several young stars just happened to be no-shows in 2004—like Brittney Spears, Christina Aguilera, and Jessica Simpson (average age, 24). Yet one can also point to a crowd of legendary old-schoolers who typically have better years than in 2004 and are expected to roar back in 2005—Rolling Stones, Bruce Springsteen, U2, Elton John, Rod Stewart, Pink Floyd, Phil Collins, and Carlos Santana (average age, 57). Not a single rap star has yet entered the ranks of the top-grossing tours.

Forty years ago, rock concerts evoked images of a youth rebellion. Today, they evoke images of midlife nostalgia, fueled by those same youth forty years older.

An aging audience is a shrinking audience. From 1996 to 2003, the annual number of concerts declined by 16 percent. Ticket sales fell in tandem. Meanwhile, to sustain total revenue, promoters like Clear Channel raised the average ticket price by 8.9 percent per year (versus an inflation rate of only 2.3 percent). The highest price for an all-day ticket to Woodstock was $6.50, most attendees paid nothing, and everyone sat wherever they could find a spot. Today, a premium seat for acts such as Paul McCartney or the Rolling Stones are listed for $250 to $400, and on-line brokers often ask $1,000 or more. In the past year, promoters have cut ticket prices in an effort to stem the decline. Even so, the year 2005 is likely to register double-digit percentage declines in ticket sales.

As the rock concert has aged, its economic function has changed. In its early decades, the concert was largely a promotional device to push album sales. Today, its main purpose is to make a profit on its own ledger. Its image in the eyes of youth has also changed. Today, Millennials kids are more likely to go (or be reluctantly persuaded to go) to a concert to see what their Boomer and Gen-X parents once enjoyed than to go see something they have discovered on their own.

The rock concert cannot forever sustain itself on the same generational fan base, growing older by the decade. To re-energize, it needs a new youth fan base—and to find that, it will have to be freshened, teched-up, and retooled.

Table 6.2: Top Grossing Touring Artists of 2004		
Rank	Artist	Age
1	Madonna	46
2	Prince	46
3	Shania Twain	39
4	Simon & Garfunkel	63
5	Metallica	41
6	Bette Midler	60
7	Sting	53
8	Kenny Chesney	36
9	David Bowie	57
10	Toby Keith	43

But this doesn't compensate for the overall decline in youth interest. The live concert industry cannot indefinitely keep raising its ticket prices for an aging audience.

Every available indicator—from the downloading of song files and the aging-up of rock concerts to the new youth revival in musical theater—suggests that this generation will democratize and technologize the music culture in ways that will rock the industry. The tremor has already hit. The reshaping of the industry is about to begin.

Film and Television

Movie producers and the TV networks, seeing that they aren't suffering as much as the music industry, may suppose they're doing a better job connecting with Millennials. To some extent, they are. But neither movies nor TV can afford complacency. Given the size and spending power of the Millennial youth market, the long-term revenue trends are disappointing—and the most recent news is downright worrisome.

In the movie world, there have been positive trends. Many of the highest-grossing films of recent years have been family-friendly and kid-oriented, including such box-office giants as *Harry Potter*, *Monsters, Inc.*, *Elf*, and

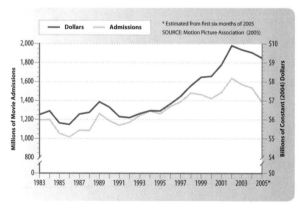

Figure 6.3 ▶

Gross U.S. Box Office Receipts and Movie Admissions, 1983–2005*

Finding Nemo. These films continued the decade-long golden age of children's film-making, which began in 1989 with *The Little Mermaid.* In 2004, nine out of ten of the highest grossing films were Millennial-targeted—from *Shrek 2* and *The Incredibles* to *The Polar Express* and *National Treasure* (the only exception being *The Bourne Supremacy*). Many teen films like *Save The Last Dance* have ridden a strong wave of interest in confident and take-charge

Millennial girls. The *Spider-Man* series has started (with a lag) to extend the same kind of anti-slacker persona to boys.

Once vibrant Gen-X film styles seem increasingly nostalgic and risky at the box office. In action-adventure films, directors are replacing lone-wolf male leads with "family men"—who are usually accompanied by children. As genres, slasher films and super-edgy teen comedies (like *American Pie*) appear to be weakening.

Meanwhile, "R" ratings have been in steep decline since 2000. Although movie studios still produce plenty of R-rated stuff, it no longer sells nearly as well. In 2003, R-rated films accounted for 7 in 10 new releases, but only 2 in 10 of the top-grossing hits—and R-rated films do even worse in the DVD after-market. Millennials are an important reason for this decline. Fewer teens want to see or (as carding gets stricter) are allowed to see R-rated films, and fewer families feel comfortable watching them together.

Fortune magazine writer Granger David, after summing up the stark mismatch between the R-rated tilt of Hollywood output and the G-rated tilt of everything that makes money, recently de-clared: "If Hollywood were run like a real business...where things like return on investment mattered, there would be one unchallenged, sacred principle that studio chieftains would never violate: Make lots of G-rated movies." Fortunately, studios have produced enough good G-rated movies— along with good PG- and PG-13-rated movies— to keep the movie theaters filled. Or at least they have until recently.

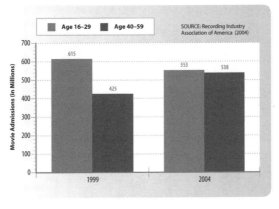

◀ **Figure 6.4**

Total Movie Admissions by Selected Age Brackets, 1999 and 2003

Just as Millennials are entering the prime Hollywood-targeted age bracket (remember, this starts later for movies than for music), there are signs that the film industry faces serious new challenges—even in the PG category. In 2003 and 2004, annual admissions and constant-dollar ticket receipts in U.S.

movie theaters experienced modest declines, followed by a double-digit percentage decline during first half of 2005.

The major studios might dismiss the theater business as a mere media-marketing sideline for an industry that now makes 80 percent of its global revenues off DVD sales (to rental chains and homes) and off TV rights. But as movie demand keeps shifting from the theater to the home entertainment center, studios should worry that their product may soon be redefined and repriced as a just another "console" activity. In 2005, moreover, even DVD sales have decelerated sharply, with some evidence that the recent cooling both in ticket and DVD sales is coming disproportionately from youth.

In its relation to Millennials, the movie industry may be nearing the same point where the music industry was in the late '90s—the point of maximum collision with the breaking wave of this generation. If so, the stakes will rise for movie executives, making this an important time to re-examine their approach to the youth market to see how they might strengthen what they're doing right and eliminate what they're doing wrong.

For television, less is immediately at risk. Millennials are years away from making their major mark on TV since they are currently at the younger edge of the age 18 to 34 bracket most desired by advertisers. However, the apparent youth indifference to this medium—and their facility with DVRs like TiVo and other ad avoidance technologies—might warrant some fundamental rethinking of the long-term future of the industry.

The youth market situation in television is a mixed one, with cable generally doing better than the broadcast networks. In some areas, TV has been responding well to Millennial tastes—for example, in the thriving fortunes of the two premier kid networks, Nickelodeon and Disney, and in the production of smart new teen-oriented programming on several other networks (WB, Fox, and UPN). Quality shows about family life, high school, epic adventure, and superheroes have done well with 'tweens and teens. The occasional risqué film or show finds an audience too, but many of the shows that once had large teen followings, from MTV to cable comedy shows, now have aging Gen-X audiences. Even wrestling, a '90s-era staple with 'tween and teen males, is starting to lose its youth audience. A large, yet-to-be-filled programming gap is emerging for first-wave Millennials in the late teen and early adult age brackets.

Nielsen Research, confirming the magnitude of that gap, recently found that prime-time TV viewing by males age 18 to 24 dropped ten full percentage points between 1999 and 2003, with the steepest fall during evening prime time. This loss was only partly compensated by a gain in late "night owl" viewing between 1 and 6 AM. Nielsen found that the 14- to 17-year-old viewership has also fallen. The "nostalgia" shows still draw teens, but new scripted shows aren't reaching younger audiences, especially young males, as effectively as they once did.

This recent decline is a continuation of a longer trend. Over the last fifteen years, the rate of TV watching has been falling in every youth age bracket just as soon as Millennials have entered that bracket—making this the first-ever teen generation to watch less TV than the one before it.

Why is overall teen TV time declining? Millennials are much busier than earlier generations. They have less "free time." When they do have time, they have many more hi-tech leisure options available to them—from sending IMs to their friends and playing video games to going on the Internet. In hours per week, according to Harris Interactive, the Internet (16.7 hours) now actually exceeds TV (13.6 hours) among youth aged 13 to 24. Even when they do watch TV, Millennials are likely to multi-task, which means that they're watching with less focus. Shows like MTV tend to resemble digital wallpaper in their eyes, a bit like the animated portraits on the stony walls of Hogwarts Castle. They have it on, but they aren't really paying attention.

Raised with computers since birth, Millennials expect to interact with their media. But TV can't really offer interactivity, which may explain the well-researched finding that there is a directly inverse relationship between computer time and TV time among teens. Interactive shows like "American Idol" offer a partial response to this new youth desire (and to their equally strong desire to "fire" many pop celebrities). But, clearly, this is only a stop-gap. As Millennials mature, some merger between TV and Internet entertainment seems inevitable.

Both visual media, movies and TV, are discovering that file sharing is not just a music problem. It is also their problem. As more Millennials gain access to broadband Internet, more of them are able to fiddle with video files—downloading and uploading, sampling and watching. Portable entertainment players (like the new iPod) will soon be filling up with both legal and illegal video downloads. Once again, the public hears the familiar heated rhetoric and witnesses the familiar legal antics and legislative hoopla.

Thus far, the movie industry, like the music industry, is holding firm to existing business models, and is using courts and legislatures to bolster that defense. TV networks are responding with much greater urgency and creativity, no doubt because they are feeling the heat from DVRs, from slack demand for TV ads, and from the rapidly growing flood of ad spending pouring into the Internet (expected to reach $13 billion in 2005). They are doing their best to diversify, with pay-per-view, programs on DVD, and a steady migration of content to Internet formats.

Millennials, once again, are on the cutting edge of this shift. They are the viewers most attracted to such newfangled attractions as *maniatv.com*, a 24/7 live Internet TV "network." They explain why cable networks (with younger fans) are rushing in this direction much faster than the old broadcast networks. Several of them are already putting ad-supported episodes of popular youth shows on the Internet. Soon, most of the networks are likely to approve a system offering Internet-searchable, pay-for-view programs. This approach is a good fit for the fragmented and serial nature of much TV programming. It's also a good fit for Millennials, as hands-on video consumers and "indie" video producers.

These young video producers are themselves becoming a force that is growing by the year. Hundreds of colleges and high schools now have built-in video studios and offer digital video (DV) courses taught by instructors with substantial real-world experience. Outside school, many young people are buying digital videocams and sophisticated editing software. You see evidence of this in network news "disaster" footage from local amateurs, and in the recent boom in local newspapers and Webzines soliciting stories from young "citizen reporters." Al Gore's new Internet-based "Current TV" network intends to rely on audience-generated programming for at least a quarter of its material. In time, this will happen on a much broader scale, on the Internet and elsewhere, where teched-up young indie filmmakers will start offering inexpensive and professional-looking program segments and even full-length movies.

When Millennials see the future of their pop culture, they see that it is democratized not just on the consumer side, but on the producer side as well.

The Internet and Video Games

The Millennial Generation has never really known a world without the Internet. It's been with the oldest Millennials from middle school forward. And it's been with younger Millennials (today, through high school) since forever. The percentage of families with home-based Internet, and the percentage of young people with their own email addresses, skyrocketed during the late '90s. By contrast, most Gen Xers first encountered the Internet as young adults or just coming out of college, and most Boomers first encountered it in or entering midlife.

This location in history has given Millennials a very different attitude toward the Internet than that of older generations. For them, it's like what a pencil and paper were for Boomers—an extension of a person's voice, thoughts, and dreams. Millennials use the Internet to communicate, play games, meet friends, ask questions, research issues, confess secrets, wonder about stuff, and just while away the time. In recent years, according to the UCLA World Internet Project, Internet use by 12- to 15-year-olds has reached 97 percent, compared to 75 percent for their parents.

With each passing year, young people are taking advantage of widening online opportunities for networked group participation—whether in discussing, gaming, or organizing. Even when Gen-Xers and Boomers do feel entirely at home with the Internet, it's mainly as a solo-empowerment tool. Only Millennials intuitively grasp its capacity to empower teamwork.

For today's young people, the Internet is a force multiplier for community action. They use it this way in group organizing, in community outreach, and in political mobilization. "Swarming" is a colorful illustration of how it works. In campus towns and urban areas, college-age students and young singles organize "smart mobs" through the Internet (or cell phones), and then use this rapid-fire form of chat to arrange very quickly to go to some pre-set location where they do something goofy but legal, very briefly, and then disperse.

The risk is very real that the Internet, in Millennial hands, could marginalize important segments of the entertainment industry, stripping companies of control over content, over distribution—and over revenues. With each passing month, Internet entrepreneurs are making daring new incursions into traditional media categories—from full-length music videos and weekly TV shows to online music stores and video-rental services, university courses and museum galleries, pop culture quizzes and current events, and interactive advertorials and infomercials. Dozens of small video producers are now swarming to produce serialized Web movies, supported entirely by advertisers and subscribers. To date, most entertainment companies have responded in only very limited ways to this new challenge—with experimental trials and promotions that have secured at best only tentative footholds in this new medium.

As more Millennials come of age over the next decade, the era of experimentation will end and the era of full-scale adaptation will begin—all under the heat of the digital IT revolution. Entire forms of entertainment will make the Internet their permanent media home, beginning with music videos, news shows, documentaries, and old movies, and then with TV serials and sporting events. Advertisers will have to harness the Web's interactive potential and not just offer Internet versions of TV ads (just as, in the early days of TV, ads had to get beyond the talk-driven ad format of radio). Every form of entertainment will come under growing consumer pressure to move to the Internet. Multi-tasking Millennials, in particular, will wonder why they have to watch a dumb "channel" or hear a generic "station." They will ask why everything can't be customized to their own preferences.

Some companies, finding themselves unable to adapt, will be desperate to find ways to retain youth interest in their broadcast-type media in the face of the Internet challenge. A successful strategy may be to emphasize how well their "mass" media projects an aura of national community and big branding—attractive images for Millennials. Some marketers believe that commercial TV ads retain a legitimacy edge among young people for just this reason: They appear on a medium that's public and national and standard—something that young people may continue to savor in the midst of personalized on-demand entertainment. A smart executive will exploit such opportunities.

Video gaming in recent years has become one of the entertainment industry's major success stories. Among the major forms of pop culture, it is also the newest, the most comfortable with the Internet, and the most dominated by Millennial consumers.

Total U.S. video game sales, hardware and software, have nearly doubled in constant dollars since 1997 and reached $9.9 billion in 2004. Even this figure doesn't include the most recent and explosive gaming category, online game subscriptions, which now amount to about $500 million and are expected to hit $1.5 billion by 2007. Roughly 40 million households include at least one person who plays online games, double the level of just five years ago.

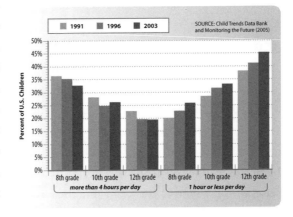

SOURCE: Child Trends Data Bank and Monitoring the Future (2005)

◄ **Figure 6.5**

Daily Hours of TV Watching in Grades 8, 10, and 12

These sales figures put video games ahead of movie theater revenues, and on track to pass recorded music sales in just two or three years. Computer and gaming magazines have grown in circulation and ad revenues even as other teen-targeted publications have suffered advertising slumps. Console games have come to dominate sales growth, with new sales surges arriving after the introduction of each new level of technology (most recently, Sony's PS3 and Microsoft's Xbox 360). These two companies have tooled these networked devices to be useful not just for gaming, but also for channeling and organizing all kinds of household media. Game capable cell phones (like Nokia's N-Gage gamer's phone) are becoming popular among young people and may soon compete against consoles.

Led by creative strategizers, the video game industry has entered a partnership with the professional sports leagues and has thereby created a whole new cross-platform business model. For years, game companies have obtained the exclusive rights to pro sports trademarks (including digital images of recognizable players), enabling gamers to play complete virtual branded sports games like Electronic Arts' Madden NFL. The more realistic these games become and the more widely they are played, the more they will add to the revenue of both sides of the entire sports "experience"—video game companies and professional sports leagues.

The average age of videogamers has steadily risen over the past decade, warping the demographic breakdown, which now features a concentration of young Millennials and then a wide age scattering of older people. According to the industry's own reckoning, 35 percent of "serious" gamers are 18 and under, roughly another 10 percent are college-aged, and then the other 55 percent are distributed among older Gen-Xers and Boomers.

Video game producers know that a new game is more likely to become widely popular if it does well with the concentrated mass of young Millennial consumers. At the same time, they are aware that half of their core customers are over age 30—many of them Xers and Boomers who have aged with gaming over time and are often still attached to the gaming styles of an earlier era. "Edgy" and anti-social game themes were once associated almost exclusively with youth. Today, however, they are at least as popular among young adults in their late-20s and 30s—a good example of how distinctive tastes can "age up" over time.

Although serious gamers tend to be mostly male across all age brackets, there is an emerging generational difference among female consumers. Relatively few older women played games as teens, while Millennial girls have dominated certain popular games (like *The Sims*) from 'tweenhood on. Women of all ages have become very strong participants in the fast-growing "Massively Multiplayer Online Games" (MMOGs).

Millennial Downloading

The unpaid "downloading" (or file sharing) of digital music arose as a concern for the recorded music industry shortly after the emergence of Napster in 1999—and in the midst of a long decline in music sales to teenagers. A brief sales rebound and a successful legal assault against Napster calmed industry nerves somewhat, but not for long. Since then, three consecutive years of double-digit sales losses, combined with lost court battles against file-sharing Web sites Kazaa and Morpheus, led the Recording Industry Association of America (RIAA) to counterattack against music fans who download.

In a speech at the 2002 Grammy awards that many young people recall unfavorably, recording industry executive Michael Greene delivered a lengthy and pointed accusation against a "young generation" he described as "oh so criminal." In the spring and summer of 2003, RIAA tried to police, or at least deter, collegiate downloaders by enlisting university administrators—with mixed success. Soon thereafter, industry lawyers filed suit against 261 Web-linked persons who had each downloaded more than 1,000 music files on their computers, trying to instill fear of punishment in countless others through the publicity generated by the action. Additional mass lawsuits have been filed periodically ever since.

In their newly recorded CDs, the music industry is also experimenting with a variety of software "locks" to limit the number of time buyers can reuse the CD files. Their purpose is not so much to prevent file sharing as to help deter it by making it more troublesome. Meanwhile, as broadband spreads to a larger share of households (and "super broadband" to many colleges), the film industry is beginning to worry about downloading, as well. Thus far, movie studios are following the music industry's steps—warnings, then lawsuits, followed by more sophisticated software locks.

Despite this industry resistance, lateral file-trading networks are likely to be around for a long time. To date, roughly 10 billion audio files have been traded by persons 14 years and older. As Millennials age, and more in this generation reach their teen years, that number will surely keep growing.

The main short-term consequence of the industry's current strategy has been less to stop non-revenue downloads than to push Millennials toward low-price on-line stores that mimic file sharing. This era officially began late in 2001, when Apple Computer introduced iTunes and the iPod. It has been gaining strength ever since, with a growing variety of software and hardware vendors.

The main long-term consequence, which should be of great concern to industry leaders, is to reinforce the widespread youth view that large entertainment companies—and the music industry in particular—are adversaries, not allies, of today's young people.

There are three common myths about downloading:

■ **Myth One:** *Teens download because they care less these days about stealing or breaking the law.* That is Michael Greene's argument, but there is no evidence to support it. It is contradicted by the fact that rates of violent and property crime among have fallen dramatically over the past decade. It also disregards surveys showing that most teens who download are uncomfortable that what they are doing may be illegal. Teens download not to be openly defiant, but because the technology makes it practically effortless. For young Boomers, who certainly were not above "ripping off the man" in their heyday, the art of copying a song or movie was difficult and inexact, and required equipment that was expensive and hard to find. For Millennials, the art of copying is simple,

exact, and requires equipment that is relatively inexpensive and owned by nearly everybody.

■ **Myth Two:** *Teen downloading is a major reason for the music industry's fall-off in CD sales.* This is implausible for the simple reason that the first big drop in CD sales occurred in 1997, when hardly anybody yet knew about file-sharing. The first file-sharing service used by significant numbers of teens (Napster) was not available until the fall of 1999. Young people are quick to say that the main reasons they are buying fewer CDs are simple: They do not want to buy music in CD format—and, given the choice, they do not want to pay for songs they don't want to hear.

■ **Myth Three:** *File sharing will eventually be driven out of existence.* This is not going to happen. In any generational battle involving technology, Boomer CEOs and lawyers cannot possibly defeat Millennial consumers and the Gen-X entrepreneurs who will invent and sell them the tools they want. What will happen, instead, is that new forms of media delivery (such as single-song on-line stores) will start seriously competing with free downloads. "File sharing is a reality, and it would seem that the labels would do well to learn how to incorporate it into their business models somehow," posted Moby, a genre-busting DJ and recording artist, in a post on his Web site. "Record companies suing 12-year-old girls for file sharing is kind of like horse-and-buggy operators suing Henry Ford."

Compared with older generations—including Gen-X—Millennials are far more facile with emerging technologies, far more tempted to buy them and use them, and far more inclined to discard "old" entertainment media that don't fit their emerging lifestyle. With the Internet and video gaming as with all other forms of entertainment, Millennials share a collective sense of entitlement. They are the first generation that expects to control the media they consume. They understand that entertainment is going digital—and, as a group, they sense the power to steer new digital technologies in the direction they want.

PART TWO

THE POP CULTURE

THE POP CULTURE

We now consider the various forms of youth-targeted entertainment in terms of the seven core traits of the Millennial Generation. At the start of each chapter, we'll identify four key strategies. We'll then address trends that suggest these strategies, in each media. At the close of each chapter, we'll discuss implications for pop culture aimed at the older generations.

Some of these trends are very apparent today, some are just starting to be visible, and others have yet to arrive. None of these trends has reached its point of maximum impact. Those days are yet ahead.

7 | STRATEGIES FOR A SPECIAL GENERATION

"'Smallville' is easy to criticize. It's hokey, often contrived, and far tamer than most teen-oriented shows.... But 'Smallville' works because it plays like a comic book come to life: it's grand, mythical, and action-packed, ...a familiar journey with a preordained conclusion, so the show is all about the struggle to get there."

— TV reviewer Mary Colgan (2003)

STRATEGIES FOR A
SPECIAL GENERATION

Collectively, Millennials have grown up as the special object of parental and public attention in ways that Generation X did not. The difference can be traced back literally to birth. In 1979, according to the Yankelovich Monitor, 45 percent of women aged 20 to 40 agreed that "having a child is an experience every woman should have." By 1999, that percentage had risen to 68 percent.

Gen-X grew up during an passionate era in which society turned away from kids. Many Xers absorbed the lesson of the child of divorce writ large—everyone was happy until we came along. Millennials, by contrast, have grown up during a backlash era in which society rediscovered kids. From birth onward, a sense of wantedness has accompanied their growth, from grammar school through college.

In this respect, Millennials have something in common with young Boomers—who also arrived in a post-crisis era when America yearned to reclaim some sense of hearth and family. Yet there is a critical difference. Young Boomers grew up in schools and neighborhoods that were often more comfortably child-focused than the

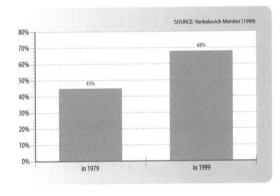

SOURCE: Yankelovich Monitor (1999)

◀ **Figure 7.1**

"Having a Child is an Experience Every Woman Should Have." (Share of Women Aged 20–40 Agreeing)

families. National policies and big institutions and social habits hugely favored kids, to be sure, but many parents felt a deep dissatisfaction with the roles of mother and father as then defined.

Millennials, as a generation, feel a specialness that started with the devotion of families and parents and that has only belatedly worked its way out into our national civic life. More than Boomers—and very unlike Gen Xers—Millennials sense they are the *personal* focus of adult aspirations. Few were procreated out of habit or by mistake. Most feel their parents chose to have them for a reason. Now growing up, these Millennials expect the popular culture to treat them the same way.

Here are four key strategies that address Millennials as a *special* generation.

* **Present a purposeful world.** Most Millennials believe that, collectively, they are here for an important purpose. They don't yet know exactly what that purpose is, of course. It might be building better communities, cleaning up the environment, ridding the world of terror, paying back the national debt, or some combination of the above. But everything they do—even the jokes they laugh at or the "downtime" cartoons they watch in their college dorms—is framed by an overarching sense that the direction of history depends in some way on what they do. This is a special new turn in the youth mood.

    When Boomers were young, the world seemed overloaded with "great society" adults who were sure they had all the Big Solutions. Boomers thought the world would be better off if they could deflate the hubris of such earth-movers. So that's what they did. Gen Xers arrived when all that hubris was imploding. They came of age during the Seinfeldian '90s, when some of the most popular entertainments involved people whose personal styles and ironic attitudes were more important than any collective plans or deliberate actions. Gen Xers never had the sense that they were here for a larger purpose. For Xers, only individuals have purpose—and that purpose is typically to keep off the radar screen of big institutions and to try to avoid the accidents of history.

Millennials are turning another corner. Boomers gained fame as the generation that asked "why?" Gen Xers earned theirs as the generation that made ironic fun of such big questions ("why ask why?"). Millennials are showing themselves to be the generation to ask the question "why not?" They assume that the big questions will require big answers—answers that work, answers that they themselves (more than other generations) will have to implement.

* **Harness the high Millennial regard for their own generation.** Far more than Gen Xers, and differently than Boomers at the same age, Millennials have a high regard for themselves, not just as individuals, but also *as a group*. Wherever they are—college, high school, sports team, theater group, student government, clubs—they are more inclined to think of anything done by their youth peers as competent, effective, and promising.

As older critics point out, this high self-esteem is not always a positive trait. Many teachers and employers are complaining about naive kids who have been so spoiled and praised, so showered with rewards both verbal and material, that they will never be able to cope well in the ego-bruising "real world." Yet this very criticism highlights a big difference between Millennials and Gen Xers. Fifteen years ago, older critics tore into young people for the opposite reason—for being cynical "proto-adults" who had been "abandoned" by their parents and schools and had been "rushed" through childhood. Whereas today's Millennials are sometimes panned as coddled and overstructured, Gen Xers used to be panned as neglected and unstructured.

Entertainment needs to shift its focus accordingly. You could not effectively target young Gen-X as a "generation;" with Millennials, it's now possible. It's harder to sell today's youth on a social environment in which young people obsess only about their personal goals—or lack thereof. It's easier to sell them on a world in which young people acknowledge all the attention they've received and probe for ways in which they can collectively pay the world back. The alienated slacker will no longer be taken seriously, except as an off-beat or humorous foil. The overprogrammed spoiled kid will be fresh new presence, both in serious drama and in comedy.

* **Depict Millennials as better-behaved than older people.** In the Boomer era, teens and collegians were often depicted as outwardly prepared, but, like Dustin Hoffman's Boomer-era character in *The Graduate*, as inwardly messed up. The new image for today's Millennials is that of Harry Potter — a child wizard who navigates a stormy childhood full of outward dangers, but who is inwardly marked by determination and greatness. Hoffman's worldly parents live comfortable lives. Potter's magical parents sacrifice their own lives for their child's. For young Boomers, behaving badly around such complacent adults was a way to redeem society. For young Millennials, that makes no sense at all. Today's Boomer and Xer adults have enough trouble behaving well themselves. Why add to the mayhem?

Hank Stuever, cultural critic for the *Washington Post*, describes the Potter phenomenon as "a symptom of what happens when every child is told that he or she is very special." What does this mean for entertainment? "Kids who are this self-satisfied," notes Stuever, "cannot be good news for the future of angry art...." True, but it can be good news for the future of un-angry art, which can be just as creative.

Up to now, showing teens and young adults in a negative light, or treating them as targets for sarcasm, has worked fairly well. Millennials still buy, and listen to, plenty of angry music. They still buy tickets to, and watch, plenty of angst movies. But, for the most part, that music, and those films, speak of an anger and angst they don't feel. The experience of the G.I. Generation, as the flaming-youth '20s evolved into the good-kid '30s, suggests that this veneer will wear away. In time, Millennials will expect their entertainments to reverse negative images of youth and replace them with positive ones, as occurred in the late 1930s.

* **Make the audience feel as special as the star.** Pop-culture "stars" were, in many respects, an invention of the 1920s. Ever since, each new rising generation has built up, torn down, or entirely redefined what "stardom" means. When Boomers were growing up, the prevailing stardom was bland and its cultural hold on America seemed relatively weak and superficial. Boomers changed all that. As they reshaped the pop culture in a more aggressive and "meaningful" direction, they witnessed the reputations of pop stars grow to mythic proportions (along with their wealth and glamour).

Millennials have been growing up in the shadow of this Boomer infatuation with pop stars as culture heroes. They are inundated with news about the lives, styles, and fortunes of "stars" of all ages. They see their parents fussing over old rock memorabilia or video clips and sometimes even share these obsessive hobbies with their parents. But Millennials do not, on the whole, like the crop of pop-culture celebrities that older people tell *them* to admire and emulate. Rather, Millennials feel special when they can choose artists for themselves—and choose them for reasons that put the whole overhyped pop culture back in its place. TV shows featuring *non*-celebrities (witness the success of "American Idol") are popular among this generation. When asked to name their personal heroes, Millennials seldom mention celebrity athletes or entertainers. A recent Yahoo youth survey revealed that celebrity product endorsements are among the least important influences on teen purchase decisions.

When Millennials think about the entertainment industry, they are more inclined to see an enemy intent on getting teens to buy whatever their stars produce than a friend interested in what teens actually like hearing or seeing. The efforts of the music and film industries to stop file-sharing via lawsuits have reinforced this adversarial feeling. Millennials think that aging Boomer and Gen-X stars get plenty of special treatment already. They think it's time that teen audiences got more of it themselves.

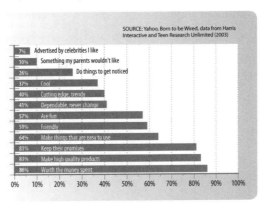

SOURCE: Yahoo, Born to be Wired, data from Harris Interactive and Teen Research Unlimited (2003)

7% Advertised by celebrities I like
10% Something my parents wouldn't like
26% Do things to get noticed
37% Cool
40% Cutting edge, trendy
41% Dependable, never change
57% Are fun
59% Friendly
64% Make things that are easy to use
81% Keep their promises
83% Make high quality products
86% Worth the money spent

◀ **Figure 7.2**

How important is it to you that the brands you use be the following?

Implications for Music and Live Entertainment

Young Boomers embraced pop music that gave expression to the profound distance they felt from the values and lives of their parents and thus to their discovery of generational alienation. Young Gen Xers, sensing the alienation without the discovery, often described their own generation as simply "lost." Young Millennials, by contrast, are gravitating toward pop music that acknowledges a new-found closeness to parents and thus to a fresh feeling of generational specialness.

The new sensibility originated with the singing stars themselves. Back in 1997, the early boy bands mesmerized teen audiences with surprising interviews about how close they had always been to their moms. Ever since, a growing range of stars have joined in these pro-mom testimonials, from Britney Spears and Avril Lavigne to Kanye West, Beyoncé, and Ashanti. Even the most hardened rappers have started to "pay back" respect and support to the mom and family. Song lyrics now make more references to family in tones of love and respect and fewer (as was once common) in tones of hostility and distance.

Increasingly, teens bring their moms along to music concerts, and the stars oblige them by singing songs "just for the moms" or even by bringing their own moms out on stage. Some venues have parent rooms, and authors of parenting books urge moms and dads to buy tickets and come along. "Going to a concert, even if it means driving a few hours, shows your adolescent that what's important to her is on your agenda," writes Margaret Sagarese in *iVillage*. "You've put your money where your mouth is."

In their homes, parents do what they can to foster and participate in the musical activities of their special kids—buying them Internet access, music software, drums, keyboards, lessons, even mini-recording studios in finished basements. The lucky kids get to go to expensive summer camps (an ad for one promises, "No Canoes—Lots of Rock") to learn how to play their parents' old songs. Meanwhile, youthful garage bands are moving from the fringe of family life to its epicenter. Most of today's most hyped teen rock bands have been organized, and smartly promoted, by Boomer parents in the music business. The sons and daughters of entertainment scions will use their connections to launch careers that reflect the form, but not the substance, of what their parents once did.

Today's 19-year-old rock 'n roller is thus very likely to bask in parental approval. This has obvious implications for themes and lyrics. They can no longer attract most teens by urging defiance against an abusive or neglectful society. *Pink*-style music celebrities—unconventional outcasts and self-proclaimed freaks—will run the risk of being seen as "losers" who never themselves managed to obtain the family security Millennials feel. At best, their performances can be widely appreciated only as jokes, or just words.

Youths who enjoy the spotlight so often in their daily lives are also becoming less tolerant of media producers who prefer that the spotlight shine only their own stars. Hold on, these kids are saying, we are the consuming audience. We want the spotlight too. We want choices in how we listen to music. We want to enjoy one song without paying big bucks for promotions or for the entire CDs. We want to be able to reshape our music for our lifestyles and friends. We want to listen to it when we want, where we want, how we want. We want to be respected for our mastery of digital technology and our ability to organize instant fan communities. Most of all, we want to listen to music *about* ordinary kids like us and *by* ordinary kids like us.

In short, Millennials want to be competed for, and genuinely served, as if their idea of what music is or could be is as important as the industry's. To date, these special consumers have driven the rise of file swapping and download sampling, the iPod craze and podcasting, song remixing and song sharing. They have created a sudden demand for venues that invite unknown young people to perform—from the stage of "American Idol" to such newly hyped Web sites as MSN's "garageband" (featuring free unsigned indie artists). Millennials want a music industry that really listens to them and respects them, *all* of them. Sooner or later, they will get it.

Implications for Film and Television

Cinematically, the entire life story of the Millennial Generation to date has given top billing to the special child—the innocent child who needs the love of others, who offers love in return, and who ends up in some sense saving the world or at least the world of everyone in the show.

The special child debuted with a bang in the early '80s with *Baby Boom*, *Raising Arizona*, and *Three Men and a Baby*, about infants and babies that gave new and positive meaning to the lives of older people. It gathered momentum in the early '90s with *Sleepless in Seattle* and *Searching for Bobby Fischer*, about young kids whose behavior shames parents into becoming better people. It reached fuller fruition, with yet older kids, in the Harry Potter and Spider-Man movies, about youths literally marked by destiny to live up to higher standards of conduct and achievement and thus to become society-saving heroes.

Over the last few years, it is no accident that the special-hero motif has broadened into a explosion of epic movies—popular among all ages, yet especially older teens and young adults—about civilization-founding or civilization-saving heroes. These range from pure fantasy like *The Lord of the Rings* series, to historical fantasy (like *Troy*, *Alexander*, and *King Arthur*), to more realistic history (like *Saving Private Ryan*), to world-shattering sci-fi (like *Deep Impact* or *The Day After Tomorrow*). Many of these movies feature young heroes whose deeds or safe return is critical to the entire plot.

This theme of cosmic and positive specialness is rarely if anywhere to be found among the movies and TV shows made for young Boomers and young Gen Xers. And now that these two generations monopolize the ranks of producers, it is sometimes difficult for them to grasp why the specialness trend is so consequential. Increasingly, the ascendant story lines are about great challenges or hard luck afflicting cared-about young people, *good* young people, reminiscent of the plots of the 1930s and '40s. Older characters will protect, guide, or defend them. Villains will seek to subvert them for personal, ego-driven ends. Youth will accept and welcome help from older people—in contrast to Easy Riders of the '60s, breakaways struggling to "get inside their heads," or the Breakfast Clubbers of the '80s, throwaways struggling to make it on their own.

The specialness theme need not be treated in a deadly serious manner. Some films are succeeding with a more whimsical or even comedic approach, often about "golden youth" that don't defeat corrupt older people, but reform them (*Big Daddy*, *About a Boy*, *Elf*). A complementary plot line shows a worldly-wise older sibling guiding an innocent Millennial through sticky situations (*10 Things I Hate About You*, *Orange County*).

On TV, Millennial children have grown accustomed to seeing countless young prodigies endowed with special powers and special responsibilities—from the anime figures of Pokémon to the superheroic Powerpuff Girls to the uniformed guys in Power Rangers. In recent years, we've seen older special kids star in lower-key drama, for example, in "Smallville" or "Sabrina the Teenage Witch." In each case, we see decent kids who try to live normal lives while coping (sometimes humorously) with vast powers they know are designed for larger purposes. Throwaway kids are on their way out. A TV series about young mutant turtles who suffered radioactive poisoning after being flushed down the toilet—the premise of an '80s-era animated favorite—would be unthinkable today.

Special Millennials also appear with rising frequently in TV commercials, with plenty of images of parents taking time from a busy work schedule to call or see a child. Over time, these images will evolve into story concepts which extend the notion of a "special" child or young adult, without the irony or self-referential snicker one commonly encounters in today's network shows.

Implications for the Internet and Video Games

Millennials feel a unique generational connection to the Internet, as they acquire the training and obtain the access to exploit it as a broadcast and entertainment medium. Thanks to the Web, they are the first youth generation to be routinely asked by businesses for suggestions about information technology. These suggestions are then taken very seriously. Web sites like *firehotquotes.com* attract, analyze, and report youth opinion in ways that are of interest to young people—and to those who wish to sell to them.

By celebrating the opinions of this special generation, along with the artist, the Internet can make or break markets for any entertainment—TV, film, music, games. It can also offer a distribution platform through which Millennials can bypass traditional broadcast networks and become the producers, directors, and "stars" of their own Web sites. In response, the networks are now actively seeking out new Internet platforms that happen to attract young users and just buying them up—which is how MTV acquired *neopets.com* (for $160 million) and how Rupert Murdoch's News Corporation acquired *myspace.com* (for $580 million). Each time, the purchaser solemnly vows not to alter the participatory flavor of these sites. The old media's not-invented-here attitude is rapidly disappearing.

Businesses are finding many ways to tap into this Millennial sense of personal technological empowerment. Digital devices are increasingly named after the "self"—from iPod to Microsoft's "My Music" and "My Video" in its Portable Media Center. To reach them via the Internet, entertainment companies are learning not to use passive tactics (like ads, especially those that annoy users) but instead to try engaging young people, individually and in groups, through interactive Web sites. Offer them something of real value—something useful, convenient, or fun—and they will keep coming back.

In the video game world, the hero is overtaking the celebrity throughout the interactive media. Many game site creators are giving Millennials the sense of personal control—and then defining game-play missions to cast them as heroes, even superheroes, who can join real-life heroes like firemen and eco-activists in quests to do great deeds. A few years ago, Hollywood experimented with celebrity-driven gaming titles. In the end, these titles have all but disappeared, even as the overall market for games has continued to grow. In a game, it's the Millennial player who is special. He or she is the "celebrity."

Implications for Older Generations

Gen-X styles remain dominant in today's popular culture, and a significant fraction of youth entertainment is still aimed at twenty- and thirtysomething Gen Xers. Those days can't and won't last. Whenever one generation is displaced in youth by another, its first reaction (especially among those who have little contact with kids) is to avoid or resist the new tide. Gen Xers in their thirties did not personally experience the shift in the youth mood, seldom have teens or collegians either as siblings or children—and, therefore, face a real challenge in interpreting and adapting program content to the special self- and group-regard of the generation rising up behind them.

Boomers and Gen Xers will retain interest in entertainments that feel familiar, recalling their own childhood and coming of age years. As Gen Xers age into their peak earning years, themes from their music and films will be heard and seen at executive conferences, on elevators, in ads for cars, insurance, and (eventually) pharmaceuticals—as has occurred for some time now with classic Boomer entertainers and their songs. Gen-X is already dipping into nostalgia via 'totally '80s" stations on pop radio.

A fresh new genre of drama can be made from Gen-X's new midlife plights and quests, as was done in the 1930s and '40s with the middle-aged "Lost Generation" in film. Classic crisis-era films like *Casablanca* featured midlife characters lost in a world without rules, while a younger generation fights and an older one commands. Similarly, the "casting out" of Gen-X 40-year-olds caught between pompous oldsters and straight-arrow youngsters will allow for the exploration of intriguing and amusing new story lines. The focus of self-mocking evil will shift steadily upward along the age ladder. Think of *Spy Kids* or *Big Fat Liar*, in which 'tweens or young teenagers defeat corrupt thirtysomethings with the aid of their parents—a plot line unimaginable twenty years ago.

Entertainments geared toward the specialness of small children will find additional adult support in the years ahead. As Gen Xers become parents themselves, many are becoming "X-treme" advocates of their own kids' specialness. Many won't dare allow what happened to them ever to touch their own children. The new Gen X-parented child and associated teen story lines can include some aspect of the aging Gen-X persona—for example, alienated loners who become ultra-protective parental figures. On the flip side, midlife Gen Xers will enjoy satire, sarcasm, or other cultural broadsides on the golden youth culture. Done right, Millennials will laugh at that, too.

8 | STRATEGIES FOR A SHELTERED GENERATION

Marlin: "I promised I'd never let anything happen to him."

Dory: "Well you can't 'never let anything happen to him.' Then nothing would ever happen to him. Not much fun for little Harpo."

— Finding Nemo (2003)

STRATEGIES FOR A
SHELTERED GENERATION

Millennials have grown up watching perimeters rise around all aspects of their lives. For many decades, Americans simply assumed that each new generation would be raised in a more "hands off" manner than the last. This newest generation is breaking the trend. In 2003 *American Demographics* surveyed parents of 'tween-agers and asked them if they allowed their kids to do a variety of outdoor activities (for example, bike to school or take a public bus alone). It then asked if they (the parents) were themselves allowed to do each activity when they were that age. By large margins, the parents reported that they were giving their own kids a lot less freedom than they had enjoyed.

By now, Millennials are used to this growing stress on protection. They expect it and, in some ways, they count on it. Today's collegians and teens

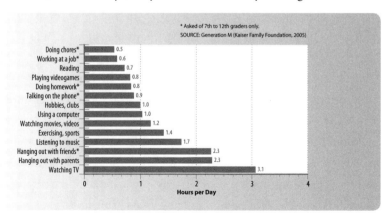

* Asked of 7th to 12th graders only.
SOURCE: Generation M (Kaiser Family Foundation, 2005)

◀ **Figure 8.1**

Daily Time Spent in
Selected Activities,
Age 8 to 18, in 2004

compliantly go along with adult intrusions that Boomers or Gen Xers, at that age, would have assailed as arbitrary, interfering, or violative of their rights. Indeed, they trust their parents and other authority figures to an extent many older people find hard to believe. For these (and other) reasons, Millennials are becoming more risk averse, more careful, more confined, and more sedentary than young people used to be.

Here are four key strategies that address Millennials as a *sheltered* generation.

✳ **Understand that Millennials tend to avoid needless risks.** For Millennials, foolhardy behavior is no longer cutting edge. It's been done by older generations, so there's nothing fresh about it. Millennials are more likely than Boomers or Gen Xers were at the same age to be disturbed by song lyrics or story lines that support risky behavior whose only purpose is to test boundaries.

Even if they aren't turned off by it, they will regard it as a formulaic repetition of a tired idea, as for example the film *XXX*, whose characters flout safety without reason. A profitable story line about youths who take over-the-top risks should either (a) target older generations who remain fascinated by youth dysfunction, as did the movie *13*, or (b) make it wickedly humorous, the way many teens listen to rap music. Far more than youths of two or four decades ago, today's collegians and teens will be inclined to view older people who tell younger people to take risks as unreal, even foolish, whereas those who help craft smart, even "hip" ways of avoiding or getting out of sticky situations will be seen as plausible mentors.

To be sure, worried parents are amplifying the same message. During the Boomer youth era, adult society eased restrictions on the culture available to children (most notably, with the discarding of the old Hayes Movie Production Code in 1968). During the Millennial youth era, adults have been trying to impose new restrictions. For the recording industry, the turning point was 1990, with new advisories inspired by parental activism led by Tipper Gore. For the emerging video game industry, it was 1994, with a brand-new rating system. For TV, it was 1996, with the v-chip and "TV Parental Guidelines." For Hollywood, it was 2000, when the industry agreed to better box-office enforcement of rules barring under-18 viewers and new restrictions on movie ads and trailers.

Well over half of all parents in 2004 say they try to rely on these advisories and restrictions. Even so, a whopping 63 percent remain "very concerned" about their kids' access to risky sexuality and violence in the media. Millennials may respond by sighing and rolling their eyes. But most do not resist their parents' passion for protection. Special teens want to treat themselves as special—as if they mattered to themselves and to the friends and family who love them.

* **Co-market to both Millennials and their parents.** The new buzzword in selling goods and services to families is "co-marketing" to parent and child "co-purchasers." With an unprecedented share of teens saying they share their parents' values and tastes, a growing number of businesses are selling to parents through kids, to kids through parents, or to everyone together through collaborative family marketing. Product surveys reveal that, in recent years, a rising share of teen purchases have involved parental input—and vice-versa. This is happening for everything from soda and sneakers to vacations, from cell phones to major technology purchases, even the family car.

It is also happening—or will soon be happening—for entertainment. Millennials want to discuss and share entertainment with their parents, whose tastes usually overlap with their own. While mom's or dad's approval of small purchases is not often necessary, it is nearly always appreciated. The more expensive the purchase or ticket, the more likely parental approval will be required. Far more than in the Boomer or Gen-X youth eras, a young person's choice to adopt a particular music-related look (e.g., a "hip-hop" wardrobe) requires parental acquiescence, if not overt approval. When parents are also buyers, parents need to be sold.

The positive flip side of the co-purchasing equation is that Millennials can be very significant influencers of parental entertainment choices. If you sell a movie ticket or rent a video to a Millennial, the odds are better than in years past that you'll soon be doing the same to others in the family.

* **Assume that youths value parental (and other) adult involvement in their lives.** Millennials will not be drawn to entertainment styles, personalities, songs, and stories that disparage close family ties. "It just continues to amaze me how much kids that age really, really love their parents," said Todd Cunningham of MTV. "They are their heroes. I never would have called my parents heroes. It was all about being away from them."

Depictions of parents are becoming more important in all media—songs, movies, games. For Millennial audiences, parents can be portrayed as objects of affection, not enemies. But hovering mom and hyper dad can also be targets of humor, as long as it has a plausible Millennial-era punch line. Obsessive and overprotective parenting styles can be (and already are) the font of many youth-targeted jokes, but they do not breed rebellion, slacker-style rejection, or media-created "alternative" role models. When Ozzy Osbourne sets rules for his own kids that he never would have followed, Millennials view this as a joke at one level—and, on another, as correct behavior, even *comforting* behavior, on his part.

* **Create messages that address the Millennials' new health problems.** Thanks to the growing protectiveness of parents, schools, and communities, today's Millennials have the lowest rates of mortality and disease of any generation in history. Compared with young Gen Xers, many fewer of them are victims of accidents or violent crime, commit suicide, overdose on drugs, or get pregnant. Certain health-related story lines and character concepts that worked well for Boomers and Xers (substance abuse, for example) are less relevant to Millennials.

As certain health issues recede, however, others are rising to replace them—most notably, obesity, asthma, ADD, sleep deprivation, athletic injuries, and all the related health-care interventions (and medications) they involve. Most of these new issues arise from the very protectiveness with which kids are now raised. At least one of them is a major challenge for at least one member of every circle of friends. In today's youth environment, it is as common for a collegian or high school student to struggle with body-altering issues as it was for a Boomer to struggle with mind-altering ones.

As in other eras, young audiences will be drawn to watching people their age who are attractive, and who can be dreamily imagined as girlfriends or boyfriends or fashion-trend role models. However, the definition of attractive can change over time — and, always, reflects a generational base line. To Millennials of either gender, being five to twenty pounds overweight is far more normal, and socially acceptable, than at any other time in the modern history of youth. In any mix of friends, these days, there will very likely be one or more persons who are overweight — and, less visibly, someone with an eating disorder. At many colleges and high schools, this has become as significant an aspect of "diversity" as skin color or ethnic origin.

Implications for Music and Live Entertainment

During the Boomer youth era, kids cheered as rock stars staged rebellions against the protective authority of adults — which, in time, collapsed. During the Gen-X youth era, parents did not figure as strongly in the songs and the rebellion theme ebbed. Instead, by the early '90s, song writers won youth over by attacking parents for their disinterest or outright desertion. Today, a number of Gen-X stars (Christina Aguilera, Eminem) are still hammering this theme home. But it no longer connects the same way. It sounds more amusing than real, telling tales about the singers' own youth, not about the youth of today's teen consumers.

Anti-adult themes don't connect the way they once did, partly because parents are clearly becoming more engaged in the lives of their kids and more protective of them — starting, often, with their choice of music. Parents are fussing more, poring over warning labels and logging in to rating Web sites. The 2004 Super Bowl, featuring Justin Timberlake's gag with Janet Jackson, catalyzed parental anxieties and triggered policy changes that are still reverberating across the cultural landscape. Edgy TV ads that might have been approved five years ago are getting canned—or, at a minimum, toned down. More live interviews are going on tape delay. More shock jocks are being ushered out of the mainstream—some, like Howard Stern, finding refuge in satellite radio. Sexed-up images like Britney's Pepsi ads and the A&F catalogue have been quietly dropped. Political pressure is now building on the cable industry to self-regulate its youth content and allow easier blocking of edgy networks like MTV.

Most Millennials do not relish these new restrictions, of course, but they do not seem to mind them much. Young people are not rallying behind Ms. Jackson, Mr. Stern, and others like them. Nor do they protest when governmental authorities want to punish the media for the unscripted events that happen on their programs. The adult furor mirrors back to them their own sense of being worthy of protection. Among older teens, it also jibes with their strong belief that younger kids ought to be even more heavily sheltered.

As more Millennials grow beyond adolescence, they will be even less drawn to stars who pick fights with their parents. As they start becoming parents, they will be more inclined to tune in to themes about the sheltering of children. Among female teen fans, Eminem's most attractive quality is not his resentment of his parents, but his fiercely protective attitudes toward his own 6-year-old daughter Halie, who is only allowed to listen to heavily censored versions of dad's music.

Safety worries are contributing to the decline in youth interest in rock concerts. On the whole, Millennials like entertainment sites to be reasonably wholesome and totally safe, not places where young people go to get drunk, stoned, or worse. And as they reach drinking age, they will avoid night clubs where people are at risk of being trampled or incinerated. Concert promoters and theme park and night club owners will need to emphasize safety and security features. Concert promoters can benefit themselves by maintaining Web data bases—as some now do—that show the safety record of each band and by publishing crowd safety guidelines. Keep in mind: The higher ticket prices rise, the more likely it is that mom and dad will have to approve.

Much of today's hip hop is adapting. Many of the best-selling rap lyrics are less about rage and wanton destruction than back in the heyday of "gangsta" rap, and more about building and enjoying the good life. Corporate sponsors of hip hop events are more worried about staying in bounds. The organizer of Toyotas' national DJ-and-dance party tour to promote the Scion reassured parents there would be "no naked women, no drugs, no swearing."

The debate over rap lyrics is becoming more intense as we move deeper into the Millennial teen era. More than ever before, leaders in the black community are coming together to tell hip hop producers to clean up their act. Citing academic studies on the link between disrespectful lyrics and low self-esteem among girls, *Essence* magazine launched a "Take Back the Music" campaign against brutal and misogynistic word play. Coeds at Spellman College organized a protest against a visiting performance by Nelly, inspiring others by their example. Al Sharpton recently threw down his own gauntlet before the media moguls: "If they've got the right to call my daughter a bitch, I have a right to say 'boycott.'"

Implications for Film and Television

Stories that feature Millennials receiving passionate, close-in support from parents and community will strike a generational chord. As Millennials grow older, getting this theme right a will be important.

Special kids seem worthy of protection—and the twin themes of special-ness and sheltering have been complementing each other, often in the same "cuddly baby" and "good kid" shows, from the time the Millennials first appeared in the early '80s. Occasionally, the urge to shelter dominates the story line—resulting in some of the most memorable movie hits of the last twenty years. *The Hand That Rocks the Cradle* was a clarion call to young parents to close the wagons tighter around their families. The laugh of Glenn Close had a similar impact in the 1996 live-action remake of *101 Dalmatians*. *In Monsters, Inc.*, the need to stop terrorizing kids requires an entire society to restructure its economy and technology—and thereby redeem itself.

What is sometimes arresting about the protection theme is how it suddenly recasts unlikely adults, especially Gen-X celebrities, in the role of protector. Arnold Schwarzenegger, the pitiless terminator, becomes the baby-sitter in *Kindergarten Cop*. Vin Diesel similarly goes from hardened criminal to family bodyguard. Eddie Murphy, the edgy-mouthed comedian and hustler, becomes the befuddled nice-guy dad in his *Dr. Doolittle* and *Daddy Day Care* movies.

Another layer of complexity is added in *Finding Nemo*, in which a single father must overcome is own fear of loss, and in *Lilo and Stitch*, about a parentless teenager trying desperately to raise and keep her younger sister. The challenge of making broken families functional and protective remains a strong Millennial-era plot line.

For this generation, the main threats to the teen world come from outside, not from the peer group itself. The drama unfolds when supportive adults, who desperately want to intervene, are for some reason unable help. The situation was different in the Gen-X youth era. Back then, serial *Halloween*-style teenagers could attack and kill other teenagers, *Heathers*-like girls could commit serial suicide, and high school students in *Dazed and Confused* could organize massive beatings of middle-school students. Meanwhile, the adults—even the well-intentioned ones—simply stood by and did nothing. A comparable story line today, featuring threats on Millennials, would feel out of joint to teens and parents both. The in-school TV drama *Boston Public*, featuring largely unprotected kids in dysfunctional environments, has fared poorly among teen viewers for just this reason.

Parents, often cast as protectors, are another growing presence in Millennial-targeting film and TV. For young Boomers, parents were often cast as powerful but distant; and for young Gen Xers, as nice but generally not around. For Millennial kids and teens, parents play—indeed, sometimes overplay—central roles in the lives of their kids.

In movies, a straight line can be drawn from the *Barney and Friends*, *The Lion King*, and *Rugrats*, featuring parent-figures who dote on little kids, to movies about 'tweens and teens locked in intimate and intense relationships with their moms and dads—as in *Cheaper by the Dozen*, *Bend It Like Beckham*, *What a Girl Wants*, *Anywhere But Here*, or *Freaky Friday*.

In TV programming, the trend began in the late '80s, when Nickelodeon brought parents back into their child programming. In the '90s, new cable stations like Disney and WB did likewise with teen programming. Along the

Millennials and Censorship

The mounting efforts of the past two decades to censor child-targeted entertainment show no signs of abating. From Tipper Gore and Senator Joseph Lieberman on one edge to evangelicals like Dr. Dobson on the other, the complaints of the 1980s grew into the laws and regulations of the 1990s, which are bearing fruit in the front-page culture-war headlines of the mid-2000s.

Over the past few years, the American Family Association has pressured Marriott International to remove adult films from their family hotels. Pepsi-Cola of North America dropped its television spot featuring rapper Ludacris, largely due to parental complaints about his profanity-laden lyrics. Jesse Jackson and Al Sharpton called on MGM to remove a scene from *Barbershop* in which a barber derides Martin Luther King, Jr., and Rosa Parks. Wal-Mart and Best Buy have voluntarily agreed to restrict the sale of M-rated video to customer age 17 and older. Networks have been caught off-guard several times, as various incidents have led to waves of complaints, Congressional hearings, and new legislation to boost fines for programming deemed indecent by public authorities.

These well-publicized actions may ultimately be less important than the accumulation of small acts of censorship by individual parents. Many Gen-X moms and dads want to protect their own kids from the kind of edgy fare they remember watching, in their own latchkey childhoods. In 1998, when the *Titanic* videotape was released, Sunrise Family Video began marketing a slightly cut version of the movie—thus creating the first "e-rated" movie. In 2002, the Albertson grocery-store chain began renting them. Today, hundreds of e-rated movie titles are marketed and rented in all fifty states, despite threats of lawsuits. For Gen-X parents who would rather do the censorship themselves, new tech-smart products are available to assist them—including a new Trilogy Studios product that lets consumers use their own computers to edit out unwanted scenes.

Given the close bonds between Millennials and their parents, attempts to "market around" parents—as the music industry is often accused of doing—or to ban personal editing products are likely to run into a wall of resistance. An alternative industry tactic would be to work with, not against, the needs and desires of Gen-X parents, to enable them to be and feel in control. The simplest way to do this is to provide maximum information—including well-crafted warnings, with very specific descriptions of content—in as many media as possible.

timeline of teen dramas, parental presence is the single biggest difference between the Xer-targeting classics of the early '90s ("Saved by the Bell," "Doogie Howser," "Beverly Hills 90210," "Melrose Place") and the Millennial-targeting shows of recent years ("Dawson's Creek," "Gilmore Girls," "Everwood," "Reba," "7th Heaven," "8 Simple Rules for Dating my Teenage Daughter").

In some new dramas—"The O.C.," for example, or "Everwood"—the common story line weaves together the lives of teens and adults in two co-equal subplots, erasing entirely the cultural barrier between older and younger generations that Hollywood has enforced since the late '50s. Now, the young man worries about dad's new job, and the mother worries about her daughter's new car. In a world of parent-child co-purchasing and multi-generational living, the dynamics of the collaborative family will only become more powerful and multilayered as Millennials grow older.

Implications for the Internet and Video Games

In recent years, politicians and parents have raised frequent alarms about the diverse risks that the Internet poses for kids—ranging from email-triggered solicitation and commercial fraud to stalking and exposure to pornography, violence, and every imaginable depravity.

To suppress these risks, politicians have imposed legislative and regulatory remedies that have either been largely ineffectual or have been nullified as unconstitutional. Parents, with more success, have been fueling the growth of a net-nanny industry, which offers spam blockers and Web filters against a selectable variety of offenses (violence, sex, religious bias, politically incorrect words). Some software goes further. Microsoft's Kids Passport enables participating services to obtain parental consent to collect, use, or disclose a child's personal data. Web sites (like *visabuxx.com*) give parents control over teen Internet spending. In the years to come, Gen-X parents can be expected to apply such aggressive parental controls even more aggressively than Boomer parents ever did.

The alternative to home filtering and blocking is for institutions caring for kids to develop their own restrictive, controlled-content systems. Many schools, camps, churches, and community centers are already taking this approach. Public "social software" sites for Millennials nearly always try to build barriers against outsiders—like *bolt.com*, which provides an easy way for young people to hang out and meet new friends, or like *Yahoo Personals* and *match.com*, for young singles looking for partners. Web systems that Millennials themselves create (for instance, *cappies.com*) often come with carefully controlled usernames and passwords, blocking access to outsiders. Over the next decade, an interlocking world of "closed" Internet sites for young adults is likely to compete with the wide-open Web.

Millennial attitudes toward Internet privacy are complicated. Most try hard to avoid revealing embarrassing personal facts to their own peer community. On the other hand, most have no problem revealing vast amounts of (what they consider) "neutral" information and images on their Web pages, blogs, and *facebook.com* sites for all the world to see—a degree of personal exposure that strikes many older adults as equivalent to living in fish bowl. At the exhibitionist extreme are the growing number of "camgirls" and "camboys" who install Internet-enabled cameras in their rooms and sometimes solicit gifts from strangers. Perhaps because today's kids are so used to being sheltered, they figure if *they* don't feel any discomfort about it, there must be no problem. Their parents, of course, will think otherwise.

Violence and sexual themes have made the video game industry a target for parents and political leaders ever since the mid-'90s—that is, ever since Millennials began to play them in significant numbers. Industry spokesmen have responded, correctly, that children are not their primary market: The majority of violent and sexual games today are sold to the 25-and-over market.

Even so, the standards are changing. What was uncontroversial for young Gen Xers is widely deemed unacceptable for young Millennials. The Gen-X software designers who puckishly inserted secret sex mods into popular games probably thought it was harmless fun. Now they know better. The shortcomings of the current system—industry labels and age-targeted ad restrictions—might be addressed as more tech-savvy Gen-X parents become the parents of Millennial teens. Gen Xers are more adept at using the technology that allows them to control child gaming experiences. In time, parents will demand and get filters allowing them to pre-set and control of the level of violence and sex in the game.

Criminal mayhem games like the *Grand Theft Auto* series (soon to be joined by such competitors as *50 Cent: Bulletproof* and *Fear & Respect*) will continue to find a youth market, especially among stressed-out boys and young-adult males who want to release some easy adrenalin. However, they will no longer feel cutting-edge. For all of their ineptitude at allowing hot-key pornography into their game, *Grand Theft Auto* designers made a smart move by constraining their music and fashion to the "Miami Vice" '80s and "gangsta rap" early '90s. It enables Millennials to feel like they're exploring some wild semi-historical fantasy. In the years to come, game violence will feel more contemporary when aimed at a civic purpose, when done for a good and noble cause, which Millennial game players, young adults as well as teens, may find more acceptable.

Implications for Older Generations

The classic Gen-X-era (Outback Steakhouse) slogan was "No Rules, Just Right." The new Millennial-era youth mindset is "No Rules, Watch Out." Given the current post-9/11 adult mindset, older generations are going along with this—so long as it does not interfere with their own cultural choices.

As Gen Xers enter middle age, some will continue to want to test the limits of edginess, and will appreciate a hint of danger lurking beneath the most mundane activities—but millions of others will not, especially parents. Thus far, the Gen-X pattern has been to be very libertarian before having kids and then very protective after having kids. According to pollsters, the "family gap" in attitudes toward politics and culture is wider among today's Gen Xers than among people in any other age bracket. This hugely separates the sensibilities of Gen Xers on the far side of 35 from those on its near side, and it tells us how even those younger Gen Xers are likely to behave as they grow older and become parents. Remembering their own latchkey-era youth, Gen-X will be even more protective than Boomers were when today's collegians were small.

In the years ahead, Gen-X parents may organize grassroots networks against teen entertainments they perceive as harmful—and, in doing so, could spark plenty of heated arguments with their own peers. This intra-Gen-X split is already apparent in the difference between fans of pop-rock and fans of country music, and will reach film and TV in time. The two sides may coexist thanks to an emerging division of the national culture into different radio formats, separate cable channels, "adult" versus "child" game titles, and the like.

TV's efforts to target Millennial market may widen the schism between network and cable programming that began in the Gen-X youth era. As more Gen Xers become parents, they are likely to demand stronger controls on what their kids see and hear. Edgy programming will continue its retreat from the broadcast networks and onto cable channels and satellite radio stations and "adult" podcasts, many of which will become the Gen-X equivalent of *Nick at Night*. As the first Millennials start becoming parents themselves over the coming years, they will accept strict controls as natural—but, as they grow older, they may favor offering new freedoms to their later-born children.

Boomers, meanwhile, will watch their last-born Millennial offspring embark on careers and marriages, and will realize that these grown up children are no longer little kids who need parental protection. A new stock Boomer character and story line could emerge, about semi-retired older people looking for new crusades—and perhaps finding them in new forms of idealism or stewardship that leads them on exotic and risky escapades. *Independence Day* featured an aging hippie warrior with a nontraditional but close American family, whose 'tween-aged kids who help him cope with alcoholism and a gift of prophecy. Now, it may be time to try this formula with hippie-ish elders and their young-adult children.

9 | STRATEGIES FOR A CONFIDENT GENERATION

"I know I can
Be what I wanna be
If I work hard at it
I'll be where I wanna be"

—Nas, "I Can" (2002)

STRATEGIES FOR A CONFIDENT GENERATION

Far more than today's older generations, Millennials are inclined to assume that, as a group, they can meet any standard and beat any challenge. On the whole, the members of this generation—especially girls—feel less doubt about themselves than young people used to feel. There's a new youth attitude that is gradually transforming into a strong collective assurance. Even when the world has problems, and even if those problems deepen, Millennials have faith that everything can be fixed. The worse the problems may seem, the more buoyant the youth response could be.

No doubt, this growing confidence is being encouraged by parents, teachers, and leaders who want the next generation to be more positive about life. Even the warnings and prohibitions are being reworked. "This is your brain; this is your brain on drugs" was a line in a famous early '90s anti-drug ad targeting Gen Xers. "Tell me you're proud of me" is a line from a recent ad targeting Millennials. The logic of the old message was damage control: Tell teens about the horrible things that will happen if they don't do the right thing. The logic of the new message is positive reinforcement: Tell teens about the great things that will happen if they do the right thing.

Here are four key strategies that address Millennials as a confident generation.

* **Tell stories within the framework of an optimistic future.** More than previous generations, Millennials have grown up expecting good outcomes, for themselves and others. They have also been raised in environments in

which people are expected to demonstrate good behavior and do good things. This is a turnaround from the days of Gen-X youth, and it affects a range of choices in the entertainment industry—from the look of ads and movie trailers, to the covers of CDs, to the harmonies and tonalities of pop music, to the desired outcome of computer games, and more.

This does not mean that Millennials demand stories that have a happy ending. Their shared belief in a basically purposeful world can set up heart-wrenching tragedies, when bad things happen to good people. They also enjoy nonsense comedic stories whose purpose is sheer fun. What's a harder sell for Millennials is entertainment that pretends to be meaningful yet has no clear resolution, that delivers ambiguous messages, that affirms nothing, and that in fact offers no real closure.

* **Craft stories about ambitious young women.** To date, girls reveal far more of this distinctly Millennial confidence than do the boys. It was no coincidence that the first Millennial musical tremor (in 1997) was driven by the new tastes of 'tween girls. Across the nation, in nearly every social realm—with technology a key exception—girls are doing more than boys to develop a new cultural style. At universities, in politics, in professions ranging from law to health-care, girls are assuming reputations for achievement and leadership that transcend age-old gender roles. Indeed, Millennial women may be America's first post-feminist generation, in the sense that they are first-ever to launch into adulthood without the slightest presumption of inferior capability. If anything the presumption is reversed, as evidenced by the dismissive references to boys in periodicals and Webzines for girls or by such wickedly popular 'tween t-shirts as "Boys are stupid. Throw rocks at them." Both genders are well aware of where they now stand on the scale.

This opens the door to new kinds of cultural messages, addressing a new set of issues. How will Millennials of both genders balance career and family? Surveys suggest that they are better prepared for careers yet also more attracted to a stable family life. Will this mean they might marry earlier than their Gen-X predecessors—or not? Will gender roles revert to something more traditional as they become parents and enter positions of leadership in business and politics—or not?

Today's young women (and men) want to probe these fundamental gender questions. They are too invested in their future to be satisfied with the sex-crazed media obsession with spaghetti straps, navels, low-rise pants, or ankle tattoos. The libidinal sap of adolescence flows, as it always has and will, but "hooking up" is not topic A to the female half of this generation. Sexual risk-taking is declining. Millennial girls look upon themselves (and, usually, expect boys to look upon them) as busy people interested in many things. When Millennial girls wear suggestive clothes worn by older celebrities who are sending out sexual messages, many of these young girls tend to think of it as just joining a fun trend or simply looking mature.

✳ **Craft stories about a newly confident male style.** While rising confidence among young women is now a surging trend, rising confidence among young men is just beginning to show itself. Part of the obstacle for guys is school, whose rule-bound structure puts them at a perceived disadvantage to girls. As more young men graduate from high school and college, Millennials will begin to establish their own male style—probably starting in the military, the technology sector, and small businesses.

The Millennial young-adult male style will be a break from the Gen-X male style—either of the tough-guy "retro" or the urban chic "metro" variety. The new standard will be both clearly male but also sociable, bland but smart, a new amalgam of the classic yet modern man.

"Age aspiration" is, as always, quite important—but it needs to capture what Millennials want to be, not just portray what the next-older generation is presently like. For guys, even more than for girls, effective entertainment role models need to be several years older than the target audience. To appeal to Millennials of college age, the best role models are Gen-X celebrities who are around age 25 or 26. It's not easy to find many of the current crop of young-adult stars who embody the positive traits Millennials want to emulate. Having grown up with zero tolerance, having taken so many tests, having focused so much on grades and college admissions, Millennials are not impressed by programming that features dull, disinterested, yeah-whateverish, distinctly unbusy twentysomethings. Young Millennial males aspire to an image that's more accomplished, engaged, and directional.

✱ **Treat Millennials as active users of culture, not just as passive consumers.** Each generation finds its own way to participate in its entertainments. Far more than was true for today's older generations, most Millennials desire—many even require—a direct interaction with their culture. Their favorite CRT screen (computer, not TV) is one that responds to their key and mouse commands. Their most rapidly-growing form of entertainment (gaming) is one that responds to their joystick or gamepad commands. Millennials resist being passive purchasers of entertainment, and would far rather craft something on their own (or with others) than buy something totally prepackaged for them.

Where they can, they adapt or invent technologies to enable them to do this. If they like songs, they want to remix their own. If they like movies, they want to produce their own. Maybe they can bill their own friends as leading divas or actors. And maybe then they can set up a Web site to allow other friends to edit or comment. The creative permutations are endless.

Sometimes, Millennials are bothered by entertainment that tries to do too much. They're not interested in media which tries to hold their attention for hours on end (the dream of film directors during the 1970s!). Rather, they feel more in control when media tries to do less. Whether relaxing or having fun, IMing or doing homework, driving or jogging, eating or trying to fall asleep, Millennials often see and use entertainment as a form of multi-tasking, something that enables them to do other things better or more enjoyably. In the new youth mindset, the purpose of pop culture is not to demand total viewer concentration but rather to provide a friendly environment for doing other things. It doesn't stir up whole new feelings and attitudes about life, but just provide a baseline to help people live their lives or maybe just give them a break from stress.

Portraying Millennial Teens

Age aspirational programming is a sound concept, but it's hard to get right—especially when portraying (or targeting) teenagers.

For legal, commercial, and artistic reasons, it's common for films about high school and college to cast actors who are significantly older than the characters they play on screen. During periods like the 1970s or '90s, having older actors portray teens was fine, since they are part of the same generation whose mindset, manners, and mores they are trying to convey. During other periods, however, older performers can impart a discordant slant to their younger characters. This happened in the early '60s, and from the late 1970s to the early '80s. It's happening again now.

Millennial film-goers and TV watchers are quite aware that teen roles are not played by teens. In recent years, they have seen many of these teen roles played by older Gen Xers who made their reputation by crafting characters who were conspicuously Gen-X-like—which has led to audience complaints about how age-miscast performers, especially males, can spoil a film. This may explain why "teen" films featuring twentysomething Gen-X performers have underperformed at the box office in recent years.

This may also explain why Millennial 'tweens appear to be relatively less attracted to programs or formats that focus exclusively on older teenagers. The way a 10- or 12-year-old might see it, if the stars aren't exactly our own age, we might as well skip all the way up to adult celebrities who may be ten or fifteen or more years older—as old as the stars in *Friends*, or perhaps as old as their own parents. In recent years, most age-aspirational "teen" magazines (from *Tiger Beat* to *Seventeen*) have seen a flight of young readers to regular celebrity magazines (like *Us Weekly*) that cover people of all ages.

This problem should abate, in the years ahead, as Millennials age. Much as John Hughes unveiled a new Gen-X "brat pack" in the mid-1980s, a new cadre of A-list Millennial stars will surely emerge over the next several years. When Millennial actors and actresses in their early- to mid-20s portray teenagers, they will be more personally persuasive to those younger than themselves. In all likelihood, they will show an ease in interacting with older adults that was seldom displayed by Boomers or Gen Xers at the same age.

Implications for Music and Live Entertainment

Happy. Sweet. Upbeat. These were the adjectives they most often used to describe the new sound, back when media critics first encountered the boy band craze of 1997, triggered by such out-of-nowhere groups as BackStreet Boys and 'N Sync. Today, as Millennials move from middle school through high school and college, the darker, edgier, and grungier genres of popular youth music in the early '90s are receding ever further from memory. To be sure, the new sound has also been frequently criticized as "bubblegum music," "formulaic," "ear candy," and the like. But even its severest detractors agree that the new sound has been a trend-changer. More than their parents at the same age, Millennials are partial to music that energizes, soothes, entertains, and delights.

In their own music, Millennials sing less often out of desperation and puffed-up hysterics, more often out of calm self-assurance. Their preferred music is moving away from goth and "loser" lyrics and toward the upbeat styles of retro-'60s male bands, with their tame and laudatory lyrics, or the confidence of the new breed of "perfect girlfriend" songsters. "I hope that people can look to me as a positive role model," says 13-year-old JoJo. "I think I'm real for real girls."

As they age, Millennials will be looking more for artists who reach out to the crowd and give expression to their audience's hopes and dreams—and less for those who are breaking beer bottles over their heads to demonstrate the depth of their introspective selves. Angst-prone, dour lead singers, and songs that use the word "I" in every line, will clash with this new youth mindset. In-your-face lyrics, near-death sports experiences, punk rage, and gangsta threats could feel outdated, even old. At best, those styles may be seen as pure entertainments, no more creative than lip syncs, where all the bluster is regarded as marvelous fun or even (when the gangsta pose is over-the-top) uproariously funny. At worse, they seem to be the stuff of bullies who need to trash-talk to conceal a real or imagined inner weakness.

Already, Millennial consumers are beginning to warp received pop genres to fit their new tastes. They've pushed grunge music into steep decline, indeed, toward virtual extinction. They've redirected the momentum of alt-rock, with punk moving away from "hard core" toward something a bit smoother, easier, more euphonic. The epithets ("punk light," "sell-out," "poseur") that get hurled at popular performers like Avril Lavigne, Ashlee Simpson, and Green Day testify that the center of gravity has shifted.

Millennials are also transforming hip hop. The raw brutality and grievance-laden desperation of the early gangsta rappers like NWA has given way to the more assured, sumptuous, and sometimes humorous celebration of bling-bling, as rendered by classy button-down vocalists like Jay-Z. Merging with rap, and enjoying meteoric recent growth, is what the late Aaliyah called the "street but sweet" sound of R&B, considered mainly female territory until the huge success of Usher. Youth-fired growth in Christian rock and the mainstreaming of Latin and Asian pop point to a similar stylistic shift—toward music that is mostly hopeful and aspirational.

As these trends deepen over the next decade, we can expect girls, as ever, to remain at the cutting-edge of their generation's new confidence. Girl pop is here to stay, as young artists follow the recent wave of new girl vocalists with a more mature but equally upbeat message. In time, a new type of romantic song may emerge, sung by a girl more cute than sensuous, someone boys would really like to have as a girlfriend—less a sex partner than a friend you can tell your troubles to or a prom date you can proudly bring home to meet mom and dad.

Where Millennial male music will go is a major question. It could combine an upbeat attitude with a new masculinism, a baritone sound, and a talent for story-telling. It could bring a modern "baby, you're hot" twist to the styles and attitudes of the romantic crooners of the late 1930s and early '40s. There may be one kind of male music that will appeal to male fans, and another kind for female fans. A wide gap between the male and female sound, today found mainly in black and Latino urban music, could spread and become a general norm. The deeper the impact of world events on this generation, the more assertive Millennial males will be in crafting new musical styles.

Implications for Film and Television

In recent decades, many films have depicted teens as shuffling aimlessly through a decaying, broken-down world: The kids are full of imagination but unable to control whether, in the end, they will get lucky or wash out. This story line no longer speaks to a rising generation of youths who, for the most part, trust in good outcomes and whose childhood has often featured busy calendars, protective parents, supportive schools, and a relatively kid-friendly film and TV culture. Millennials prefer their plot lines to be straight and linear, not random, accidental, or "ironic" as Gen Xers might interpret that word. If something is wrong, a Millennial audience will expect someone to fix it.

That someone will be a protagonist who exudes confidence. And very likely, that someone will be female, since girls and young woman have thus far personified the cutting edge of the newly confident Millennial—from "The Powerpuff Girls" and "Kim Possible," to *Mulan* and Lara Croft, to the self-assured leads played by such Millennial starlets as Lindsay Lohan, Anne Hathaway, and Hilary Duff (or the only slightly older Natalie Portman and Julia Stiles).

Confident young guys are emerging, but lag behind. They are still struggling, still a bit gawky, however well intentioned. (It is difficult to imagine, today, a female equivalent to Jon Heder, the male star of *Napoleon Dynamite*.) An interesting and open question is how the collective persona of this generation will gather strength once boys gain the same confidence of the girls. Judging by the rising number of "Dork Pride" t-shirts is any indication, one senses it is likely to include lots of guys who aren't too cool to hide their smarts or credentialed achievements. If "Revenge of the Nerds" was a cinematic rallying cry for many male Gen-Xers, "Triumph of the Nerds" might someday become the Millennials equivalent.

Male or female, the personas Millennials like to watch are robust characters inclined to take action, more than insecure people who hide behind blustery exteriors. Trash-talking *South Park*-style braggarts are being replaced by characters too self-assured to waste time insulting each other. Mean-teen or damaged-teen concepts, like those of *Cruel Intentions*, are being eclipsed by the concept of teens who rebel (or express anger) through constructive deed-doing. Self-referential irony, familiar to watchers of films like *The Princess Bride*, is fading. Millennials enjoy watching cynical, alienated characters with low self-esteem go down to defeat.

With Lemony Snicket's *A Series of Unfortunate Events*, Millennials are triggering a thematic inversion of the whole gothic horror genre. For Boomers and Xers, gothic horror featured flawed protagonists who find themselves powerless to resist malevolent forces hidden beneath a conventional surface. For Millennials, it features flawless protagonists with the pluck to overcome malevolent forces bristling everywhere around them.

In the future, new plot lines will include the kid (or collegian) who is *too* confident, the unsinkable kid who sinks anyway, or the unstoppable character who steamrolls the way to a perfect personal future, as in *Election* or the *Legally Blonde* films. Meanwhile, comedy will lose its satirical and ironic edge while gaining silly exuberance, a trend observable in such celebrity fests as *Spice Girls* or *The Lizzie McGuire Movie*. These confident young people will find ever-more laughs out of classic slapstick, full of pratfalls and deadpans, if one can imagine more mature versions of such surprise hits as *George of the Jungle*, the Austin Powers movies, *Shrek!*, or the recent TV series "The Amanda Show." And then there's that wacky and incurable optimist, *SpongeBob Squarepants*—surprisingly popular not just among small kids, but among teens and college students.

On TV, collegiate and teen audiences will expect people their age to be presented more positively in the years ahead. By the time the first wave of the Millennial generation enters its mid-twenties, later this decade, it will become more controversial to depict them on television as aimless (as in "Real World"), leave them crying on stage as losers ("American Idol"), make light of their romantic impulses ("Bachelor" or "Bachelorette"), or let them make fools of themselves ("Jackass"). By then, memories of the Miss America Pageant, which no one will any longer bother to satirize, may inspire a very new and upbeat type of "reality show."

Most successful Millennials will prefer to look upon their current phase of life as a time in which good things can and do happen to well-raised young people, regardless of their backgrounds, when they fall in love, start careers, soldier great causes, or try to do good deeds. Those who face big obstacles in life will be acutely aware of what their better-off peers are doing. Regardless of background, Millennials will be drawn to stories that address the real challenges confronted by the mainstream of their generation, in a truly contemporary (Millennial, not X) context. It may take awhile, but Millennials may gradually push television toward a new "reality show" genre of a more mutually supportive, less survivalist nature.

Implications for the Internet and Video Games

As Millennials come of age, they will use the Internet more than any other medium to express their new attitude of personal confidence. During the Xer youth era, Web sites were often depicted as a sort of Dodge City frontier, full of risk and fraud and anonymous cyberpunks. With Millennials, they are becoming the building blocks with which they construct positive social and professional identities.

At ever-younger ages, Millennials are constructing personal Web sites—as resumés, blogs, photo albums, or launch pads for successful entrepreneurial dreams. These personal Web sites can provide Millennials with online identities, even a high profile and pseudo-celebrity status in some circles. In doing this, they are assisted by Web sites (like *subprofile.com*) that help them build online IM identities and choose avatars, and sites (like *myspace.com*) that allow them to see their social networks. Girls use Web sites (like *gurl.com*) to promote female self worth and confidence in ways that were never available for young Boomers and Gen Xers.

The challenge for media companies is to tap into this youthful can-do attitude toward the Internet. The best plan—and not an easy one—is to entice young Web site creators to link their own sites with those created by the media companies, whether of an upcoming film, a concert tour schedule, a new game release, or anything else a Millennial tech maestro may wish to post and share with friends.

Having stepped uneasily into video games with dark survivalist styles—with players taking on the role of lone survivor (*Doom, Unreal, Tomb Raider, Myst*) when they are not outright anti-heroes, psychopaths, or pranksters—Millennials are looking for ways to give the protagonist a clearer and more constructive mission. In the new-style game, enemies are more likely to represent the forces of disorder, and the goal is less to take them out one by one than to establish a new world (perhaps organizing other players online for this purpose) where such enemies can no longer exist. In such over-the-top mayhem hits as *Grand Theft Auto*, young players are less interested in offing anonymous victims than in acquiring social "respect" through the building of criminal careers and empires.

Gradually, the Millennial influence will lead to further changes in game content, even as Gen Xers still rule production and distribution. As Millennials assert themselves, games with dark or horror themes will still have their appeal, but in changed form. Games may still take place in creaky settings—as in Hogwarts castle, full of wizards, potions, spells, black cats, and creaking doors—but will be less likely to convey the classic goth theme of the present being in the thrall of the past. According to the new youth mindset, the present can *do* something the past couldn't. The leading characters in games they play don't get scared and run, but instead team up and face their adversaries.

As girls continue to enter the gaming market—and when they start entering the industry itself— "girls' games" will shift from a novelty to a major source of revenue. To the surprise of many Gen-X game developers who speak contemptuously of "pink powder puff," it won't all be sugar and spice. Girls are already driving a new market for Habbo Hotel and Sims-style games of social interaction and social engineering that, while lacking overt violence, retain the potential for more subtle conflict. During the Gen-X youth era, dominated by the male video game consumer, players interacted but treated the game environment as unchangeable. As more games simulate a social system that can itself be changed through discussion, persuasion, and networking, Millennial girls will start intruding.

Implications for Older Generations

Boomers, who once had their own reputation for cockiness, are often charmed by this Millennial confidence, especially among the new young adults they now encounter as students, customers, interns, or employees. Caught in between these two more collectively assertive generations, Gen Xers will be more likely to interpret Millennial confidence as presumption (especially among boys)—or naiveté (among girls). Many middle-aged Gen Xers will see Millennials as soft, exactly the kind of young people who were at gravest risk back during their own circa-'80s high school and collegiate era.

These Gen-X anxieties could get reinforced by new generational plot lines. Old-young story relationships will be very different from what those old John Hughes films showed in the '80s. Imagine a graying, middle-aged Ferris Beuller having to deal with an ultra-assured young boss who wants to keep him from having a day off. (*In Good Company* anticipates certain elements of this story.) Plot lines could appeal across generational lines if they include older characters who step in when young people grow too trusting or foolhardy, or if the stories combine a headstrong optimism among the younger characters with an ironic or skeptical sensibility among the older ones.

The discomfort of older generations over their own new life phases will provide many new plot lines, character devices, and opportunities for humor. The Gen-X "midlife crisis" will involve slowing down and taking fewer risks, not speeding up and taking more risks—a story that will appeal most to Gen-X parents with families. Boomer aging offers countless opportunities for making jokes at about their hypocrisy, for revealing the difference between an old Boomer's self-perception and the reality perceived by others.

The Boomers' own G.I. Generation parents, as elders, were distinctly inactive in the pop culture, especially after the Vietnam War and Watergate. The Boomers can, and probably will, be far more culturally assertive as they pass through their sixties and seventies. Likewise, middle-aged Gen Xers can, and probably will, pull the culture toward a new definition of grown-up decorum, exactly the opposite of what the Silent Generation did at that age.

10 | STRATEGIES FOR A TEAM-ORIENTED GENERATION

"We're seeing a huge cultural shift away from the word 'I' to the word 'We' in this new generation of young people coming in. And that's to be celebrated."

—General James Jones,
U.S. Marine Corps Commandant (2002)

STRATEGIES FOR A TEAM-ORIENTED GENERATION

Being together with one's group (or groups) is as central to the Millennial youth experience as being a "together" individual was to the Boomer youth experience. Boomers personally witnessed, and in many ways propelled, the triumph of individualism over community, the triumph of markets over government, the triumph of "choice" over authority. To Millennials, this is an "older generation" phenomenon. They wonder how the negative side-effects of all this free-for-all can be contained—the splintering of the culture, the loss of neighborhoods, the glorification of lifestyle extremes, and the widening gap between rich and poor. Perhaps, they sense, older generations should adopt some of the same group virtues that young people already practice in their daily lives.

The 2002 Bayer Science survey asked college students nationwide if "I think my generation will be known as the 'Us Generation,' meaning that we'll be more oriented toward community well-being than toward ourselves." Nearly two-thirds agreed; only one-quarter disagreed. At military academies, counselors are reporting a sharp drop in incoming recruits who say they want to "be the best" or "be number one" and a sharp rise in those who say they want to "serve their group" and "be able to do what my team requires." If Gen Xers used to say "just do it," the new Millennial motto is "let's do it."

The implications of this strengthening community focus reach across all aspects of entertainment—how to market to young people, how to identify their new stars, to how to tell stories of interest to them, and how to adapt to way they use technology.

Here are four key strategies that address Millennials as a *team-oriented* generation.

* **Market to, and portray, Millennials in groups.** Technology is intensifying this generation's natural inclination for teamwork. Instant electronic communication creates a opportunity for (at times even a *need* for) consensus that was lacking in earlier generations. Mass fads ripple through Millennials quickly, propelling or repelling new entertainment products. With e-stores, chat rooms, and buddy lists, this is the first youth generation to keep up-to-the-moment contact with the opinions and tastes of friends, classmates, and peers across the nation. Right after the lights go up at a concert or movie theater, they speed-dial their friends, who IM their friends, and word—good or bad—goes out at digital speed.

  Story lines and characters can be crafted around the drama (and comedy) of teams, casts, unions, and other organized groups, telling about their creation, workings, deeds, and legacies. Heroes won't bear the burden alone, and certainly won't gather the glory alone. In schools, the new motto is "no child left behind"—and the credit, following the shared-valedictorian trend at many of today's high schools, is to be distributed among many. Instead of a lone *anti*-hero, the new Millennial-era *proto*-hero will turn to a mutually supportive peer group to team up against both challenges from outside and unreasonable orders from above. This has been a common feature of war stories, circa 1930s and '40s, involving mutiny against corrupt or incompetent leaders. Presented in either classic or modern contexts, it will feel fresh again.

  In marketing entertainment, the challenge is to get enough young people excited about something to get the peer-to-peer information networks rolling. High-cost ad strategies can establish a product as a "player," but beyond that, saturation ads can yield a very meager return. The typical 21-year-old has already seen an estimated 23 million ad messages in his or her lifetime and thus has become ad-resistant. Millennials prefer entertainment choices based on comments from friends they trust—or, short of that, from like-minded peers whose opinions seem authentic.

Millennials also enjoy helping other people make up their minds, which is why so many get busy with cell phones just after (or during) concerts, movies, or new TV shows.

* **Mainstream Latino, Asian, and mixed-race characters and themes.** When speaking with teenagers about entertainment, one often hears complaints about how older generations handle race in awkward or self-conscious ways. Girls feel especially strongly about racial typecasting—for example, the depiction of African-American girls as quick-tempered or troubled, of Asian-Americans as brainy and aloof, of Latinos as domestic and emotional, and so on. These type casts strike many teens as twentieth century stereotypes that linger in the minds of people older than themselves.

Diversity is, of course, important for a generation having the most multiracial and multiethnic heritage of any generation in U.S. history. Much of the new flavor of the Millennial youth culture, and its new norms about family and community, will come from second-generation immigrants from around the world who have been—Latinos and Asians, especially—largely ignored in recent programming. Mixed-race characters and issues, a matter of key concern to this generation, are also seldom seen (except, in a manner speaking, in sci-fi shows like *Battlestar Galactica*, where Millennials get to watch a variety of races and even species mingle without comment). Up to now, the emphasis in ethnic programming has been on *George Lopez*-style shows that depict upbeat and wholesome story lines, but in mono-ethnic family environments. In time, as Millennials age, this is likely to evolve to reflect new interest in multiethnic, racially blended families.

A new, Millennial-friendly genre will emerge in which attitudes, behaviors, and cultural styles will be treated not as separate multicultural fragments, but rather as ingredients in a "melting pot" that involves and affects young people of all ethnicities. Some may misread this as cultural conservatism, when in fact young people will regard it as a freshly modern and community-minded approach. Among Millennials, Latino and Asian strains are as mainstream (and fully American) as Italian, Polish, and

Jewish strains were among G.I. Generation youths in the 1930s, and Millennials expect them to be portrayed as such.

✴ **Take on issues of money and social class.** Money and its attendant desires, foibles, and vices have been a centerpiece of American entertainment since the earliest days of Tin Pan Alley. But the significance of wealth has changed, from one generation to the next. In the '60s, though Boomers championed a youth culture that would focus on values over materialism, the middle-class "establishment" they attacked actually kept a decent check on the role of money. The older generation was then known, and chided (in Melvina Reynolds' famous lyric), for their "little boxes made of ticky-tacky, little boxes all the same." Not many pop stars had a great deal of money or social influence—and when they began to gain it (as the Beatles, Rolling Stones, and other pop music icons did by the early '70s), Boomers hailed them for planting a lonely counterculture battle standard and for daring to take on "the man."

Today, by contrast, young people look upon entertainers (and other culture creators) as extremely wealthy, period. They are "the man," since there is hardly a corner of the media, society, or even politics that doesn't acknowledge their influence and sway. They live in world that hardly resembles the Millennials' own, though on MTV's "Cribs," Millennials can take a lurid peak. Entertainers are no longer on the outside looking in, rallying youth to their rebel cause. They are on the inside, where they already have everything they need.

In recent years, the pop culture industry has been more a target than an inspiration for Millennial thinking on issues of economic and social class. Today's young people notice the growing inequalities between rich and poor in their school districts and on their campuses. What they don't see first-hand, they get from the news—like how high-rolling CEOs walk away with millions, while shelf-stockers struggle for a living wage. Restoring a decent sense of proportion, reviving a sense of community in the workplace, and strengthening the middle class (which they perceive as weak and endangered) will be a lifelong agenda for this generation.

✳ **Tell stories about the defense or restoration of civic life.** For decades, entertainment has challenged the social order—and has celebrated challenges posed by the enlightened and creative individual willing to thwart the will of the team or group. That day is passing—or, at least, transforming. What will feel more on point to the Millennial mindset will be entertainment that celebrates social order and defeats the forces of chaos and disorder, which are led by disruptive (or evil) individuals. The fresh story lines will involve the rescuing, restoring, and rebuilding of a society, which (again) reinforces the Millennial fascination with great myths and epics.

There can be considerable violence and mayhem in these stories, as young heroes use moments of epic crisis to forge cooperation out of anarchy and construct a new civic order. Polls reveal that Millennials do not look upon current pop-culture violence levels as excessive. What's important, for them, is that violence be used as a restorative force, that it not be merely chaotic or random or vengeful. One person's psychosis carries less meaning than the problems afflicting the world. Their mindset (and era) is less that of *Taxi Driver* than of *The Day After Tomorrow*.

Implications for Music and Live Entertainment

Picture the image of hi-fidelity sound that's been around for thirty years—an isolated individual with stereo headphones, lost in a private universe. While this approach sold music to Boomers and its echo still resonated for Gen Xers, it doesn't work nearly as well for Millennials. It says nothing about downloading, about interactivity, about sharing songs with friends, about using music to help build communities, inspire peers, and change the world.

Thanks to the group orientation of their information technology—the IMs, the emails, the chatrooms, the networks, the online gaming—Millennials are much more likely than older generations to regard choosing and arranging and listening to music as social activities. As such, one's personal reaction to a solo digital experience becomes less important than its social "staging," that is, the total context of friends and other digital elements surrounding the experience.

Millennials and the Price of Pop Culture

Many young people today think music, movies, games, and entertainment in general are priced too high—and some in the industry believe this perception contributes to illegal file sharing. In a 2003 Harris Poll, 7 in 10 teens said that "there would be a lot less downloading" if CDs were "a lot less expensive." Citing consumer objections to high prices, the music industry has been pulling back on CD prices and concert ticket prices since 2003, though so far these price cuts have failed to turn sales around.

All this raises a question: After adjusting for inflation, is the price of entertainment higher for Millennials than it was for their parents at the same age?

For most products, in fact, the answer is no. In 2005, an average U.S. movie ticket cost $6.39. In 1970, the average ticket cost $1.55, or $6.51 in 2005 (inflation-adjusted) dollars—almost exactly the same.

Music is a more complicated to compare by price, over time, but today's bottom line is even more favorable for today's young consumer. In 2001, near the recent high point for music prices, the average CD retailed for $14.64. When CDs were introduced, in 1983, the average price was $21.50 ($38.23 in 2005 dollars). By 1990, CD prices had fallen to a bit less than $13—which, adjusted for inflation, was higher than in 2001 and far higher than in 2005.

Measured in terms of cents per minute of playing time, and adjusted for the rise in overall prices, today's recorded music is cheaper than ever. Today's CD album is the inflation-adjusted equivalent of a Boomer teenager paying $3.50 for a vinyl LP in 1970, or $2.75 for an LP in 1960, which is less than the price most of

today's fiftysomethings will recall having spent for Beatles or Elvis albums back then. A single-song cost of 99 cents is less than half what Boomer teens paid for the small vinyl "45." Even when you add in the "flip side" second song on those 45s, today's iTune purchase is a bargain.

Other media show a mixed trend. TV is now more costly. Most Americans pay regularly, through monthly cable or satellite fees, for video service that used to be entirely advertiser-supported and free to the user. Yet consumer electronics are now far less expensive. The hand-held radio or cassette recorder, a significant purchase back in the 1960s, is a mere stocking-stuffer today. The performance of sound and, even more, video systems has risen enormously. Today, one can buy a superb audio-video entertainment system for the inflation-adjusted equivalent of what a basic color TV cost in the 1960s.

On balance, Millennials (and their families) pay more for some things, and less for others, than their parents did at their age. Overall, it is likely that they are paying less per song or movie—meaning that the pop culture has become more accessible and affordable than ever before.

Yet a "high" price is not just a number, but also a perception. A look beneath the numbers reveals three basic reasons for the widely-shared Millennial impression that pop culture is too expensive.

Inflated prices at the high end.

Thirty or forty years ago, it was very hard for anyone to pay more than the average or median price for a song, a movie, a football game, or a concert. Today, a person can pay far more, and many do. Taking advantage of the widening distribution of household incomes and enabled by endless improvements in digital technology, the entertainment industry now markets to individuals willing to pay hundreds or thousands of dollars yearly for everything from wall-size plasma TV and media centers to premium cable and radio subscriptions to super-luxury seats at sporting events and concerts.

The changing price of rock concerts is a good example. The cost of attending the legendary 1967 Monterey International Pops Festival (offered at two and only two prices, $3.50 or $6 for the entire day) would be the equivalent of $16.70 to

$28.60 today. The best ticket for a top-line rock concert now often costs around $500—and even more in the online market that did not exist back in the days of illegal "scalpers."

Astronomical prices at the high end allow the industry to make more money off the wealthy, but also set an unattainable—and, at times, demoralizing—standard for quality entertainment in the eyes of young people. No matter how much money they can expect to earn, Millennials conclude that the price tag for what's best in entertainment will always be far beyond their reach. For many, high-end prices are also a painful reminder of the growing spread between wealthy and middle-class families that they encounter in other areas of their life, from schools and cars to vacations and careers.

Higher relative prices.

While average pop culture prices have risen no faster than prices generally, they have risen much faster than the price of travel and communication, which many young people naturally regard as a relevant standard of comparison. Travel is a staple ingredient of family leisure, and communication the lifeblood of modern digital media. Millennials understand that the price of both has been plunging over their lifetimes, making the pop culture seem more expensive by comparison.

Young Boomers looked upon culture as cheap, communication as costly.

Millennials look at communication as cheap, culture as costly.

For a Boomer collegian, an hour-long LP music album cost about ten times less than an hour-long call home. For a Millennial collegian, an hour-long CD costs about ten times *more* than an hour-long phone call. (If that phone call is made at night or on weekends on a cell phone, it's free.) For a Boomer collegian, a ticket to a rock concert could cost anywhere from 10 to 100 times less than a coast-to-coast plane ticket. For a Millennial collegian, a ticket on eBay for a top-name rock concert can actually cost more than a ticket from New York City to Los Angeles and back.

Shifting social perspective.

When Millennials look at the pop culture, they see it playing a different role in America's social life. This also affects perceptions of price.

In the Boomer youth era, the most exciting pop culture experiences were free or near-free, and even low-income teens could participate in nearly anything they wanted. Most adults viewed youth entertainment as "kid stuff," and few regarded it as a major industry or serious national activity. Faced with little cultural competition from their (G.I. Generation) parents, Boomers felt free to experiment with their new youth culture in ways that seldom required money.

In the Millennial era, teens find it hard to separate their own pop culture from all of the quality-graded price tags that they find attached to pop culture in general. Millennials are surrounded by Boomer and Gen-X adults who take entertainment very seriously—and who are often highly knowledgeable about it and quite eager, and financially well-equipped, to

engage in it. This results in very high and expensive adult-set standards about the "right" way a person can see a celebrity performer or even watch a movie. Young Boomers could not have imagined using NASA-scale computer power to remix an audio recording—or taking a graduate degree in film to write authoritatively about Elizabeth Taylor.

Given the economic growth of entertainment over their lifetime, moreover, Millennials are very aware of how entertainment works. Few young Boomers knew anything about what it cost to make an LP, from studio recording to the pressing of the vinyl. Millennials know exactly what the raw materials for a CD cost. Nearly all have burned a CD and have a good idea what it costs to produce and market an album. They know how big the markup is. When Boomers were in college, there was little talk about who made how much money from which album. Now, in the Millennial college era, that's talked about all the time.

In principle, many have no problem seeing celebrities keep what the market will bear. But having been raised on VH1 and MTV, they've seen the "real lives" of rock stars in programs that show them living in beautiful "cribs," buying "bling bling," decorating walls with expensive art that bears no connection to their lives, perhaps even self-destructing on drugs they have no problem purchasing. Many Millennials feel qualms about steering more of their own (or, often, their parents') income to artists who, in their eyes, already have more money than is good for them.

Will youth still spend the money on pop culture purchases? Yes. But when asked if they think the price they see at Best Buy is fair, many of them will say no. Here again, fairly or not, large entertainment companies find themselves in the unwanted position of being cast as adversaries of the young people they are trying to serve.

A parallel shift can be witnessed in live performances. From their young-est years—from their first glimpse of Barney and their first visit to Disneyworld to their first TV glimpses of boy bands—Millennials have grown accustomed to front-stage rows of cute boys and girls dancing "in sync." Today, in part as a result, teens prefer watching a group perform together rather than an isolated singer standing in front of the shadowed band. Ensemble music is on the way back, along with fancy footwork. Large casts and tight scripting is already back in high school theater. This trend will continue. As in the 1930s, bands of all kinds will get larger and more elaborate, with each member contributing to the overall jam.

Other group trends are in store. As more Millennials become performers, we will see more performers join forces, collaborate easily on both digital and live productions, and avoid egotistical competition. (A leading indicator here is today's hip hop scene, where joint CDs are becoming more common and "battle rapping" is getting friendlier.) Performers will build a fan base through casual performances that invite audience participation. Grass roots bands will play more to local audiences, thereby finding it easier to make ends meet and putting extra pressure on pricey star-venue concert acts that appeal mainly to graying audiences. In the digital era, fans won't just recom-mend songs to their friends—they'll *sell* them directly to their friends. *Burnlounge.com*, a network marketing franchise that lets anyone set up their own on-line music store, has placed itself at the cutting edge of Millennial efforts to democratize and decentralize the selling of entertainment—a trend the industry will have to watch carefully.

As the personal cult of the artist wanes, Millennial performers won't mind accepting distinct roles for singers and songwriters. Rather than contracting with producers to sell CDs or songs one-by-one to individuals, more artists will build careers by licensing into movies and games, by enlisting ad spon-sors, or by going directly onto a media company's payroll.

Expensive CDs will be history. Through digital technology and direct marketing, manufactured music products could become little more than tickets paid to access a branded digital music community, enabling perform-ers to build direct and enduring links to fans—bypassing traditional labels, distributors, and retailers. Marketing and promotion will switch to interactive formats, taking cues from instant messaging 'bots—software programs that mimic IM conversations to pitch products or services, publicize concert tour dates, show album liner notes, and allow free downloads of selected songs.

Racial and ethnic boundaries will continue to blur rapidly, as Millennials produce new white rappers as their update on Eminem, and as they expand such overlap regions as Latino urban (Hurban) or Asian pop (Mando- or Canto-pop). Genres that are today overwhelmingly Caucasian, or only white-and-black—like country music—will eventually need to find some young Latino, Asian, and mixed-race stars. The grown-up children of immigrants may import traditional ethnic dance into their popular music, with new dances combining formality with friendliness, the classic with the original. Creating a new dance step may once again be the ticket to a hit single.

In live theater, Millennials will press for racial cross-casting, or—more to the point—race-irrelevant casting. Many of the most creative and artistically skilled Millennials are the offspring of immigrants from around the globe—from all parts of Asia, the Islamic world, former Soviet republics, many nations in Africa, and every latitude of Central and South America. Many others are mixed-race. To them, Huckleberry Finn doesn't need to be portrayed by a Caucasian, any more than he has to be portrayed by a redhead. When a publishing house tried to insist otherwise, in a recent high school production of Big River, they ran into major youth resistance and had to back down. To the Millennial eye, having a Pakistani, Latino, or African-American girl playing Maria Von Trapp will not be a statement or a breakthrough. It will simply be no big deal.

Girl power will assert itself in musical styles. Much as key Boomer music trends (and other youth behaviors) were male-dictated in the '60s, key Millennial trends have been and will continue to be broadly influenced by females. The dominance of Millennial women in college and professional schools indicates what lies ahead for young-adult trends. As with race, gender cross-casting could create some interesting new entertainment concepts. In their twenties, Millennials might be fascinated to encounter classic songs, musicals, TV sit-coms, and films with gender roles exactly reversed. They might find new meanings or great comedy in old classics when presented in a modern gender context.

Similarly, Millennial consumers will erode today's boundary lines between musical genres, as part of their effort to craft a newly mainstream cultural community. What Gen-X groups now find daringly experimental, like the county-rock crossover or the country-hip hop ("hic hop") crossover, Millennials will come to accept as the new synthesis. Everything will seem a bit more pop, yet also a bit more hip hop and gospely.

The desire for a stronger sense of peer community will revive excitement about music with a real-world agenda. From the Woodstock '60s to the Live Aid '80s to the Live 8 '00s, Boomers have set the political ground rules for mass-concert formats, a fact that is bound to change. For charity concerts, instead of selling tickets for a mere cash return, the new Millennial approach is to engage young audiences in concerts that require civic participation—which is how the Boost Mobile Rock Corps issues concert tickets to youth who "do your four" hours of urban community service (their motto: "you've got 2 give 2 get"). In time, Millennials will want to hear new economic and social themes in song lyrics. Ballad-like songs about stark differences in class and wealth—about star-crossed lovers pulled in conflicting directions by love, family, and the marketplace—could strike a new chord.

Implications for Film and Television

Group and community ethics have been missing from film for over 40 years—ever since the '60s propelled the lone anti-hero and counterculture into battle with the supposedly faceless and soul-less "system." This Boomer-targeted anti-hero genre replaced the hero films that were popular from the mid-1930s through the early '60s. The civic-hero genre was defined by Frank Capra, whose films depicted ordinary people fighting the good fight for the benefit of the public, alias the "common man."

Millennials are poised to turn away from anti-heroes and celebrities, in favor of a modern update of the civic teamwork genre. In the *Spy Kids* series, a family "team" (the ultimate Millennial formula) hunt down global evil-doers, often with the help of other kids. In the *Agent Cody Banks* series, teams of kids from around the country become dutiful agents of the U.S. government. The updated *Spider-Man* series shows ordinary citizens helping the reluctant hero—assistance that the purely *anti*-hero Spider-Man of the '60s would never have received.

This penchant for teamwork has been building for years and can be traced back to some of the earliest Millennial cartoon classics, from the paramilitary "Barney" kids to the herd of kid dinosaurs in *The Land Before Time* series. Teamplay is now a staple theme in many teen movies. In *Varsity Blues*, the hero decides that loyalty to his team trumps loyalty to his coach. In *Mean Girls*, the heroine breaks up her prom crown in the last scene and gives pieces to both her friends and her enemies.

The tight relationship between Millennials and their parents can allow any group to be recast as an impromptu family, as was done in *The Fast and The Furious* and its sequel, whose racer groups stood in sharp contrast to the isolated racers in Boomer-era cult films like *Vanishing Point* or in any of the *Rambo* films. Many of today's reality TV shows ("The Apprentice," "The Amazing Race," "Extreme Makeover: Home Edition") portray everyday—and competent—people achieving things in teams.

Surveys show that youth do not hold entertainers in the same high regard they hold parents, close friends, police, or other public servants. This suggests that Millennials will be drawn to story lines involving groups (like athletic teams, show casts, or soldier squads) portrayed as permanent and fully functional families. The lone-wolf hero, even the impromptu hang-out gang, is less appealing. Coming of age in a post-9/11 world, they believe that victory or defeat has long-term consequence, not just to individuals, but to society at large.

New story lines will show the community or group doing battle to protect itself. This could include severe class conflict, resistance against cultural icons, and mutinies against oppressive leaders. These plots will feature teams (unions, political parties, extended families, military units, sports teams) prevailing over corrupt individuals. In an era when individualism is allowed fullest expression in the marketplace, the Millennial focus on peer solidarity will show up in shows that highlight issues of class and inequities of income and wealth. Indeed, this is already happening in movies like *Bring It On*, *Save the Last Dance*, and *Maid in Manhattan*.

Game shows will inexorably change. The ruthless, scheming, vote-your-buddy-off-the-island competition so popular among 30something Gen Xers will decline in popularity. Instead, rising Millennial adults will want to watch "ordinary" people get rewarded for their ability, or even just their decency, with minimal competition—in a kind of game that would resemble the "Queen for a Day" show of the early '60s, when the woman who told the best hardship story would be awarded a refrigerator. Teens are attracted to "American Idol," in part, for this reason: The contestants are ordinary well-adjusted people, success depends solely on talent, and the audience at large has a say in the outcome. The winner becomes a democratic everyman with whom everyone can identify.

Implications for the Internet and Video Games

Millennial teens are using information technology to build a sense of group participation far beyond the imaginings of Boomers, or even Gen Xers, at that age. Many teens keep their computer IM and cell phone on nearly all the time that they're not actually with their friends, giving rise to the most 24/7-peer-to-peer connected generation in world history. Saatchi & Saatchi has come up with a new term for this technology-enhanced social cohesion, "connexity." Among this generation, according to *American Demographics*, 47 percent own a cell phone, slightly below the national average of 55 percent—but where older people are more likely to use their phones for business, Millennials use them to "connex," and integrate them into their social lives.

Figure 10.1 ▶

TV and Videogame Use in Last Year of High School, Annual Survey of College Freshmen, 1987–2004

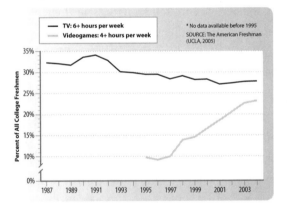

On cell phones or at computer consoles, 74 percent send and receive Instant Messages, allowing groups of people to chat in different locations all at once. Many of today's young people walk around with IM-enabled cell phones, tapping out messages to friends. Through Web sites (like *AIM.com*), they can construct platforms enabling them to communicate with their personal "team" through many different digital devices—and, if they wish, to take part in more than one conversation at a time. Those who use America Online for IM (roughly half of all teens) can now find out where they stand in the social pecking order by going to *aimfight.com* and finding out whose name shows up more (to the third degree) on *other* people's buddy lists.

"Social media" is on the rise. Hugely popular Web sites have arisen to help Millennials create virtual communities—for example, *myspace.com*, which has 18.5 million users age 16 and over, or *facebook.com*, used by 2.5 million college students on 600 campuses. Some sites (like *buddyprofile.com*) create networks of "people who care"—who are always available online to help a young person through personal troubles. Other sites (like *ratemyteachers.com* and *noindoctrination.com*) enable them to express opinions about teachers. They can share their personal calendars and photos, meet others who share their interests—and rate "hot" guys and girls on campus. They can go into each others blogs and trade opinions about the topics of the day. A growing number are turning to "community search" portals (like *shadows.com*), which rank search results according to what users think about the sites.

College campuses are seeing a growth in online community and political forums (like *citizenchange.com*). The Web is rapidly becoming a vehicle for rising Millennial participation in politics. Just type the words "youth vote" on a browser, to see how rapidly and broadly interest has grown in civic issues. More consequentially for the entertainment industry, collegiate artists and peer reviewers are using sites (like *acidplanet.com* or *sonyconnect.com*) to publish their songs and have them reviewed and ranked by their peers. They can turn to other sites (like *cdbaby.com*) to publish CDs as independents. Soon, this is likely to happen with films, also.

Thus is the Internet fueling the impulse of this generation to democratize the culture. Media companies need to find ways of inserting themselves into these peer group technologies, by providing young people with tools for creative team projects. Otherwise, they risk getting marginalized in the Millennials' digital world.

The game world is changing too. Gen Xers have played video games of the one-on-one conflict variety during their entire lives—ranging from the abstract arcade games of the '80s to today's high-resolution blood-and-guts battles, in which gamers have competed in an individual, gladiatorial combat style. By contrast, the more Millennial-friendly multiplayer game environments (in the teen hit *Halo 2*, for example) put much more emphasis on getting along with and caring for others. The key is less to kill your enemy than to form alliances, to take gradual steps to marginalize your adversary, and then to strip him of legitimacy in the eyes of other players.

As console-only games become the domain of an aging population of male Gen Xers, Millennials will be drawn to multiplayer games—especially to Internet-based "Massively Multiplayer Online Games" (MMOGs, which have also proven to be popular among Gen-X moms). This trend will be hastened now that major game box makers have introduced Internet uplinks for their game consoles. The group-oriented MMOG dovetails with the same mix-and-match, sampled, file-swap approach Millennials bring to other entertainment and communications media. Many youths will expect email, cell phone access, and instant messaging to become default game features. In the years to come, four out of five mobile phone users in the United States and Western Europe are expected to play mobile games, paid for through sponsorships, pay-to-play charges, and subscriptions.

Implications for Older Generations

Pay It Forward is a movie about a kid who, to carry out a school assignment, thinks up a wonderful neighborly idea for improving society and actually sets out to implement it. The tragic way in which older people react to his efforts reminds us that older generations do not always welcome the Millennial focus on teamwork and community. Some older people refuse to acknowledge it. Others will be troubled by what they do see, having been so steeped themselves in a culture of individualism.

Those who have kids of their own are usually the most supportive. Yet even some Gen-X parents will often prefer to set themselves apart, seek out the "anti-group," and feel drawn toward story lines that sort out winners from losers. Most Boomer parents will thrill to seeing their communitarian visions embodied in their grown-up children, but many will still will worry about the authoritarian and collectivist tendencies of the new youth culture.

If the national mindset becomes less playful and more serious—for example, at a time of war, terrorist threat, or economic crisis—adults of all ages will feel a greater sense of duty. In such times, the new Millennial attitude of civic commitment may usher in a new attitude of purposeful (even propagandistic) culture. Meanwhile, probing the dangerous dark side of "group think" will be a task left mostly to older generations.

11 | STRATEGIES FOR A CONVENTIONAL GENERATION

"In some ways they are as wholesome and devoid of cynicism as the generation that wore saddle shoes."

— *New York Times* (2000)

STRATEGIES FOR A
CONVENTIONAL GENERATION

Millennials push toward the center harder than toward any edge. This center can be powerful. It can be greatly influenced by peer, family, and societal pressures to make smart choices. And it can often take older generations by surprise.

Back in the late '60s, many young Boomers laughed at a futuristic *Mad Magazine* spoof about the American family around the year 2000. It showed "hip" middle-aged parents rage with frustration over their earnest and straight-arrow teens. Now fast-forward to the real year 2000, in which a New York Times-CBS poll appears showing that half of all teens trust their government to do the right thing "all or most of the time," versus only one-fourth of their own parents. Shortly thereafter, a UC-Berkeley poll found that teenagers are significantly more conservative than adults on abortion, school prayer, and faith-based charities. Boomers might wonder: Did *Mad* have it right all along?

Millennials cannot be described as "conservative" in any political or ideological sense. "Conventional" fits them better. Most Millennials believe strongly in institutional trust, community standards, and personal responsibility. Few want to experiment with lifestyles or test the merits of cultural relativism. They typically like to focus on what they have in common, which helps explain why "social norming" campaigns (on substance abuse and sexual behavior) seem to work for them.

This trend has important implications for the producers of pop culture. On the one hand, Millennials perceive their outlook as distinctly modern, a fresh way to overcome the ennui and social exhaustion they sense around them. On the other hand, they have a classic bent, and widely share a desire for moving the culture in more serious and decorous directions.

Here are four key strategies that address Millennials as a *conventional* generation.

* **Respect the new norm, and beware pushing too hard toward the "edge."**
When assessing the dress, language, and mannerisms of today's youth, people often make the mistake of trying to compare them directly with those of youth twenty or forty years ago. Such comparisons are out of context. It's much more meaningful to compare how each crop of youth is situated relative to the prevailing pop culture of its own time. During the '60s, for example, teenagers were less vulgar in speech and attitude than they are today—but young Boomers were clearly *more* vulgar than the adult pop culture, which was then chastised as a "vast wasteland" because of its dullness. Millennials, on the other hand, are significantly *less* vulgar than the pop culture they encounter. Pushing the edge is not new to them; it's something their parents once did and (often) still do.

Obscene lyrics elicit a "so what?" response among teens more than any desire to take them further. Teachers report that the vast majority of schoolyard profanity is simply the repetition of lines they hear in the media. Youth magazines like *Teen People*, with their frequent features on parents, community service, and religion, have grown noticeably blander

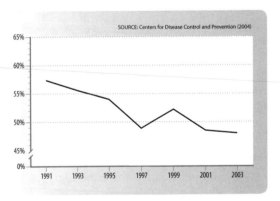

Figure 11.1 ▶

Percent of male high school students who report having had sexual intercourse, 1991–2003

SOURCE: Centers for Disease Control and Prevention (2004)

than stories in the adult *People*. This same path holds for fashion and sexuality. Dress styles are very casual, but they are moving in a classic, preppy, or retro direction. Many high school students are sexually active, but "True Love Waits" attracts more interest than any other slogan on the subject. It's not unusual, in fact, to hear women in their late teens voice disapproval and concern for the "inappropriate" behavior of younger girls.

Despite the efforts of their parents (and others) to wall them off, Millennials are stepping into a pop culture that is laced with a broader range of sexual expression, from innuendo to in-your-face grossness, than anything today's older generations confronted at like age. They are reacting (according to *Seventeen* magazine, in a recent feature story on "Miss Modesty") by choosing styles that are "just a little more covered up." There will continue to be a youth market for nasty-but-nice story lines like that of *American Wedding*. However, the youth markets for these entertainments will be buoyed more by curiosity than commitment. This genre will be perceived, by youth, as having been coined by older generations—and, as a consequence, as no longer occupying society's creative cutting edge.

* **Tell stories that define or reinforce societal norms.** Raised mainly by a Boomer Generation that broke the rules, the first half of the Millennial Generation will be inclined to translate their parents' moral discoveries (and behavior) into a new system of rules. Time-tested themes of individualism and institutional decay will not resonate as much as they did forty years ago, when Boomers were the same age. Smashing societal norms, or fomenting chaos out of order, will feel like over-used themes—while creating norms, and establishing order out of chaos, will feel fresh.

In their schools and communities, Millennials have already been growing up with an abundance of adult-imposed norms and standards. Over time, they have learned to feel comfortable with rules—even to flaunt their rule orientation a bit as an acknowledged contrast between themselves and older people. In recent years, the rule-abiding kid and the unruly adult ("wear your bike helmet, dad," or "buckle your seat belt, mom," "that's a bad word, dad") have become standard movie and TV gags. They wouldn't have made sense in the '80s or '60s. Over time, Millennials themselves will begin to adapt and apply these rules on their own to deal with problems. As young adults, they will enforce these rules through a peer consensus on norms of acceptable behavior.

Millennial stars will take less interest in setting their own criteria for success by leading unusual lives that either pretend to be more meaningful and fulfilling (the pattern for many Boomer stars) or are marked by an abundance of glitz and high-end play (the pattern for many Xer stars). They will have fewer quarrels with parents, teachers, and other aspects of the adult world. Among both stars and fans, some of the new Millennial norms will seem like throwbacks (like the trends toward decorum, family, traditional weddings), and others will not (netiquette, group dating, gay marriage). Either way, year by year, young people will seem ever less interested in rule- and taboo-breaking as a central focus of entertainment.

* **Focus on the entertainment ahead of the artist.** Millennials will re-define the role of art versus artist, focusing more on the technical quality of the entertainment, with less regard to its back story, context, or credentials. During the Boomer era, the subjective experience became all-important, and the artist's vision and creativity was paramount. Too much polish was often actively avoided. During the Gen-X era, personal authenticity (as revealed in the proliferation of "uncut" and "unplugged" releases) became the touchstone of true art. An artist could be authentically good or bad—or a sell-out. Millennials are moving back to objective production value. They are beginning to focus less on an entertainment item's intrinsic elements or credentials (including "street cred") and more on the extrinsic attributes of the finished item itself.

Entertainers assembled by corporations, singers who don't write, and formula films will be acceptable if they're good. Whether a product includes a celebrity "superstar" will matter less than before, unless that superstar can in fact perform at a superior talent level. The full legacy of

Forbidden Fruit?

Over the last twenty years, perhaps the most durable argument against parental advisories or explicit censorship of any kind—for films, music, or Web content—was that such notices had the unwanted consequence of enticing youth to seek out the "forbidden fruit" they were not supposed to see. Many pop culture producers have used this concept to justify marketing campaigns designed to make their product appear intentionally shocking or offensive to parents.

As Millennials replace Gen-X in the youth age brackets, the concept no longer finds much empirical support. In 2005, a Gallup Poll asked teens aged 13 to 17 the following question: "In general, do you think a warning label on a CD makes you more or less likely to buy it?" The results are shown in the table below.

Notice that "Less Likely" beats "More Likely" by over 5-to1 among younger teens, by 15-to-1 among older teens. The lesson is clear: Respecting parental opinion has become the new Millennial norm—quite a distance from the defiant youth attitude so common two generations ago.

Age	More Likely	Makes No Difference	Less Likely
Age 13–15	5 %	58 %	28 %
Age 16–17	1 %	84 %	15 %

the pop culture—along with literature, history, and news events of the past few decades—can be used as a Millennial playground, whose bits and pieces matter less for their original meaning than for the tableaus they provide for stories, characters, and jokes.

* **Help Millennials democratize the culture.** Compared with Gen Xers, Millennial audiences, as they mature, will show more appreciation for "ordinary" music and musicians. By valuing the wedding singer, the songster with the acoustic guitar, and the local musical theater, they will be part of a growing democratization of music, with an assist from advancing technology. In music and film, Millennial audiences will want to take part, to interact, even to be included as co-creators of the song or story of the moment.

The music industry will have to adjust to the idea that every Millennial has the power to be a producer as well as a consumer of music. Sitting alone and listening to "important" music is a relic of the Boomer and Gen Xer past. The political opinions of superstar musicians are unlikely to inspire young activists, or sway youth voters, to the extent they did in the '60s. More in keeping with the Millennial style would be amateur musicians who personally rally and energize the political movements they've joined and the leaders they've chosen.

Instead of trying to lecture, intimidate, and file lawsuits against tech-skilled Millennials, the industry should encourage them to participate in the production and distribution of music. For example, a daring artist might request re-mixed versions of their music from fans. In time, Millennial cultural aspirations will bind artist and audience together, and usher in the sort of popular editing, reinterpreting, and sharing of tunes in a manner traditionally associated with folk music.

Implications for Music and Live Entertainment

School of Rock is a movie about a burned-out (Gen-X) rock star who tries to teach his craft to a class full of (Millennial) middle-school kids. He finds it's tough work. The kids need careful coaching on how to scream and jam and rip their shirts and raise their fists in defiance of the system. But ultimately he succeeds, and this hilariously on-target show ends with the kids performing flawlessly for their adoring and applauding parents.

For decades, a central theme of American pop music has been the misfit between kids and adult society and their need to rage against convention. Now we're finding out what happens to pop music when, across all ethnic and socio-economic lines, young people are becoming more inclined to "fit in." Today's typical teenagers sense that they lead reasonably pleasant and untortured lives, get along fine with their parents, and generally trust the powers-that-be. In the years to come, we'll find out how pop music can reinvent itself to keep the attention of a conventional generation of new consumers.

One way it can reinvent itself is to put more emphasis on the quality of the song or act and less on the authenticity and self-styled creativity of its artists. With a conventional generation (as with conventional societies), doing something entirely new is not as prized as doing something tried and true, and doing it very well or in a fresh and appealing way. Millennial listeners think nothing of turning on "oldies rock" from Led Zeppelin to ZZ Top (with or without their parents) nor Millennial musicians of reverentially studying the Woodstock "classics." Today's teens rave about new pop hits (both on CDs and in movies) that are merely remixes of old songs, about rap commentary on old rock recordings, and about spliced-together videos of old music acts and parodies of such acts. They care less about the original artistic vision behind the act, and they care more about the style and context of its performance.

Older generations have mixed feelings about this youth comfort with retro styles and reruns. While they may see it as leading to shallow artistic plagiarism, they also acknowledge that it celebrates their own cultural achievements. From veteran stars in their fifties breaking rock concert sales records to mom rockers in their thirties banging drums at Mamapalooza festivals, Millennials look up the age ladder and salute. They then move on, worrying not about how to create something yet newer but how to make it all work for their own lives and technologies.

Another way pop music can reinvent itself is by putting more stress on affirming norms and values rather than breaking them. Over the last decade, youth has driven a steadily rising market for religion-infused music—not so much for the traditional "Christian" or "Gospel" genres (whose growing market share has been driven by all age groups), but for new Gen-X rock groups like Switchfoot, Jars of Clay, and MercyMe that have been introducing Christian themes to mainstream youth audiences. For evangelizing Millennials, the new trend is to reach for the mainstream and to try to mix inclusively with the "secular" world. As the *Village Voice* (sarcastically) describes it: "From hardcore punk to hip-hop, die-hard young Christians have turned to what were once the most heathen niches of pop culture to express their faith, minister to marginalized cohorts, and spiritually seduce new groupies."

A surprising number of "American Idol" stars—Clay Aiken, Ruben Studdard, George Huff, and RJ Helton—have proclaimed their religious beliefs and later released gospel songs. Country music (as embodied by the 2005 Idol winner, Carrie Underwood) has recently been gaining market share, thanks to the appeal of solid values and "real people" artists for the under-35 consumer. Hip hop is responding to the same trend, with "Mary is My Homegirl" T-shirts selling briskly in urban areas while Kanye West's "Jesus Walks" became one of the top-selling rap songs of recent years.

With Millennial influence, the favored new forms of music over the next decade will have purposes more reminiscent of the 1930s (storytelling, entertainment, and moral uplift) than of the '60s (prophecy, rebellion, and soul-baring). The cultural shift from the 1920s to the '30s is instructive. In the late '20s, the multiracial crowds gathering to hear "hot" jazz in urban centers from St. Louis to Harlem could hardly have imagined a future in which popular music would not forever get hotter and wilder. But by the late '30s, with the advent of swing, mainstream jazz evolved into a friendlier and more upbeat sound—something far less wild, less hot, and (one might say) more conventional.

Implications for Film and Television

If ever there were a cinematic archetype for the conventional side of the Millennial Generation, it's Harry Potter. The typical news film shot of Harry shows a bright-eyed boy in glasses looking very proper in a uniform dress shirt and tie, part of a group of kids who struggle to excel and have fun in a very structured institutional environment where they worry a lot about grades and exams and punishments and penalties. Yet they also, from time to time, band together to save the universe from destruction. No one feels fundamentally alienated or oppressed or scorned, except very evil people, and there is no ambiguity about who those very evil people are.

The first Potter readers are in college now, of prime film consumer age, so it's timely to ask what made the Potter books and movies so popular among them. The answer lies partly in how the author, JK Rowling, gets Millennials so right, and also in how adroitly she characterizes older generations. Think about the midlife Boomers who today run England or America—and then picture the middle-aged teachers and directors at Hogwarts, those individualistic, weirdly dressed, spiritually obsessive, perfectionist egotists who feel more at home lecturing than governing. Think about today's young adult Gen Xers—and then picture the kind-hearted giant, Hagrid, who has to carry out the bidding of older wizards while fighting bravely to overcome his checkered past.

To be conventional, one must *trust* conventions and believe that they work, that they bear fruit over time, and that they lead to the ultimate triumph of good over evil. Just as Gen Xers were once taught to be skeptical, Millennials are taught to be trusting. Think of the core message of *Polar Express* or *Big Fat Liar*. As teenagers, the same kids who at age seven enjoyed such Disney classics as *Lion King* and *Mulan*, starring youths who live up to society's timeless tests and challenges, are today avidly watching movies and TV shows that hang their entire plot lines on the glitzy prom, the championship game, the big exam, or the epic battle. Conventional outcomes matter. If you trust and try, you may win or you may lose in a Millennial plot line, but you will not be a loser or sucker. If you try hard and fail, at great cost, you will be celebrated for your sacrifice.

In the visual realm, as with other media, Millennials are pulling away from the cultural "edge." In recent years, there has still been plenty of R-rated and youth-targeted sex and violence out there, along the lines of *American Pie 2*, *Scary Movie 3*, or *Kill Bill*. But these "edgy" genres were already well established among Boomers and (especially) Xers before Millennials came along. One reason they get made is because older generations of producers are familiar with films of this kind and find them easy to make and market.

When sex and gore work for Millennials, moreover, the film's purpose is typically not to "shock" viewers out of their comfort zones, but rather to provide the grist for pure goofball humor or to advance the tried-and-true plot mechanics of an action movie. Genuinely disturbing, convention-inverting messages rarely work well with teens—and within a decade, they won't work with young adults either.

To discover what's fresh among young Millennials, you have to take a look at what's new in today's youth world. Some films and TV shows are doing this. In the title-teasing *What a Girl Wants*, what she wants is her father. In *Ella Enchanted*, what makes a girl enchanted is that she always obeys whatever she is told. In "Joan of Arcadia," the popular TV series about an otherwise normal teen, what makes a girl special is that she regularly talks to God.

Had these story lines appeared before the mid-'90s, they would have seemed out of joint.

In the future, sexual content will have its place, as it will always have in cinematic story-telling, but it will need to be either more romanticized (and less glaring) or more slapstick to appeal to the emerging Millennial mindset. On the whole, today's young people are uncomfortable with the sort of hippie-era naturalism that has always resonated with Boomers. Millennials find nakedness embarrassing and seldom welcome it other than as a theatrical tool to humiliate the villain.

Sexual orientation is less of a "big deal" to Millennials than to older generations, in part because they have both heard and talked so much about it. Revelations about gay lifestyles don't feel as new to them as they once did to older generations, in youth. Millennials believe that all conventional couples—gay or straight—merit equal public recognition, which is why they are much more supportive than older generations of gay civil unions and gay marriages. On the other hand, Millennials are not attracted to the more daring and provocative ways that older generations often like to depict sexuality—gay or straight. (Most would be shocked to learn that the "sexual revolution" of the '70s was all about destroying marriage as an institution, not about giving everyone an equal right to get "hitched.")

TV and film violence will remain popular for young-adult Millennials, as long as it serves a civic purpose, with "good guys" beating "bad guys." They won't be satisfied with just a huge body count and a lot of dark ambiguity, except if the purpose is entirely comedic. Should real-world events turn in a violent direction, the youth interest in cinematic violence will diminish, as it did from the mid-1930s into the '40s.

Implications for the Internet and Video Games

With their frequent complaints about illegal file-swapping among teens, many media industry leaders have implied, and some have directly stated, that freebooting criminality is rampant in today's youth generation. This generational accusation sidesteps the obvious point that the young people of every era, given the same technology, would have done the same thing.

Lots of Boomers and Gen Xers tried to pirate. It was just too difficult to do very effectively. Before confronting today's young people over file swapping, music and film executives from older generations should ask themselves whether, had it been possible, they would have done what Millennials are doing. The answer, probably, is yes.

File-swapping, alias "piracy," is common, but not the norm. Surveys show that most Millennials—even those who download for free—have misgivings about it. They are only slightly more likely than adults to say that file-sharing ought to be totally legal. Millennials just wish there were a cheaper and simpler way to purchase exactly what they want. With the huge success of iTunes and video game music, they certainly show they're willing to pay to hear the music they want, if the industry readjusts its approach to fit the purpose and way that they listen.

Millennials are not a wild and lawless presence on the Internet. On the whole, and in contrast with young Gen Xers a decade ago, they are making the Internet a lot tamer. Today's young people often seek out the mainstream by identifying for each other the popular new spots on the Internet where they can congregate and hang out. Many Millennials are comfortable relying on their "top ten" lists to determine where they should Web surf next, and several Web sites (like *newtopsites.com* and the Yahoo buzz index) have stepped in to help.

Every media company should set the goal of having its Web site make one of these "top ten" lists. The challenge is to find some unmet need and fill it, or to address the true cutting-edge taste-makers of this generation in novel ways. On the Web, as elsewhere, this generation perceives its tastes as classic, modern, and eclectic. The advantage will go to those who get there first and best.

Millennials are showing signs that they will, in time, round the corners of today's edgy video game industry. Playing video games is already a common recreational activity among college and high school students. It's likely to become even more popular once the industry more broadly targets their emerging mindset. Millennials of both genders will be drawn to a widening range of games that combine challenge, conflict, violence, realism, morals, and storytelling. Companies that persist in stubbornly pushing the edge of acceptability and tolerance will increasingly find their market limited to middle-aged people. Meanwhile, Gen-X parents (especially dads) who grew up with video games can be expected to share their passion with their own sons and daughters. Gaming centers aimed at the younger set would do well to have well-defined kids and moms-and-dads areas.

To attract Millennials as they age, video game story lines can follow a more conventional and classic plot line. Beyond all the battles, games can increasingly involve progressive play, often for positive ends—for example, establishing peace and prosperity throughout the virtual empire. Violence will often be a restorative force. Winning will often require constructive activity. Players may rack up points for building, not blowing up, gleaming virtual towers in the game world. Clues, puzzles, and spatial problem-solving common in early video games may enjoy a new popularity.

Millennials will not avoid violent games. Rather than wage battles on isolated consoles, they may want to start collectively waging virtual world wars. Their interest in the military is already developing far beyond the mere pulling of triggers. As children of parents who can no longer tell them much about military service, Millennials want to know about what it's like as a lifestyle and career—where you live, who gives you orders, how you advance in rank, when you retire, and what you do then. After the U.S. Army uploaded its new recruiting game, *America's Army*, 400,000 people downloaded it within its first week—most of them youths of recruitment age—and more than 240,000 players completed the basic training portion of the game to qualify for online play. In the game, a player who breaks the rules suffers a severe penalty. Shooting one of your fellow soldiers, for example, lands you "virtually" in Leavenworth prison.

Millennials will accelerate the trend to making video games pay, at point of purchase and as an after-market. Already, people buy and sell game "powers" acquired in online games. In the future, a virtual economy will appear in these virtual worlds, which teens and collegians will find and exploit.

Implications for Older Generations

As a generation drawn more to the center than to the fringes, Millennials will be more inclined to visit the main tent than to gawk at sideshows. Because they are more likely than Gen Xers to see the world as ordered and rational, rather than fractured and irrational, they will be more attracted to stories affirming deep meaning in the world and events, like *Lord of the Rings*, and less attracted to random, no-rules worlds so common in '90s sci-fi films. Genres like the moody horror movie, gritty urban drama, or dystopian science fiction will still find their niches, but these will more likely be popular with aging Gen Xers than with Millennials. Audiences for the more outrageous game, talk, and reality shows will gradually age. Many cable channels will find their racier programming confined to an increasingly narrow and middle-aged demographic.

Many older people, taking pride in their own "unconventionality," will view these new youth trends with a mixture of surprise, disdain, and backhanded admiration. They may look upon the generation the way *Washington Post* reviewer Allison Stewart did the young singer Clay Aiken: "almost too square...excessively mild-mannered...a defiant embrace of the middle... [with] no discernible sense of irony." The next decade will feel like a cultural inversion of the '60s, when the skeptics and rule-breakers were young, the trusting souls middle-aged.

Many Boomers and Gen Xers who have "pushed the edge" all their lives will persist in trying to prod younger people to rebel in ways that will rekindle thoughts of their own youth. Some will find niches where they can do this, but others will lose their audiences. Cultural institutions that came of age with Gen X—like MTV, BET, and Comedy Central—will face a stark choice: whether to abandon the old style and target the new youth attitude, or keep the style and retain their original audience. Some may be tempted to do both—but, in time, the new youth attitude will be so flagrantly non-X that this strategy will not work. Institutions that choose to age with Gen-X will need to re-define exactly what "pushing the edge" means for a moms and dads in their forties.

Many Gen-X and Boomer parents will feel conflicted. First-wave Xers with kids are perhaps the most defiantly pro-family age-group in America today. This is revealed most strikingly in country music, whose mostly Gen-X male singers (many from the heralded Gen-X country "Class of '89") are writing one ballad after another proclaiming their love and fidelity for their wives, their duty to their families, and their adoration for their children. Yet many of these same parents watch Tarantino films late at night and like to listen to Nirvana when they go driving alone. While Gen Xers may try to shield their growing kids from their own nostalgic artifacts, Boomers will continue to be more willing to share and pass on their cultural memories. Entering old age, Boomers will widely regard their contribution to the pop culture as one of their generation's most enduring achievements.

12 | STRATEGIES FOR A PRESSURED GENERATION

"Sometimes I feel more pressure than maybe I should, because I know there are so many people who want me to do well."

—Sarah Hughes, age 16, on her 2002 Olympic gold medal victory

STRATEGIES FOR A PRESSURED GENERATION

Coming of age is stressful for every generation. For Boomers, apart from those who had to confront Vietnam or the draft, the stress commonly came from within, in the search for self-discovery. For Gen Xers, the stress resulted more from personal risk-taking in an environment of family and community dysfunction, which translated into the sort of cynicism and detachment captured in the films by John Hughes. For Millennials, the stress is more likely to arise from earnest efforts to please adults, plan ahead, fit in with peers, and satisfy the stiffening requirements for training, education, and careers. Depending on a person's age, this means worrying about grades, college admissions, a first job, student loan debt, and the search for affordable housing.

Millennial stress is compounded by the nonstop workaholism of so many of their parents, by a young person's fear of real-life failure (to get a good job, to afford a home, to make a marriage work), and by the inability of adults to appreciate the new anxieties of teen life. Among today's teenagers, 70 percent worry a lot about finding a good job when they get out of school—whereas only 37 percent of adults think that teens worry about that. Four times as many high school students worry about getting good grades than about pressures to have sex or take drugs, and six times as many complain that they don't get enough sleep.

More than previous generations, Millennials are learning to wait, defer gratification, to bottle up their feelings—and to use entertainment to help them get through a pressure cooker of a young life.

Here are four key strategies that address Millennials as a *pressured* generation.

✻ **Present realistic stories about Millennial stress at home, in school, and on the job.** Faced every day with anxieties about tests, grades, college or graduate school admissions, not making mistakes, and not letting anybody down, Millennials inhabit a world full of new stories that haven't often been told—but which easily could be. These are stories of suppressed energy held in check, told by characters who feel empowered—and stressed out—by high expectations and intense competition standing in their way. Whether Millennials like it or not, the world is sorting them in school and will continue to do so afterwards. Those who are favorably sorted will feel concerned about those who aren't. Those who aren't will have to cope and find support.

Stories of this kind can be about very ordinary and very real people—the disappointed parent, the cheating friend, the overly competitive teammate, the kid with test anxiety, the athlete who misses the cut, the actress who doesn't get a call-back, guy who doesn't impress the rich girl, the girl who can't fit in at a private school—all of whom, after initial disappointment, find a way to prevail. A favorite protagonist for young Boomers and Gen Xers has always been the underachiever. Millennials would prefer more stories about—and may feel more sympathy for—the overachiever.

✻ **Depict stories with characters who face high-stakes choices in high-pressure situations.** Themes of mounting intensity leading to a dramatic, often violent confrontation—the staple underlying many classic showdown westerns—are making a comeback. The *Lord of the Rings* and *Matrix* series and other popular Millennial entertainments follow this mold. One of the great pleasures young readers have with Harry Potter books and movies is expecting that the virtuous lad will somehow cross swords with evil, and defeat it, before the end of each adventure. And one great pleasure of following the whole series of adventures is anticipating that each duel will be bigger and more consequential than the last. It's inconceivable that Harry might one day decide he's had enough, drop out, move to Bermuda, and just decompress for a couple of years.

The heroes in popular Millennial stories do not decompress. They do not evade pressure. Instead, they suppress and even hoard pressure, gathering more of it upon themselves. In the end, they seize on it as a propellant for violence of a cleansing sort, a powerful and necessary force for restoring order. These characters are not necessarily happy, but the way in which they feel "tortured" is more external than internal, and is caused by actual danger, not by some inner neurosis or anxiety. Actions, not feelings, are what count.

✳ **Cast comedic light on the stress of life.** Each generation has its own funnybone. What makes older people laugh typically doesn't work as well for the young—and vice-versa. In many ways, one generation's punch line is the next generation's set-up line. In our lifetimes, we've seen this evolve from Bob Hope, Lucille Ball, and Abbott & Costello (G.I.s) to Steve Allen, Stan Freberg, and Bill Cosby (Silent), from Gilda Radnor, John Belushi, and Jerry Seinfeld (Boomer), to Mike Myers, Adam Sandler, and Jim Carrey (Gen X). A suggestion of where Millennial humor is going can be seen in clips of the first on-screen G.I. teenagers cast in comic roles—Red Skelton, Katharine Hepburn, and especially Mickey Rooney and Judy Garland.

When they want to laugh, they prefer something to be pure fun, not laden with meaning and context. Theirs is a humor like that of other times of civic stress, a humor that leans more toward farce and whimsy than toward cynicism or caustic comment. Recall the hallmark of films of the late '30s and early '40s: the grump (sometimes a "sad sack" soldier), constantly ordered to new tasks, who often complains in comic fashion, but who ultimately does not rebel or refuse to work, and who in the end contributes to a good outcome.

The early indications are that Millennial comedy relies on a more scripted, goofball, timing-is-everything kind of humor. The joke is broadly accessible and has no subtext, yet the comic's own point of view remains concealed. It gets funnier with repetition—as well-timed anticipation is half the pleasure. It can look mean, but it's not. There's nothing that hurts or clings about it, unless you happen to get your eye poked or land in a bucket of water.

* **Target Millennials as multi-taskers.** Millennials are superb multi-taskers. They cope with the busyness of their lives by doing many things at once. They excel at giving each chore just the right amount of attention; many even take formal "time management" lessons to refine the art. All this means that effective Millennial entertainment must be multi-task-friendly, made of bits and pieces that make sense separately or together. These young people grew up with hand-held clickers capable of muting, fast-forwarding, channel-changing, or turning off devices, enabling them to edit out any bit of content that isn't of interest. They like employ technologies for this purpose—to extract just one song from a CD, browse the added elements of a DVD, or watch a football game while avoiding the ads.

When they want a larger entertainment experience, they prefer to combine fragments of this and that into their own self- or group-constructed show or CD mix. It's far more important that the total experience be fun (and a stress reducer) than that it have any meaning.

Reaching Millennials with pop culture products—or any commercial messages—requires strategies and platforms that adapt to their ways and connect with their styles. To get this TiVo-inclined generation to listen to an ad, it must be either deftly targeted, possess some entertainment, or enable some promotional use. Most of the rest gets tuned out.

Implications for Music and Live Entertainment

In recent years, the teen taste in pop music has moved toward sounds and lyrics that are tightly wound, tense, and wired. Teens are tuning in to fewer songs about aimless lives, hopeless fantasies, or an unrestrained id or libido—and tuning in to more songs about complicated real lives suspended between competing personal loyalties. Choices must be made, promises given or taken back, people hurt or comforted, parents reassured or offended, friends or siblings helped or left alone.

In their high-stress world, Millennials see music as a realm where these choices can be negotiated—or, alternatively, where pent-up frustrations and energy may be safely released. Either way, the goal is to affirm or fix things rather than reject or destroy them. One avenue of release for boys is offered by 100-decibel music of bands like Linkin Park, with lyrics that reveal almost no sign of irony or despair, but plenty of pressure-cooker statements about obligations to other people. Groups that offer a pure release, with simple lyrics and retro-style singable melodies, are likely to replace the Korn-style wails about societal abuses.

Others are moving toward music that is personal, informal, and low-tech—from acoustic guitars to plain old pianos, which are enjoying a new surge in popularity. Still another youth avenue is silly music, including cheerfully goofball novelty songs and "chip music" composed out of sounds extracted from old video games. In the years ahead, hip hop and punk will open itself up to increasing humor and brighter colors, often using the old dangerous images as a foil.

Young Millennials are already hearing plenty of this happily off-beat music at home, where Gen Xers are adapting edgy musical styles into a smarter kind of kid's music that the whole family can enjoy. Kids albums by They Might Be Giants and the Waco Brothers' Jon Langford bring to mind the mood of the classic Looney Tunes of the 1930s and 1940s. Those albums are clean and non-rebellious, but retain just enough of "the edge" to work for parents and children alike.

The music industry will also have to adapt to the ever-busier schedules of youth. The rock-concert circuit needs to jettison any vestigial assumption that kids find chaos appealing. Events should be advertised well in advance, with travel and show times made as predictable as possible. Over-long events, or horrendous traffic jams, will be major drawbacks for teens—and their clock-watching parents.

In their daily lives, Millennials have become multi-taskers. So long as an activity does not require their full attention, they often do several activities at once to save on precious time and to keep themselves stimulated. Producers of Webcast music or TV music videos need to understand that their content is often little more than background noise to teens who may be focusing entirely on something else.

Radio, with its ubiquitous presence and background role, is an ideal multi-tasking medium. Unlike other media, it has not lost audience to the Internet. Instead, it has become the number one simultaneous activity for Web surfers. Radio may be a prime area for growth, but only if play lists are re-targeted to Millennial tastes. When Boomers were growing up, radio had auto audiences all to itself—and usually was the only entertainment medium available in teenagers own bedrooms. This helps explain why most radio formats are defined for Boomers and Gen Xers.

The time is ripe for better Millennial-targeted programming by broadcast radio, satellite radio, and Internet Web- and pod-casting. Ideally, it would let young people sample diverse musical styles in a less commercial-saturated setting. They could also provide a venue for Millennials to find out their peers' musical tastes, since MTV has de-emphasized music in favor of programming and the largest music publications (*Spin*, *Rolling Stone*) target older audiences. Programming (like satellite radio) that involves regular user fees will visibly split Millennials between those with money and those without. Imagine how Boomers would have felt, back in the '60s, if good radio stations were freely available only to teens with affluent parents. In the Millennial era, this is an accepted feature of the youth landscape.

Radio can pivot more quickly than other entertainment media, and is in a better position to "democratize" the pop culture by including, in play lists, high-quality cuts made by young performers who live and perform in a station's listening area.

Implications for Film and Television

Movies that worked well for young Boomers typically featured youths who sought less social pressure and found salvation when they escaped it, as in *The Graduate*, *Goodbye Columbus*, or *Easy Rider*. For Gen Xers, we recall cinematic youths who never experience much pressure and show great creativity without it, as in *Risky Business*, *Ferris Bueller's Day Off*, or *Slackers*.

The story lines for Millennial-era youth are turning another corner. In an increasing number of hit shows, youths are thrust into urgent situations, accept the challenge, and perform well in pressured environments. Animated superheroes nearly always work feverishly under pressure. The popular *Spy Kid* genre of live-action movies for 'tweens depicts ordinary kids thrown into life-and-death situations. *Matrix*-style epics feature young adults who fight knowing that civilization hangs in the balance.

Many Millennial-targeted films reveals the same familiarity with alarms, deadlines, dates, calendars, schedules, and digital countdowns that this generation shows in its real daily life. Two recent movies (*Clock Stoppers*, *Catch that Kid*) have depicted kids working against the literal tick of the clock. In the years to come, as Millennials reach young adulthood, Millennial-age characters in films and TV shows can show their grace under pressure in less fantastic and more real-life scenarios. More stories can emerge about young adults with long-term life

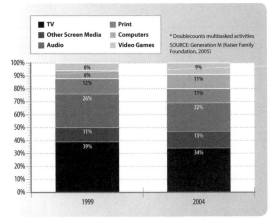

◄ **Figure 12.1**

Share of Total Weekly Time* Spent with Media, U.S. Youth Age 8 to 18: 1999 and 2004

plans who are comfortable taking step-by-step approaches to marriages and careers. In a reverse twist on the Boomer-era classic *The Graduate*, landmark Millennial films may show young people making earlier life-determining choices, including marriage, than older generations.

This new Millennial brand of grown-up behavior could produce young stars with fewer obsessions and a greater ability to multi-task, to achieve a "life balance" among their obligations. Stories featuring obsession with a single goal will remind many in this generation of compulsive, driven Boomers (alias, parents) and could be grist for comedy.

Millennial TV viewing has been in decline for many years now, at every time of day except for late-night retro shows. To keep its young-adult audience as Millennials move into their twenties, television programming will need to make numerous adjustments, to story lines, to tone, and to characters. Over the rest of this decade, networks will have to cope with young viewers who will less often be couch potatoes, and will more often be gamers or Web surfers who keep a TV on in the background or who toggle between videos and games via home theater technologies. Programs and commercials will struggle to be noticed at this diminished level of attention. In long run, the networks may all need to change their platform to the Internet—and entirely refashion the format of their sponsors' commercials and promotions.

Implications for the Internet and Video Games

In different ways, today's new digital technologies both reduce and increase the stress of Millennial lives. They make a vast array of essential tasks far faster and easier to perform—researching and writing in school, collaborating and presenting at work, and networking and sharing among friends. Yet many Millennials will freely admit that new technology, even as it saves time, often more than fills whatever time it saves by immersing them in a nonstop blizzard of messages, ads, songs, videos, games, and endless other distractions. The net effect can be to add to total stress. The temptation to "waste" time with new technologies can be a real problem in many a young life.

One solution is to do several activities at once, and Millennials are indeed avid multi-taskers. When a MTV survey recently asked 18- to 24-year-olds how many hours they spend surfing the Web, downloading music, and emailing friends, the average time totaled more than 24 hours a day. It turns out that the most avid multi-taskers are often those who feel most overwhelmed—which casts doubts on whether multi-tasking really solves the pressure problem. Another popular youth solution is to make and follow a detailed schedule of daily activities, often though organization software. Web sites help them construct calendars to plan their lives, or even allow calendars to be freely shared among friends.

With every passing year, as Millennials keep flocking to new technologies, the less-versus-more stress balance is becoming harder to assess. Cell phones are becoming pocket PCs that access the Web, send and receive emails and files, IM friends, and do just about everything that desktop computers can do. More than half of all Millennials—more than twice the proportion of adults—use cell phones to send text messages. Web sites (like *jamdat.com*) that enhance the entertainment value of cell phones, allowing downloads of films, TV streaming, and games, are becoming time savers for young people looking for handheld amusements. Small devices like the iPod, the MP3 Key Ring, and Microsoft's Portable Media Center enable young people to take their entertainment on the go.

One common theme in all of these advances is to invite Millennials to do something faster, while also inviting them to spend more time at it. New products, devices, or sites that would in fact make it easier for users to save time—for example, by allowing them to sample music and video fragments quickly or enter and exit a game in just a few seconds—could find an eager Millennial market. More than anything else, Millennials complain about the "hassle factor" in many of the available entertainments, produced by companies who apparently imagine that today's teens have endless time to spend on them.

The Millennial struggle against pressure will also affect video game content by drawing a brighter line between games that truly challenge players and games that just let them work off stress. During the Gen-X youth era, the most popular games were those that provided constant action and immediate payoffs for players with short attention spans. In contrast, Millennials may seek games with more distant payoffs, longer periods of development, and subtly changing players and relationships. "Slow build" historical and simulation games, in which players build nations and run cities, are growing in popularity.

A slowing style of game play may combine with the emerging multiplayer paradigm to create a game circumstance reminiscent of Boomer-era board strategy games. To the extent the video game industry can make classic games more Millennial in tone (smarter, group-oriented), they may find an audience.

In college and at work places, when Millennials seek a brief respite from their daily stresses, they may prefer low-tech, slow-tech, and no-tech game alternatives—along the lines of the "chill zones" colleges are stocking with pool, ping pong, old-fashioned pinball, and other diversions. Non-video games may, in time, enjoy a revival.

Implications for Older Generations

Older generations have difficulty understanding the Millennial reaction to all the stress in their youthful lives. Boomers believe Millennials should be broadly happy, even grateful, for all that compulsive parents, teachers, and legislators are doing on their behalf, no matter if this is becoming the most tested, prodded, nagged, and scheduled youth generation in history. Many Gen Xers wonder what Millennials are so worried about, anyway. So what if you miss a deadline or fail an exam? Just pick yourself up and try something new! Gen Xers are not inclined to ask why Millennials prefer to set themselves apart from the habits and tastes that underlie the Gen Xers' more risk-prone, improvisational lifestyle. Boomers and Gen Xers may think they know all about youth angst, but what they know is linked to the '60s or '80s, eras whose youth mindset, and problems, were very unlike those of today.

Over the next several years, as Millennials find places in the pop culture where they can take refuge from pressure, many older culture creators will resist the growing youth tendency to value entertainment as diversion or stress reduction more than entertainment as message. Eventually, the pressures and anxieties of the youth experience will translate into a wholly new style that is the Millennials' own. By around 2010, a distinctly Millennial sense of humor will emerge, with preachy older people and life-worn but coyly useful middle-aged people as the source of many a punch line. To many an older person, this will appear brash—but will elicit knowing chuckles, too.

13 | STRATEGIES FOR AN ACHIEVING GENERATION

"This is the first time in the history of the human race that a generation of kids has overtaken their parents in the use of new technology."

—Peter Eio, Lego Systems (2000)

STRATEGIES FOR AN ACHIEVING GENERATION

Every year, the highest-achieving Millennial youths astound older Americans by showing off their academic prowess. There was a time, not so long ago, when the National Spelling Bee could be won with words like *lyceum* (1992) or *vouchsafe* (1973) or *sanitarium* (1938). Consider the winning words of the new millennium, tongue twisters like *autochthonous, pococurante,* or *succedaneum.* Admissions officers at the nation's upper-ranking colleges are broadly reporting a recent rise in the qualifications of incoming freshmen—and admit that they are turning away vast numbers of applicants they could have admitted ten or fifteen years ago.

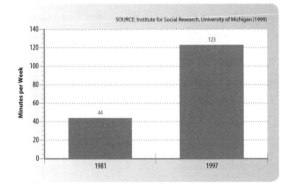

◄ **Figure 13.1**

Average Time Spent per Week on Homework by Students Aged 6–8, 1981 and 1997

A much higher share of Millennial teens say they aspire to post-secondary education than the teens of any prior generation. Over seven in ten of today's high school students say they are aiming for a four-year college degree, and at least that share of all races and ethnicities agree that a college degree confers "respect." Many of them will no doubt discover they lack the motivation or education or money necessary to get their degrees. But even these

Millennials will be more inclined to let their best and brightest set the cultural tone than was true for Boomers or Gen Xers in youth.

How do you provide entertainment for young people whose generation is achieving more, in school and out, than their parents did at the same age? How do you deal with young people who are skilled at music and drama, adept at technology, and able to communicate in media most older people can't fathom? What do you provide for teenagers who feel constantly pushed by older people to meet ever-higher standards? But, countervailing this, how do you accommodate kids who have weaker life-coping skills than young Gen Xers did, or less questioning minds than Boomers did?

Here are four key strategies that address Millennials as an *achieving* generation.

✱ **Portray the Millennial world as full of smart and aspiring achievers of all backgrounds.** Millennials respect achievement at a young age. They are faced, on a daily basis, with larger homework loads and more standards-based tests than their parents ever knew, and they know this. While the depth of this respect varies considerably among ethnic groups (young Asians the most, African-Americans perhaps the least, Caucasians and Latinos in the middle), the overall ethic of work, achievement, and reward is a striking new development among young people in every ethnic group. And it is strengthening by the year across the entire generation. Meanwhile, the appeal of aimless and unscheduled non-engagement—of "keeping one's options open" and dealing with situations as they arise—is weakening by the year.

Youth-targeted entertainment is starting to recognize this shift, albeit slowly. Pop music reflects it least, which in part accounts for the recording industry's failure to connect with young Millennials as well as it connected with earlier generations at like age. TV and film are reflecting it somewhat—you won't find any slackers at Hogwarts—but these media are still delivering plenty of Gen-X-era attitude about family, school, and workplace. More than today's older generations, Millennials are inclined to look upon the world as full of capable young people who will be, in their imaginings, even more capable when their turn comes.

* **Feature late-wave Gen Xers who embody Millennial aspirations.** Through the history of the popular culture, dating back to Tin Pan Alley, every generation has found role models from the prior generation, especially those who are just a few years older than themselves. Those role models tend to be individuals who succeed in anticipating—and coining—styles and attitudes of people five or ten years younger than themselves. The Silent Generation looked to Jack Kerouac, Frank Sinatra, and Marlon Brando. Boomers looked to Bob Dylan, Abbie Hoffman, and the Beatles. Gen Xers looked to Michael Jackson, Axel Rose, and Madonna. The leading wave of Millennials—those now in college or in entry-level jobs—will similarly feel a need for, look for, and find culture mentors from Gen Xers who are just older than themselves.

    Thus far, one can point out many late-wave Xer celebrities (born from 1976–81) who have served as role models for the next generation and whose work and image in some ways reflect emerging Millennial traits: Britney Spears, Kanye West, Beyoncé Knowles, Justin Timberlake, Jennifer Love Hewitt, Colin Farrell, Drew Barrymore, Julia Stiles, Freddie Prinze, Jr. The full roster of names from which such a list is compiled is noticeably weaker on the male side than on the female—a fact that should give producers a good idea of where they need to search the hardest. Yet the list does suggest the cultural sway that late-wave Gen Xers have had on the Millennial imagination even if some of these transitional figures are by now losing their youth appeal. The next round of youth-pop mentors will cast off all but the thinnest veneers of the old X styles and provide Millennials with articulate expressions of the new youth attitude.

* **Give focus, and voice, to the most gifted Millennials.** The rise of so many gifted young artists creates new opportunities, challenges, and perils to the entertainment industry. Never before, in U.S. history, have so many young people received so much highly specialized voice, instrumental music, dance, drama, and other fine arts training. They train at school, after school, on weekends, and during summers. Where a Boomer who was gifted at musical theater would be fortunate to be in one high school

show every two years, a Millennial who is gifted at musical theater might participate in a school musical, a one-act play, a fall and spring community theater show, and a summer youth musical over the course of a single year. College-level theater is also bristling with activity, showing a bent toward newer themes and more experimental works.

Behind all this is a cadre of mostly Boomer arts teachers and directors—and, especially, the Millennials' own parents, who range from gentle prodders to obsessive-compulsive perfectionists, always pushing their kids to advance their skill levels. Parents who make a living in entertainment and broadcast media often use their experience and connections to launch their own children down similar paths that—they hope—will lead to high-level careers. Multigenerational rock 'n roll families, once almost a contradiction in terms, is becoming a reality.

Surveys show that entertainment is a very popular field (and ambition) among high school students. College fine arts programs are thriving, and many offer special pre-professional curricula. Over the next several years, there will be a multitude of young adults who are determined to sing, dance, perform on stage and TV, write scripts, and make films—and who possess the ability to justify that determination. Countless more Millennials who are not themselves artists will have known or seen college classmates with performing skills rivaling or exceeding those of celebrity stars.

* **Make use of literature, and other curricula, that Millennials have studied in school.** In this era of the *No Child Left Behind* law, curricula are becoming more standardized within each state, and—given the power of large states like Texas and California over textbook companies—over most of the nation, too. Where Boomers were given far fewer book-reading assignments, and Gen Xers were exposed to curricula that often were invented district-by-district or even school-by-school, Millennials in K-12 schools are reading far more books off similar lists. More than before, what 'tweens and teens are reading tends to resemble what peers elsewhere are reading.

Especially in high school, the new Millennial study plan also emphasizes good-to-read "literature" more and fun-to-read contemporary fiction less. The new plan stresses classics, whether by Nathaniel Hawthorne, C.S. Lewis, or Toni Morrison. Latino authors, especially from South America, are becoming popular among Millennial collegians. What is less popular—sparking complaints from the National Endowment for the Humanities that book reading is declining among 18- to 24-year-olds—are the more artistic genres and the noun-verb potboilers so often found on bestseller fiction lists. Boys in particular prefer nonfiction, but rarely get credit for reading it. In response, many students tend to focus more on what they "need to get out of it" (prompting a booming business in elaborate study guides and summaries) than on the experience of reading itself.

Changing reading patterns provide opportunities for all entertainment media, but especially for cinema. Many of the classics on those lists (*Moby Dick*, *The Scarlet Letter*, *The Red Badge of Courage*, to name just a few) were made into movie classics in the quarter-century from 1930 to 1955, but have never since inspired a top-quality remake. A number of items on their reading lists have never been filmed. To a lesser but still significant degree, the Millennial-era science and social studies curricula (and nonfiction) also point to many common story (and song) ideas.

Implications for Music and Live Entertainment

As Millennials take over popular culture, there will be more performers who are smart, get along with their parents, handle their business affairs wisely (as the Olsen twins and other recent teen stars have done), and—in many cases—benefit from a life of well-connected privilege. Performers will wear their affluence comfortably, with few signs of awkwardness or embarrassment, and their fans will mostly approve. Few will complain that lots of money somehow contradicts an artist's broader message. Promoters that specialize in "viral product seeding" among teen influencers find that most youth are "comfortable with corporate." Many admit that their jobs would have been impossible back in the heyday of young Boomers or Gen-Xers.

Fifteen years ago, rap stars bragged about toughness and tenacity more than cash and creature comforts. Today, the emphasis is the other way around. Vast wealth has simply become an assumed fact of celebrity life

To be sure, riches alone will not win fan respect. Genuine artistic achievement, rather than celebrity trappings, will be the main draw. Millennial audiences will constantly be on the lookout for new pop-music stars who are not mere media creations, but who can sing and dance exceptionally well. Skilled musicians who have overcome adversity will be especially celebrated. Instead of VH1 stories of rock stars falling into ruin, Millennials will be attracted to variations on the "American Idol" career stories, in which ordinary, hardworking individuals attain success.

The current Millennial fascination and reverence for "classic" pop genres will lead to modern updates of those styles. In the emerging youth mindset, the music with which Boomers and prior generations grew up—unlike the music of the '80s and '90s, with which Gen Xers grew up—still needs to be awarded its celebrated place in history. Many Millennial artists and performers will devote their lives to reviving aging styles (from blues and jazz and swing to vintage '60s rock) and keeping their legacies alive

Parallel developments may arise in other live performances, especially musical theater, which has a special hold on Millennial entertainments. Big-budget musicals were sorely lacking for young Gen Xers, whose early musical diet consisted mainly of song fragments from "Sesame Street." The Millennial childhood witnessed the second golden age of blockbuster animated musicals, beginning with Disney's *The Little Mermaid* and continuing through to the rise of DreamWorks and Pixar. Over the past decade, several cartoon movies with musical components have been released each year, usually to gigantic kid audiences. In those films, the quality of the songs, lyrics, and vocals typically exceeds what one hears on pop radio play lists, and their presentation is more reminiscent of the old '30s MGM musicals than of '80s MTV music videos.

As young adults, Millennials will want to sustain their strong personal connection with movie musicals, and—perhaps as an expression of their more traditional, "low-tech" side—will provide exuberant new audiences for live theater, with new tastes. Over the next decade, the new attitudes, training, and school-based experiences of young-adult performers and playwrights will begin to make a mark, heralding larger changes to follow. In the

Millennials and Sports

The Millennials' fascination with video sports games reflects their location in history. The sports playing and watching life to date of today's 23-year-old coincides exactly with the current era of commercialized and youth-specialized sports—an era that dates back to the mid-1980s, with the L.A. Olympics, the rise of Nike, and the burgeoning of free-agent sports economics.

Generational comparisons are instructive.

Boomers grew up playing work-ups, sandlot ball, pick-up football games, and table-top sports games—in which kids played with whomever was around, somewhere close and easy (often a street), improvised their own rules, played until it got dark, and then went home, with adults hardly caring what they did so long as no one got hurt. Millennials grew up playing on select teams, with hired coaches, distant fields, published rules, and publicized standings—with nearly everything obsessively administered by adults. In the Boomer child era, you'd often see children and teenagers playing a game of catch with a baseball or football, even if they weren't very good at it. Now, you see Millennials playing catch far less often—but when you do, they tend to be very good at it.

At school, Boomers had long recesses, and a small number of (male only) sports teams, often filled by kids who played multiple sports, who seldom thought of it as a ticket to anywhere, and who had at most a dim idea of how a person can become a pro sports star. Millennials have short recesses (at some schools, none at all), and a large number of (female and male) sports teams, often filled with people who play only one sport, who often see sports as a ticket to college or even a lifetime of great wealth, and who have a fairly clear understanding of how a person can become a pro sports star.

Boomers grew up watching pro athletes who stayed on the same team for years, who played in stadiums named after heroes or home towns, who earned only two or three times what school teachers earned, whose private lives stayed out of the news, whose games were affordable for the average family, and whose team merchandise consisted of an inexpensive cap or pennant. Millennials have grown up watching pro athletes who jump teams frequently, who play in stadiums named after large corporations, who earn more than a hundred times what school teachers earn, whose private lives and business deals are constantly in the news, whose games are costly for the average family, and whose team merchandise is extensive, expensive, and heavily marketed.

To Boomers, sports felt more creative, casual, and myth-driven. To Millennials, sports feel more organized, specialized, and money-driven. Today, sports appear to matter more than before to those collegians and teenagers who see it as a possible career path—but less than before to the majority who see it only as a diversion. This has contributed to rising rates of obesity (due to the larger share of youth who do not play sports at all), even while the rate of overuse injuries to the knee and elbow are rising (due to the larger share of youth who train constantly in the same sport).

The future relationship between pro sports and Millennials is open to serious question. There will surely be an ample supply of quality players, of both genders, in all sports—but the question is, will their peers show enough interest in watching them play to sustain the current economics of those sports? Given the demographics of sports audiences, two or three decades may pass before this question can be answered. The ascendance of the free agent over the team, the disconnect from civic purpose, and the overt commercialism of contemporary sports all run contrary to where Millennials appear to be headed as a generation.

When new Millennial stars emerge—like a LeBron James, Michael Phelps, Freddie Adu, Danica Patrick, or Michelle Wie—they swiftly become miniature corporations. Sports originally became a big business by cashing in on the great popularity of reticent athlete-heroes whose original dedication to sports had nothing to do with money. The open question is whether this trend will continue for a new generation of athlete-CEOs for whom money has always loomed large, from the very first peewee sports camp. The answer may depend on what happens to the nation, and economy, over the next two decades—and, especially, what new ethic of sports emerges among Millennial players and fans.

The early trends are mixed. On the positive side, Millennial boys have shown surges of interest in wrestling and X-treme sports, though both surges have recently faded. There has been an increase in teen expenditures on personal sports equipment and sports video games, and those trends—especially the latter—may be enduring. Meanwhile, teen TV viewing of most pro sports is steadily declining, as is the teen purchase of pro sports logo clothing. The ticket buyers and television sports audiences for most pro sports continues to age. Teams and networks are responding by giving the sports-watching experience a more Gen-X feel. In doing so, however, they risk making sports less Millennial in tone than they already are—which will exacerbate the difficulty of marketing sports to this rising generation.

coming era of the Millennial artist, the live concert may become less of a celebrity event than a community event. A new "middle-class" of entertainer may emerge, as young people find new ways of earning a living as performers in cities and towns across America.

Live entertainment aside, technology will be the main topic. As they mature, Millennials will take justifiable pride in their ability to use technology to transform and improve many areas of social life, including pop culture. The nature of music itself will sound more digital in its rhythms and melodies. Film and TV music will gradually move away from '90s-influenced grunge and techno, moving into a new style that will suggest game sound tracks.

The biggest licensing market for music could be in game environments. As console games give way to Internet-enabled virtual worlds, music will be performed "live" by virtual bands to global audiences, with a team of creators behind every virtual artist. Gaming music may have entered a new era of respectability at a recent concert in the Hollywood Bowl, where the Los Angeles Philharmonic played video game music from *Halo*, *Metal Gear Solid*, *Warcraft*, *Tron*, and *Myst* to an appreciative audience consisting largely of Gen Xers and their Millennial children.

Millennials are opening the door to produce a new style of "band" with studio musicians and teams of animators, splitting the identity of artists from their appearance. In what could be a precursor to a large new trend, "video mods" now take existing music videos, strip out the video, leaving the audio. They substitute popular gaming characters (from *Sims II*, *Extreme Golf*, and other games) who sing and perform on virtual musical instruments. Talent can be added to any game character by anonymous musicians and vocalists. From this, it's only a short step to "live" virtual concerts within Internet-connected games.

Implications for Film and Television

Stories about the challenge of achievement—and the rewards of success—will strike a chord with Millennial audiences. Scripts can include positive youthful characters who see a need or a problem, plan and work to make things happen, and gain recognition in the end. The worst troublemakers (or villains) can be portrayed as the anti-achievers—lazy, shiftless, in-your-face slackers, characters that would require a more nuanced treatment for Gen-X or Boomer viewers.

The most conspicuous Millennial achiever, of course, is the ubiquitous young superhero. Never before in the history of cinema, even including the hero-obsessed late 1930s, have we seen such a preoccupation with youths endowed with world-changing powers. They turn up as ants, lions, toys, and fish; as peasants, gods, magicians, and Native Americans—or as loners in uniform (Spider-Man), gangs in uniform (Power Rangers), and families in uniform (Incredibles). In the spring of 2005, there were 18 new superhero movies (animated or live-action) currently under production—ample testimony to the popularity and profitability of this distinctively Millennial genre.

In the years to come, more shows will feature the less extreme and more realistic dimensions of the achieving Millennial. One aspect of the new Millennial reality is smartness. Gen-X came of age defining a sardonically slow-witted image of youth—an image that climaxed in the *Wayne's World*, *Dumb and Dumber*, and the *Bill and Ted* movies of the early '90s. The dumb trend has since reversed itself. In recent years, cartoons have featured genius kids (like the Thornberrys and Jimmy Neutron). Articulate and high-vocabulary dialogue has been heard in such teen movies as *The Emperor's Club*, *Teaching Mrs. Tingle*, or *10 Things I Hate About You*, and in such TV series as "Dawson's Creek," "Gilmore Girls," or "The OC."

This smart trend still has a ways to go. Over the next decade, TV shows that successfully target young adults starting careers and families will have to pump up the vocabulary and play down the atmosphere of risk and dysfunction. Shows that are popular with all age brackets will have to tone down their elements of youth dysfunction. *The Simpsons* has already moved in this direction. It now shows less of Bart, and Bart no longer brags about being the "classic underachiever." Future TV ads will show less of the "Dell guy" and more of his smarter younger friend.

Contest and "survivor" shows will have to smarten up a bit to keep Millennials' attention, perhaps through a sort of creative cross between "Fear Factor," "Jeopardy," and "Scholar." As campus life attracts greater media attention, a team-versus-team collegiate brain tournament might attract attention—like the old "College Bowl" of the late-'50s. Millennial anxieties over school and money will provide new grist for programming. Donald Trump anticipated this concept in episodes of "The Apprentice" that pitted college against non-college contestants. By billing the face-off as "book smarts" versus "street smarts," he shrewdly tapped into the emerging class tensions within this rising generation.

Millennials will not be surprised or irritated by teen characters who are smart but naïve, who are overweight or medicated, and who have to encounter and overcome difficult challenges. Parental or other elder help will be expected to be available, a place to turn when things get rough.

Implications for the Internet and Video Games

To Millennials, the Internet is as an arena for personal and community achievement. They use it to play, work, and study. With a software assist, they use it to digitally simulate some aspect of the real world (or an imaginary world) for entertainment or research. They then enjoy sharing that world with others. Those youths who are learning to master the digital arts of musical, video, and game production are capable of discovering entirely new realms of profitable applications in advertising, training, simulation, management, architecture, and other professional realms. To older generations, top-quality music and video are the exclusive domain of a relatively small coterie of specialized professionals. For Millennials, these arts are rapidly democratizing, and the talents they require are beginning to become adjunct skills for a wide cross-section of creative careers.

Millennials use the Internet to upload and share their own works, and to download those of others. They like to mix and match various fragments of the culture, past and present—perhaps combining music from their parents' era with a tune from the pop charts, altering the vocals into something resembling a character of a popular video game. New software packages (like MoodLogic and MusicMagic Mixer) offer sophisticated methods of arranging song collections. Through "machinima" (narrative films that use game software engines), films will allow their content to be used in Web sites, fan stories, homegrown movies, and games, all using the plot line and characters.

This is the first generation that doesn't need to ask permission from older producers—or, even, to ask anybody for money—in order to broadcast its own songs or radio shows. They don't need a literary agent to sell a script before making, editing, producing, and distributing their own films.

Their online digital skill advantage over older generations will only grow over time. Millennials are now writing, and will continue to write, software to do things older generations find incomprehensible, taking the Web to new levels others cannot imagine. The same teens who are now collaborating on MMOGs to ward off barbarians and build castles may become the young leaders who, twenty years from now, will be organizing vast networks to overhaul economic or political institutions, and not just in America. The World Wide Web is, of course, worldwide, enabling this to be the first generation to publish its thoughts to a universal audience. This is already happening in interactive sites like *livejournal.com* and *blurty.com*.

On the whole, Millennials are inclined to see the world in terms of conquerable challenges. This attitude has recently been reinforced by digital gaming and simulation technology, which break the world down into environments that can be analyzed, manipulated, engineered, or improved. In video games, Millennial players frequently take on the role of "fix-it" engineers who resolve ordinary problems, a role that appeals to girls as well as boys. A decade ago, they were introduced to gaming with Tamagachi-style "pets" that required them to take care of a virtual creature by manipulating its environment—and, more recently, with "constructivist" games like *The Sims*, whose game ethic has nothing in common with the warrior ethic of Gen-X-era games.

Where console gaming battles offer the player little beyond racking up points against a machine, the new online multiplayer games provide more sophisticated grounds for achievement. Unlike console games, online games remain in play after a player turns the connection off. Upon returning, that same world is present, albeit with changes created by other players. Soon, new Web authoring environments will let anyone create online multiplayer games. At that point, youth won't just be collaboratively playing these games, they will be collaboratively building and improving them.

This ability to change the virtual world allows gaming scenarios unknown in the Gen-X era, enabling players, acting alone or in groups, to build coalitions to battle terrorism, global warming, AIDS, and other intractable problems. To connect with Millennials, video game producers need to appreciate the seriousness and scale of their collective ambition. Today, they can win the struggle in a game. Tomorrow, they expect to succeed in real life.

Implications for Older Generations

Imagine a revival of *Reality Bites* with fortysomethings having to deal with temp work after corporate layoffs — or *The Graduate* with the generations inverted and a 60-year-old Boomer getting a humanities degree and walking into a party full of sober young people talking about "plastics." As Millennials enter their twenties, their very modern set of capabilities will become ever more apparent to older people — who will roll their eyes a bit at their occasional naiveté and optimism, even as the nation takes pride in their upbeat, can-do attitude.

Taking cues from Millennials, smarter story lines may start working for older audiences better than they have in recent decades. Recalling the films of the 1940s and '50s, these may include more stories about good people of all ages who face difficult tests leading to personal triumph or tragedy. Classics, authentically told, may enjoy a revival, as well. The Boomer narcissist and Gen-X slacker will be more the stuff of nostalgic humor than of contemporary interest to younger people. Meanwhile, aging Boomer musicians will continue to enjoy success, as their generation remains a dominant group of music purchasers for many years.

Events of the day, and a sobering national mood, may accelerate several of these trends. If the mood darkens, entertainments — including those for older people — will tend to become blander and more escapist, much as they did during World War II. Culture creators of all ages can take cues from Millennials in learning how to apply familiar styles in engaging new ways.

14 | THE MILLENNIAL FUTURE

"It fills us with pride to know that, no matter what happens in this life, you three will take care of each other with kindness, and bravery, and selflessness as you always have. (signed) Your loving parents."

—parents' letter, in *Lemony Snicket's A Series of Unfortunate Events* (2004)

THE MILLENNIAL FUTURE

Millennials and History

To understand what the future may hold for Millennials—and what Millennials may hold for the future of the entertainment industry—a good place to start is to trace the foreseeable milestones of their lifecycle. As Millennials fill young adult age brackets over the next couple of decades, the effect on entertainment will shift from music and rock concerts to film and video gaming, then to television, and eventually to theater.

They have already started graduating from college (2004), and will soon do so from professional schools (2006–07) and Ph.D. programs (2008–09). Already in 2004, they were among our most celebrated Olympians. In the years just ahead, they will fill the ranks of young-adult celebrities in the Olympics, pro sports, and entertainment—and the military, in any wars the nation may wage. In 2007, the oldest Millennials will reach the current median marriage age for women and the birth of their first child. In 2009, they will reach the current median marriage age for men.

Later this decade, they will become the dominant consumers—and marketplace influencers—of film. Before 2010, in all likelihood, someone will make a landmark film to define the Millennial experience, just as *The Graduate* defined Boomers in 1967 and *The Breakfast Club* did for Gen Xers in 1985.

Through the 2010s, they will be the most important film audience, and their young-adult tastes will drive new directions in cinema. They will become the most sought-after—and still hard-to-reach—TV market. By now, their older cohorts will dominate the ranks of culture creators, and their younger cohorts will dominate the ranks of culture consumers.

Through the 2010s, they will be giving birth in large numbers, returning to college for their fifth-year reunions—and swarming into business and the professions, no longer as apprentices. A new youth activism, of which we got a foretaste in 2004, will begin making a real impact on national politics in the elections of 2008 and 2012.

Some will enter state houses and the U.S. Congress. Around 2020, they will produce their first U.S. Senator, and their first children will apply to college. Through the ensuing decade, they will produce the culture that will be consumed by a younger generation.

In the 2030s, their impact on the youth culture will weaken, as younger generations overtly resist their styles. In theater and other fine arts, however, they will be the dominant audience. Before the end of this decade, they may elect their first U.S. President. They will occupy the White House into the 2050s, during which they will also provide majorities in the Congress and Senate, win Nobels, rule corporate boardrooms, and fill the ranks of collegiate parent bodies. By then, they will relish what they recall of their own youth culture, and may despair at its overt rejection by younger generations.

Thereafter, into the 2070s, they will occupy the Supreme Court, be America's mature generation—whatever that will mean at the time—and provide academe with its most valuable alumni contributors. Many will still be in their nineties in 2100, perhaps venerated as part of an honored and memorable generation.

What will happen over the course of their lives is, of course, unknowable. But in all likelihood, the Millennial Generation will dominate the story of the twenty-first century in much the same degree as the World War II-winning G.I. Generation dominated the story of the twentieth.

Along the way, history will intrude on their lives. When and how, no one can say. Whatever the peril, whatever the challenge—economic, political, military, social, environmental—do not expect years of '60s-style picketing, protesting, yelling, and arguing. Instead, expect 1930s-style energizing, organizing, teaming, and doing. The graver the national peril, the more Millennials will become the center of attention. What they need will become a national priority. What they do will become controversial to some eyes, a source of national pride to others.

A major national crisis would have profound implications for how Millennials view entertainment—and for the entertainment industry generally. Recall the months after 9/11, the shows that were cancelled, postponed, or rewritten, and the effect this tragedy had on the willingness of people to attend live events (and their attitude when they did), or travel to theme parks, or visit New York City and Washington, D.C.

That mood has eased, at least for now. But the industry should learn from the Jackson-Timberlake imbroglio, or the public scolding of Take-Two Interactive over its "hot coffee" mod, that it may soon find itself in an altogether new place, where the old rules no longer hold. Additional terrorist strikes, financial meltdowns, or other events of comparable alarm could alter the popular culture landscape beyond recognition. The record of history shows that, during and after the Civil War, and again during and after World War II, the prevailing culture changed in fundamental ways, becoming simpler, less rowdy and violent, more hostile to anything that challenged the common mindset—in a word, bland.

At first thought, this seems not be good news for culture creators. Yet the new historic tableau of a post-crisis era can lead to creative opportunities unimaginable before. Without the Civil War and Emancipation, how could we have had the birth of blues (the most important single element leading to the late-nineteenth century advent of the modern pop culture)? Without World War II and the onset of the Cold War, how would rock 'n roll have been possible?

If a hard dose of history should happen—if, for example, America should face an epic crisis, like a protracted war on terror, a clash of civilizations, or a severe economic downslide, Millennials will be affected the most. The experience of similar generations at major moments in our history, suggests that Millennials will do what those times may require, with more optimism and less complaint than older people might today expect. Part of what they would do, in such times, would directly impact cultural trends, bringing change from which there would be no going back.

Millennials will know that the bulk of their lives will lie in the years *beyond* the crisis—whereas the bulk of the Gen-X and Boomer lives will have taken place in the years *before* it. And, by nature of their core traits—from their confidence to their team skills to their high-pressure high-achieving frame of mind—they may, as a group, provide just what those times will require. Many will see in it their lifetime agenda, an agenda very unlike what Boomers set for themselves back in their own youth, or Gen Xers in theirs.

The more powerful the dose of history, the more pronounced and noticeable will be the Millennial break with Gen-X styles and attitudes—and the more rapidly and fundamentally they will change the entertainment industry.

Millennials as Culture Consumers

At present, the Millennial market for youth entertainment remains overshadowed by the prevailing "of Gen-X by Gen-X for Gen-X" style, but this style is growing dated and can't last. The Millennials' close bonds with their parents will soon put the older generation on the defensive for its alienated attitude, as colorfully anticipated by Village Voice critic Eric Weisbard in his review of Election:

> *"The children of the Boomers will make common cause with their parents, a seamless transition of power, while those of us [Gen Xers] who haven't cashed in from behind the scenes shake our fists from some wretched little garret...like Matthew Broderick hurling his lunch at the limo bearing Reese and the congressman at the end of Election, smearing up the works for just a second, then running away as fast as he possibly can."*

Up to now, Millennials have shared the pop culture target market age brackets with Generation X. This will change, very soon.

Within a few years, Millennials will dominate the popular culture's target market. By 2010, a recognizable Millennial generation will have appeared in Western Europe and China, and in Eastern Europe, Latin America, and the rest of Asia a few years later. During this era, the gap will narrow between

Millennial tastes and what the pop culture will provide. The emerging Millennial culture will take fewer cues from the tastes or expectations of older people. Male Millennials will step out of the shadow of "girl power" and begin to assert their own voices.

In music and live entertainment, many of the edgier trends of the past several decades will subside. There will be new themes, new words, and new stories. Serious issues of politics and economics—some of them global issues—will rise in importance, while values issues will fade. Issues of social class (or money) will feel fresher and more urgent in the young-adult mind-set than issues of race or gender.

Millennials will rely on their electronic peer groups to relay news of hot new sounds and artists laterally, under the radar of large, centralized media. Traditional publicity and advertising will reach them less (and more expensively). Over time, Millennials will propel the digital IT revolution, determining its shape and its winners and losers. The "digital convergence" will truly arrive. TV will integrate with interactive media. All forms of entertainment, from sports to opera, will grow a "game" dimension. Businesses will patch pop culture into branded lifestyle ensembles that will often leave few traces of ultimate authorship.

For the near-term, network and large-audience cable television's programming will continue to target the Gen-X cohorts who are most likely to purchase products based on watching commercials. As a consequence, X-style entertainment is likely to retain a strong position in television after it fades from music, film, and interactive games.

Long after Millennial trends in music, gaming, and the interactive world have become the norm, Broadway will just be encountering the breaking generational wave. Historically, theater audiences tend to be older than those of other performance media. Even so, with the right choice of material and proper marketing, theater companies can turn Millennials into a robust theater audience.

The importance of theater, in understanding this generation, extends far beyond youth-cast or youth-targeted productions. In other areas of entertainment, mass markets and big-name stars tend to rule, but in theater,

Millennials can go where they wish without conforming to Gen-X styles—and, at times, by resisting them overtly. Many more high schools and colleges are putting on big and highly elaborate plays and musicals now, even as Broadway's Tony-winning shows tend to reflect stripped-down, harder-edged, parody-themed, more sardonic than singable styles. Given the diminishing relevance of well-known plays and musicals to their own experience, teenage and collegiate Millennials are writing more plays and musicals on their own than teachers recall prior generations having done.

The seeds for the Millennial cultural breakout have been amply planted in American schools over the past decade. Theater, film, and TV media are becoming mainstream activities at high schools across America, many of which are equipped with theaters, black boxes, studios, editing labs, and other equipment that never existed for other generations. While differing greatly across school systems, course offerings and extracurricular activities that teach communications and entertainment skills are, by any measure, far more advanced to what today's adults remember from their own school days—and far superior to what one finds elsewhere in the world.

Millennials as Culture Creators

Before the end of the 2010s, Millennials will become the primary producers *and* consumers of popular culture. After that time, the *next generation* will begin replacing them in the tween and lower teen brackets. Unlike Millennials, this new generation—for now, let's call it the Homeland Generation—will never have known what America felt like before 9/11 (or, perhaps, some even more decisive event yet to come).

It's possible, but by no means certain, that 9/11 has already drawn the lines between Millennials and their Homeland successors. If so, today's newborns are the leading-edge members of this new generation. Whatever the initial birthyear, we call it "Homeland" because the children appear fated to grow up in a time when the protections of a child's world will rise to the point of family (and national) obsession. As children who will not have a personal memory of the '90s mood, whose parents are overwhelmingly Gen Xers, and whose upbringing is driven in part by the post-9/11 mood change, Homelanders will grow up in an entirely new childhood environment.

By around 2020, this new Homeland Generation will reach the same point in their life cycle that Millennials occupied around 2000. In the 2020s, Millennials will begin creating popular culture for them, just as Gen-X is now doing for them. Millennial stars, many of them Latin and Asian, will reveal their generational persona on all media. In the eyes of youth, Millennial styles will start to feel as middle-aged, and replaceable, as Gen-X styles increasingly do today. By then, their generation will have become a tired subject, much like Boomers were in the late '70s, or Gen-X in the late '90s.

What will they provide, as cultural mentors, for the Homeland Generation? That's far into the future, and of not much concern to the entertainment industry of today, but one can imagine them steering that younger generation, in the 2020s, in directions they will have missed in their own culture.

While many will be the offspring of Millennials, this will be the generation shaped primarily by Gen-X parents and leaders, who will stop at nothing to prevent these children from enduring anything close to their own latchkey youth, especially in what could be perceived as more dangerous times.

The Millennials' most dominant impact as parents will be on the generation that follows the Homeland. Remembering their own youth full of stress and achievement, middle-aged Millennials will begin to loosen the restraints on youth, subtly pushing them to "question authority"—which young people will obligingly do, filling a role vacated by the mostly deceased Boomers.

Millennial Connections

By the 2020s, the entertainment industry will be entirely in the hands of Millennials and Gen Xers. They will be the stars, film directors, TV script writers, and producers up and down the age ladder. As the Millennials' own pop culture tastes become institutionalized in their own entertainment industries, what forms will they take?

Through the history of the popular culture, certain media styles, companies, personalities, bands, directors, and entertainment technologies have successfully established strong connections with particular generations throughout their life cycle. For the G.I. Generation, it was Busby Berkeley musicals, big band music, radio comedies, and 78s. For the Silent, it was jazz improv, vintage rock 'n roll, drive-time radio, PBS, and LPs. For Boomers, it was vintage TV, hard rock, protest rock, mass concerts, TV programming (like "All in the Family" and the vintage cast of "Saturday Night Live") with an edge to it, and cassettes playable in cars. For Gen Xers, it was MTV and hip-hop, New Wave and grunge, the synthesized musical styles of the '90s (whose beats can now be heard in ads, news shows, and sports highlights), the films of John Hughes and Quentin Tarantino, CDs and VCRs.

What will form long-term bonds with Millennials, in this new era of IMs, iPods and DVDs? Early indications are that it will be upbeat, interactive, and relevant to their own experience as a generation. Who will present it first and best? That's the challenging question that directors, and game designers across all media are now grappling with it. The next round of music and film creators will be seeking the answer as if their livelihoods depended on it—which they do.

Despite their current resistance to commercial advertising, this generation will, in time, show a new type of brand and product loyalty that will likely endure for decades. Those who make fundamental errors about youth tastes will trail the market, be relegated to niches. The ones who do well will be those who see the Millennial wave coming, catch it early, and ride it smartly.

15 | A MILLENNIAL REALITY CHECK

"It is imperative to remember that Millennials are an entirely new generation altogether; different from Baby Boomers and Gen Xers not just in values and ideals, but also in their experiences and activities.... Corporations are adapting their products and marketing to reflect this shift because they know that if they do not, Millennials will simply pass them by."

—Timothy Mask, in the American Outlook (2003)

A MILLENNIAL REALITY CHECK

Why is the entertainment industry's credibility so low, among today's young people?

Why is it, when you ask high schoolers and collegians who their generation's principal adversary is—and you move beyond partisan politics—you will hear so many single out the music business?

Why has loyalty to brands, stars, and genres grown so weak?

Why have we seen the recent downturns in movie and rock concert attendance, especially among the young?

The answer: There is a generational rebellion, led by "rebels" who are not really angry but clever and persistent, driven in part by what some of them see as a generational battle waged by older people bent on profit at their expense.

In a technology-driven battle between today's 50-year-olds and today's collegians, who has the advantage?

That's easy. A war against the young is a war the entertainment industry cannot win.

The industry's Boomer leaders sometimes justify their "tough love" war plan by arguing that there is no compromising with criminality. That sounds familiar—like something young Boomers heard from their own parents, back in the days of tear gas, inner-city riots, rampant graffiti, and skyrocketing youth violence. In the long run, the culture changed as Boomers wanted—a fact which ought to make them cautious about predicting victory for the "older generation" this time. As the culture changes, so do the social norms and cultural usages that define what criminality is. Boomers ought to know this better than most generations.

Whether the issue is downloading, file-swapping, broadbanding, or anything else, Millennials will build in strength, beyond where the entertainment industry can fight them in the legislatures, the courts, or even in the realm of public opinion. Millennials will win not just because they can, but because they will feel their position is right, and necessary, to change the culture—and because they will ultimately gain broad support from older generations.

The sooner that more people in the entertainment industry stops fighting high-tech Millennials and instead focus on how to monetize their skills and tastes, the better for everyone.

Lawyering is part of the problem. By persisting in legal and legislative maneuvers against teenagers who share songs, the music industry risks positioning itself as strategic adversaries in the lives and minds of a very large share of the rising generation. These are people who could and should be lifelong consumers. It could take a long time to undo any damage.

When lawyers suggest pursuing an "open-and-shut" case against thousands of young John and Jane Does in the war on downloads and broadbands, be careful to ask—as leaders should about real wars—what's the exit strategy?

Pricing is part of the problem. When Boomers were young, nearly every corner of the pop culture was affordable on a teenager's allowance. Today, entire categories of high-end entertainment are beyond the means of all but the most affluent Millennials. This makes today's teens expert at weighing costs and benefits and making quick purchasing tradeoffs—for example, deciding that a video game worth delivers more hours of fun than two music CDs or that renting a DVD for friends at home is a lot cheaper than buying five theater tickets.

This "Millennial wallet" question has enormous long-term stakes. Affordable (or free) rock concerts provided key coming-of-age experiences for Woodstock-era Boomers and Lollapalooza-era Gen Xers, which helps explain why concert tours are still so popular, and profitable, for the artists of those eras. For Millennials, however, tickets have become so expensive that not many can attend without a parent's credit card, or without bringing a parent along—and when they do, the event has such a commercial feel that, later on, it will not kindle the same nostalgic memories.

Young people who don't attend concerts today are unlikely to do so ten, twenty, or forty years from now. As Martha Randolph Carr observes, it's not just a question of paid versus unpaid downloads. It's a question of emotional bonding: "If today's rock stars and tour promoters don't get it, if they don't get past the MP3s and headphones and start playing venues where kids can feel personally connected with the band—then, when they're as old as Mick Jagger there won't be crowds of middle-aged ticket buyers lining up to see them one more time."

Marketing is also part of the problem. From TV to magazines, from ad-time creep on AM/FM radio to the ever-expanding ads and trailers at movie theaters, the Millennial world is awash with advertising, much of which they ignore or avoid—and much of which is essentially unchanged, in form and attitude, from the Gen-X era. Marketers constantly lament that today's teens and collegians are hard to reach. They are—unless a campaign targets them smartly, using cultural artifacts, humor, and twenty-first century methods that connect with them.

The best way to do that—like the best way to reach 30-year-olds, 50-year-olds, or older people—is to enlist the help of people the age you want to reach. These would be people of the targeted generation, who understand the common location in history, shared personal experiences, and powerful cultural connections that make them feel part of a generation.

In lieu of legal battles, high-end productions, and Millennial-blind marketing, the task should be to figure out what's going on in Millennial heads, and how best to entertain them. This will require thinking outside the "X box," and realizing that what used to feel "outside the box" might now be stuck in cement, quite unprofitably, within it.

What to Do

Anyone who has Millennial sons and daughters should think of this generation the way they think of their own kids and their kids' friends, multiplied many times—and then look at these young people in a new light, in the context of their own time, the behavior of other generations around them, and the larger flow of history.

Anyone who doesn't have Millennial children should not try to learn about them by watching in focus groups gathered for a client's special purpose. Focus groups have their usefulness, for sure, but they can be very misleading, especially when those assemble these groups have institutional agendas. Millennials want to please adults and can thus be susceptible to push-polling, giving questioners answers along the lines of whatever a sponsor might desire.

The best way to learn about Millennials is to watch them in their own setting, watch them doing what they enjoy doing and what they're good at doing—and watch them with an open mind.

* Go see a big high school musical.
* Attend a collegiate "indie" film festival.
* Watch (or join) a party featuring the latest multi-user video game.
* Poke through youth-created Web sites—including political ones.
* Check out Web sites featuring discussions by Millennials, often related to their favorite music, anime character, or game.
* Watch TV ads carefully, being alert to which ones cast Millennials as X, and which ones get them right.
* See movies about teens from past decades (late '80s, late '60s, mid-'50s, and 1930's) that reveal other breaking generational waves.

Of all professions, entertainment can be the most insightful, intuitive, and imaginative. There are so many stories and characters, songs and dances, artists and stars, each with a fresh Millennial flavor just ready to be written and filmed, danced and sung, discovered and celebrated.

Millennials are rising. The popular culture is changing. Twenty years from now, we'll look back, and it will all seem so obvious.

About the Authors

Neil Howe and William Strauss, best-selling authors and national speakers, are renowned authorities on generations in America. They have together written several books, all widely used by businesses, colleges, government agencies, and political leaders of both parties. Their remarkable blend of social science and history—and their in-depth analysis of American generations—lend order and meaning, even a measure of predictability, to social change.

Their first book, *Generations* (Morrow, 1991), is a history of America told as a sequence of generational biographies. *Generations* was photographed on Bill Clinton's White House desk, quoted approvingly by Rush Limbaugh and Newt Gingrich, raved over by Tony Robbins, and cited by economic forecasters from Harry Dent to David Hale. Then-Vice President Al Gore sent a copy to every Member of Congress, calling it, "the most stimulating book on American history I have ever read."

Their second book, *13th-Gen* (Vintage, 1993), remains the top-selling nonfiction book on Generation X. *The Fourth Turning* (Broadway, 1997) forecast a major mood change in America shortly after the new millennium— a change much like what actually happened, after September 11, 2001. *The Fourth Turning* reached #10 on the amazon.com list four years after its release, and its Web site (fourthturning.com) has the internet's longest-running discussion forum for any nonfiction book. "We will never be able to think about history in the same way," declared public opinion guru Dan Yankelovich,

Millennials Rising (Vintage, 2000) has been widely quoted in the media for its insistence that today's new crop of teens and kids are very different from Generation X and, on the whole, doing much better than most adults think "It's hard to resist the book's hopeful vision for our children and future," adds *NEA Today*, "Many of the theories they wrote about in their two previous books—*generations* and *13th-Gen*—have indeed come to pass."

Articles by Howe and Strauss have appeared in the *Atlantic*, the *Washington Post*, the *New York Times*, *American Demographics*, *USA Today*, *USA Weekend*, and other national publications.

Strauss's and Howe's theories and predictions are based on their profiles of generations—each reflecting distinct values formed during the eras in which its members grew up and came of age. They have observed that similar generational profiles recur in cycles driven by a rhythmic pattern of non-linear shifts or "turnings" in America's social mood. This cyclical pattern has been present for centuries, and not just in America. History shapes generations, and then generations shape history.

About LifeCourse Associates

LifeCourse Associates is a generational consulting firm developed by Neil Howe and William Strauss in response to the many inquiries resulting from their books. They offer keynote speeches, seminars, communications products, generational audits, and consultations that apply the authors' unique historical analysis to help audiences better understand their businesses, families, and personal futures. Their ideas and generational perspective can have a profound effect on strategic planning, marketing, product development, communications, and human resources.

Their books include *Generations* (1991), *13th-Gen* (1993), *The Fourth Turning* (1997), *Millennials Rising* (2000), *Recruiting Millennials* (2001), *Millennials Go To College* (2002), and *Millennials in the Workplace* (forthcoming).

In recent conferences, the U.S. Department of Labor, U.S. Department of Health and Human Services, and U.S. Central Intelligence Agency have all adopted the Howe-Strauss generational framework. Other LifeCourse clients include the Viacom, Ford Motor Company, PBS, J. Walter Thompson, Kraft Nabisco, Leo Burnett, Scholastic, Inc., Merrill Lynch, U.S. Bureau of the Census, National Workforce Association, USDA Forest Service, BBDO Detroit, AARP, and McGraw-Hill. LifeCourse has been especially active with clients who deal with Millennials and with the youth and young-adult age brackets. Howe and Strauss have spoken to the faculty and administrators of many colleges and to national collegiate organizations, such as the American Association of Collegiate Registrars and Admissions Officers (AACRAO), the National Association of College Admissions Counselors (NACAC), and the Council of Independent Colleges (ICI). They have spoken to teachers, principals, and superintendents of K-12 education in over 20 states, and have addressed the National High School Leadership Summit and the national meetings of the National Association of Secondary School Principals and the National Association of Elementary School Principals. They have also consulted often with every branch of U.S. armed services—Army, Navy, Marines, Air Force, Coast Guard, and Reserves.

Contact LifeCourse Associates

Call (866) 537-4999 or go to www.lifecourse.com.

Sources

Given the vast range of topics covered in this book—and the numberless scholarly, journalistic, and pop culture sources that bear some connection to them—there is no way we could reference everything of interest. Although much research on the demographic and spending trends of particular media markets is proprietary (and often very expensive), we have generally tried to make no claims that cannot be supported by research that is publicly available.

Virtually every one of these sources (whether studies, surveys, businesses, or government agencies) is available for inspection on the Web. Some offer elaborate on-line data centers. Readers are invited to follow up there for further detail and updated information.

For readers who wish to dig deeper into the data sources for the overall youth behavior and attitude trends described here, we urge them to consult the comprehensive bibliographic reference section we included at the end of *Millennials Rising* (2001). As a convenience, we provide below a brief list of sources (from publications and Web sites to programs and agencies) that we have found most useful in our own work.

As for readers who want to find out more about our generational perspective on American history, or about our earlier treatments of the Millennial Generation, we invite them to read our three previous coauthored books: *Generations* (1991), *13th-Gen* (1993), and *The Fourth Turning* (1997).

Readers with further questions are invited to contact us at LifeCourse Associates.

Sources on Media, Summary List

Kaiser Family Foundation Reports

Henry J. Kaiser Family Foundation, "Studies of Entertainment Media and Health";
see publications; among recent releases:
Generation M: Media in the Lives of 8-18 Year-olds (2005)
Parents, Media and Public Policy: A Kaiser Family Foundation Survey (2004)
The Role of Media in Childhood Obesity (2004)
Rating Sex and Violence in the Media: Media Ratings and Proposals for Reform (2002)

IMDB

Internet Movie Database; extensive information on individual movies, historical records,
and box-office trends; updated continuously

Informa

Informa, Telecoms & Media; nonproprietary press releases on online demographics, media
usage, and the entertainment industry

Jupiter Research

Jupiter Research; nonproprietary press releases on online demographics, media usage, and
the entertainment industry

Media InfoCenter

Media InfoCenter, directed by the Media Management Center at Northwestern University;
comprehensive public information on media and advertising industries

MPA Research

Motion Picture Association of America; *U.S. Movie Attendance Study*, *MPA Market Statistics*,
and *MPA All Media: Revenue Report*; data updated annually and available upon request;

Nielsen TV Audience Research

Nielsen Media Research; various proprietary and public reports on TV audiences and advertising

NPD Research

NPD Funworld; proprietary and public data on the computer and videogame industry

Pollstar Research

Pollstar Online; public data on music concert revenues and ticket sales

RIAA Research

Recording Industry Association of America; "Marketing Reports" and "Consumer Trends;"
updated annually

Rockonomics

Marie Connolly and Alan B. Krueger, *Rockonomics: The Economics of Popular Music*
(National Bureau of Economic Research, 2005), with analysis and historical data on the
music and concert industry

Yahoo Survey
Yahoo!, *Born To Be Wired: The Role of New Media for a Digital Generation* (research by TRU and Harris Interactive, 2003)

Sources on Attitudes, Summary List

American Demographics
Crain Communications, *American Demographics*; monthly periodical; part of *Ad Age* since 2005

Drexel Poll
Drexel University, *Drexel University Futures Poll: Teenagers, Technology and Tomorrow* (1997)

Gallup
Gallup News Service; The Gallup Organization

Generation 2001
Northwestern Mutual Life, *Generation 2001 Survey* (1999)

Harris Interactive
Harris Interactive, *Trends and Tudes*; monthly newsletter and Web site for youth research

Horatio Alger
Horatio Alger Association, *The State of Our Nation's Youth*; annual publication

Monitoring the Future
Lloyd D. Johnston, Jerald G. Bachman, and Patrick M. O'Malley (project directors), *Monitoring the Future Study* (Institute for Social Research, University of Michigan); annual questions to students in grades 12 (since 1975) and in grades 10 and 8 (since 1991); reports issued in various years

NASSP
National Association of Secondary School Principals, *The Mood of American Youth* (1974, 1983, and 1996); students aged 13-17 interviewed early in each year

PRIMEDIA/Roper
PRIMEDIA, Inc., and Roper Starch Worldwide, Inc., *The PRIMEDIA/Roper National Youth Opinion Survey* (1998); students in grades 7-12, interviewed in November, 1998

Public Agenda
Public Agenda; regular published surveys on youth attitudes and adult attitudes toward youth (e.g., *Life After High School: Young People Talk About Their Hopes and Prospects*, 2005)

Roper
Roper Starch Worldwide, "Roper Youth Report"; proprietary results published annually; public results reported irregularly (www.roper.com)

SLFC Survey
Student Loan Finance Corporation, *America's Youth Look to the Future* (2003)

Shell Poll
Shell Oil Company, *The Shell Poll* (1999)

TRU
Teenage Research Unlimited; various reports (e.g., *What's New With Teens and Teens' Take on Technology*; both for 2005 Pepsi Teen Day)

UCLA Freshman Poll
L.J. Sax, A.W. Astin, W. S. Korn, and K.M. Mahoney, *The American Freshman* (Higher Education Research Institute, University of California at Los Angeles); published annually; yearly surveys since 1966

Who's Who
Who's Who Among American High School Students, *Annual Survey of High Achievers*; "high-achieving" high school students interviewed annually since 1967

YATS
Defense Manpower Data Center, Youth Attitude Tracking Survey (U.S. Department of Defense); survey of potential high school-aged recruits; published annually

Sources on Behavior, Summary List

General
The Child & Family Web Guide (Tufts University)

Child Trends DataBank (Child Trends)

America's Children (U.S. Federal Interagency Forum on Child and Family Statistics); annual publication (childstats.gov)

Trends in the Well-Being of America's Children and Youth (U.S. Department of Health and Human Services), annual publication; website

The Child Well-Being Index (Duke University)

Demographics, Family Structure, Race, Ethnicity, Family Income
U.S. Bureau of the Census (U.S. Department of Commerce)

Economic Indicators
U.S. Bureau of Economic Analysis (U.S. Department of Commerce)

Youth Employment
U.S. Bureau of Labor Statistics (U.S. Department of Labor)

Educational Achievement
The Nation's Report Card (National Assessment of Educational Progress, of the U.S. Department of Education); regular publications

The College Board; regular publications

Schools & Colleges

U.S. National Center for Education Statistics, *The Condition of Education* (U.S. Department of Education); published annually

Children's Use of Time

Sandra L. Hofferth and Jack Sandberg, *Changes in American Children's Time, 1981–1997* (Institute for Social Research and Population Studies Center, University of Michigan; November 9, 1998)

Youth Health, Sex, and Risk Behaviors

U.S. National Center for Health Statistics

Youth Risk Behavior Surveillance System (U.S. Centers for Disease Control and Prevention)

U.S. National Institute of Child Health and Human Development (U.S. Department of Health and Human Services)

Youth Studies Group, Stanford Center for Research in Disease Prevention

Teen Births, Abortions

Alan Guttmacher Institute

U.S. National Center for Health Statistics

Family Dysfunction

U.S. Children's Bureau (U.S. Department of Health and Human Services)

U.S. National Center on Child Abuse and Neglect (U.S. Department of Health and Human Services)

Youth Drug Abuse

U.S. Substance Abuse and Mental Health Services Administration (U.S. Department of Health and Human Services)

Lloyd D. Johnston, Jerald G. Bachman, and Patrick M. O'Malley (project directors), *Monitoring the Future Study* (Institute for Social Research, University of Michigan); annual questions to students on substance abuse in grades 12 (since 1975) and in grades 10 and 8 (since 1991); reports issued in various years

Partnership for a Drug Free America

National Center on Addiction and Substance Abuse at Columbia University

Youth Crime

U.S. National Criminal Justice Reference Service (U.S. Department of Justice)

National School Safety Center